The CIM Diploma Case Study Book

The Marketing Series is one of the most comprehensive collections of books in marketing and sales available from the UK today.

Published by Butterworth-Heinemann on behalf of the Chartered Institute of Marketing, the series is divided into three distinct groups: *Student* (fulfilling the needs of those taking the Institute's certificate and diploma qualifications); *Professional Development* (for those on formal or self-study vocational training programmes); and *Practitioner* (presented in a more informal, motivating and highly practical manner for the busy marketer).

Formed in 1911, the Chartered Institute of Marketing is now the largest professional marketing management body in Europe with over 22,000 members and 25,000 students located worldwide. Its primary objectives are focused on the development of awareness and understanding of marketing throughout UK industry and commerce and in the raising of standards of professionalism in the education, training and practice of this key business discipline.

Books in the series

Behavioural Aspects of Marketing
K.C. Williams

Business Law
R.G. Lawson and D. Smith

Cases in Marketing Financial Services
Edited by Chris Ennew, Trevor Watkins and Mike Wright

The CIM Diploma Case Study Book
David J. Pearson

Economic Theory and Marketing Practice
Angela Hatton and Mike Oldroyd

Effective Sales Management
John Strafford and Colin Grant

Financial Aspects of Marketing
Keith Ward

The Fundamentals of Advertising
John Wilmshurst

The Fundamentals and Practice of Marketing
John Wilmshurst

International Marketing
Stanley J. Paliwoda

Marketing Communications
C.L. Coulson-Thomas

Marketing Financial Services
Edited by Chris Ennew, Trevor Watkins and Mike Wright

Mini Cases in Marketing
Lester Massingham and Geoffrey Lancaster

The Principles and Practice of Selling
A. Gillam

Strategic Marketing Management
R.M.S. Wilson and C. T. Gilligan with D. Pearson

The CIM Diploma Case Study Book

David J. Pearson

Published on behalf of
the Chartered Institute of Marketing

Butterworth-Heinemann Ltd
Linacre House, Jordan Hill, Oxford OX2 8DP

A member of the Reed Elsevier group

OXFORD LONDON BOSTON
MUNICH NEW DELHI SINGAPORE SYDNEY
TOKYO TORONTO WELLINGTON

First published 1994

British Library Cataloguing in Publication Data
Pearson, David J.
CIM Diploma Case Study Book. –
(Marketing Series: Student)
I. Title II. Series
658.8

ISBN 0 7506 1848 5

Composition by Scribe Design, Gillingham, Kent
Printed and bound in Great Britain by Clays, St Ives plc

Contents

Preface vii

1 CIM examiners' guidance notes for tutors and students 1

2 The June 1991 Examination Case 7
Morton Packaging plc

3 The December 1991 Examination Case 39
Brewsters Ltd

4 The June 1992 Examination Case 71
Euro Airport Ltd (EAL)

5 The December 1992 Examination Case 119
Regional Railways Central (RRC)

6 The June 1993 Examination Case 189
Royal Mail (RM)

Preface

The Case Study is the most difficult exam in the CIM Diploma.

This book has been designed to help you prepare for it. With previous cases, questions and examiners' comments, you will get a very good idea about what is required.

Along with general guidance for the Diploma Case Study, I have included examiners' comments on past case studies.

David J. Pearson

1 CIM examiners' guidance notes for tutors and students

12 MARKETING MANAGEMENT (ANALYSIS & DECISION)

Notional taught hours: 45

Method of assessment:	3 hour written examination
Number of questions:	all questions to be attempted (3 or 4)
Pass mark:	50%

Preferred sequence of studies

The culmination of the Certificate and Diploma course is the Case Study. The examination has the purpose of ensuring that those who hold the Diploma qualification have not only achieved a certain level of marketing knowledge, but also have the competence to use that knowledge in addressing simulated marketing management problems.

Any aspect of the entire Certificate and Diploma syllabus may be applicable and if you have been exempted from parts of the course you should ensure you familiarise yourself with the detailed course requirements.

This paper should be taken at the end of your course study.

Rationale

To extend the practice of candidates in the quantitative and qualitative analysis of marketing situations, both to develop their powers of diagnosis and to create a firm basis in decision making.

By the end of their study students will be able to:

(i) Identify, define and rank the problem(s) contained in marketing case studies
(ii) Formulate working hypotheses regarding the solution(s) to problems identified in marketing case studies

(iii) Assemble, order, analyse and interpret both qualitative and quantitative data relating to a marketing case, using appropriate analytical procedures and models
(iv) Describe and substantiate all working assumptions made regarding the case problem(s), working hypotheses and data
(v) Generate and evaluate the expected outcomes of alternative solutions to case problem(s)
(vi) Formulate recommendations for action and feedback on case problem(s) including their financial and human resource implications
(vii) Prepare and present appropriate marketing case reports.

Senior Examiner's comments

The CIM Diploma is recognised increasingly widely as a licence to practise. It is in no one's interests for it to be awarded lightly, as those who have striven hard to attain it will surely agree. The value of the Diploma depends directly upon the quality of the people holding it; in turn the respect earned from peers, superiors and clients depends on the value of the Diploma.

Marketing Management: Analysis & Decision (Case Study) is quite rightly the severest test in the CIM examinations. It is the only subject for which an exemption cannot be granted. The examination is based upon a real-life major case study and requires the application of theories, principles and techniques learned in the study of other subjects. It is not an examination to be passed by regurgitating knowledge.

Candidates must demonstrate beyond reasonable doubt that they are capable not only of in-depth analysis before the exam, but also are able to take decisions and write clear, concise and convincing marketing plans. These marketing plans need to show an understanding of the corporate and financial implications.

Question design

Questions applied in case studies do not have any standardised format; they may vary in number; throw up a surprise situation; they will be action orientated; but one inevitable and recurring theme will be the strategic marketing of product and services. The examiners are aware of the time constraint of three hours and the questions are designed to enable a candidate to cover them adequately, if not well, within that period. Candidates should remember that they are expected to have knowledge equivalent to the syllabus of the other three Diploma subjects. The whole course (Certificate and Diploma) is a legitimate source of questions.

Examination approach

Candidates are required to do what the examiners ask, to answer the questions as put and in accordance with any mark allocation which is stated on the paper. This means the management of the time within the examination situation is crucial. In every case, candidates have a human role to play within the structure of either the case, the examination paper, or both, to which they are expected to be able to relate. Usually, this means that they have to respond and restructure their thinking within the examination itself; this is precisely what the examiners are seeking.

Preparation

There are two basic parts to this paper embodied in its title – **analysis** and **decision**. There can be no better description of these two parts than the questions put to his students by one lecturer as follows:

- What is wrong?
- What are you going to do to put it right?

Within the context of management, marketing or otherwise, the second question is the critical one, but cannot be answered without the problem identification implicit in the first.

There will be anomalies in the case, as in real life. Assumptions will therefore need to be made and clearly stated. The CIM cannot enter into discussion on these aspects, either verbally or in writing.

Problem identification will certainly require the application of statistical and financial analytical techniques, and of organisational and behavioural understanding and marketing knowledge. The examiners must know what these problems are, what alternative solutions to them have been considered and which alternative has been chosen by the candidate, i.e.:

- What is to be done?
- In what time period?
- By whom?
- With what financial and human resource implications?
- And with what projected outcome?

There is no such thing as a right answer to these questions. Above all, sensible recommendations are required, supported by reasoned argument. *Lists of problems and regurgitated materials from the case itself do no candidates any credit.*

The evidence is overwhelming that a great many students try to seek refuge in analysis and come to their examination desks hoping that inspiration will suddenly flow to the tips of their ballpoint pens! The Case Study is issued prior to the examination date to enable students to conduct their analysis before responding to the situation posed in the examination hall. A restatement of this analysis is insufficient to pass the examination. Decisions must be formulated and clearly articulated on the exam day itself.

Decisions

There is an apt Chinese proverb which says: 'He who deliberates fully before taking a step will spend his entire life on one leg.' The question of taking decisions is a conceptual leap for many students. They need help. In the absence of full information, they have to make assumptions, use their judgement and be prepared to back it up on paper.

One of the difficulties, which the examiners fully understand, is the lack of knowledge about any particular industry used in the Case. Marketing decisions, however, are applicable in any environment based on sound principles relevant to the situation. The examiners will not tolerate academic essays; we need to see applications and this means that candidates should adopt management report style and format to maximise their chances.

Further research

The examiners can state categorically that there is no need for any candidate to seek additional information outside the Case Study. There are three reasons for this:

1 The examiners incorporate within the Case itself enough information for the candidate to work on. It is a self-contained exercise.
2 Case Studies need to be disguised to preserve confidentiality. Trying to search out the company concerned can thus not only be a waste of time but lead to confusion.
3 Access to additional research data is, particularly for overseas students, limited.

Nevertheless, candidates may be expected to be able to state within the examination what additional research information they would seek, for what reason, in what time period, at what approximate cost and by what method. There is every justification for encouraging student research during the course of an academic year in order to have the experience and be able to apply it to the examination Case. No students will earn additional marks for external research data introduced in the examination.

Creativity and innovation

The lack of imagination by the majority of candidates in this examination is a major weakness. Marketing is creative; it is one of the means by which companies distinguish themselves or their products from competition. Only on rare occasions are the examiners confronted by some illuminating or different approach and marks then have a tendency to soar!

What tutors can, and should, do

For the purposes of this section, the examiners must assume that students have, at the beginning of the year, the knowledge and skills required by the subject. What follows can also only be recommendations; there is no one way to learn/teach case studies, just as there is no one answer.

Action recommended

1. Prepare a programme of case material covering the major areas of marketing activity.
2. Issue that programme to all students, highlighting the main features of each case. Work this up slowly, either from mini-cases or parts of past examination cases.
3. Increase the complexity as the year goes on.
4. Recommend appropriate textbook chapter readings or other reading materials relevant to the part(s) being dealt with.
5. Start using at least one technique, from statistics or finance, early on, to guide decision-making; develop successively.
6. On each problem identified, force students, if necessary, to put forward at least three alternative solutions and justify each one.
7. Insist on a written report on how the selected solution should be implemented within a given time scale.
8. A clear statement of their proposed strategy is essential and an understanding of what actions will cost the organisation in real terms.
9. Where groups are working together, brainstorm creative ideas; brand name, advertising headlines, unique selling propositions for examples, to get them thinking creatively.
10. Decision-making must start early and students should be developed to plan, organise, direct, control and evaluate such decisions by the time of the examination.
11. The students, not the tutor, should be doing the work. Prepared syndicated model answers rarely succeed.
12. Subject tutors as well as students are urged to read the Examiners' Reports published twice annually by the CIM which offer more advice specific to each paper.

Future examinations

The Senior Examiner has, in 'Marketing Success', advised tutors and students that his future intentions are to include a mix of short-term tactical decisions and longer-term strategic analysis and planning in this subject's examination papers.

It has also been made clear that all plans should have time scales i.e. require scheduling and should indicate the resource implications.

In addition, the CIM wish all future Diploma students to be aware of the financial implications of their marketing plans and to be able to plan on a European, if not fully global, basis.

Tutors and students are advised that extra material may (and probably will) be included in the examination paper itself. A proportion of the total marks available (as stated in the exam paper) will be allocated for taking this additional information into account when answering the questions set. This procedure has been adopted to test students' ability to think and react in the examination hall itself rather than simply relying on their pre-prepared material.

The following notice was sent to all June 1993 examinees in advance of the examination:

Important Notice to all Case Study Examinees

The copying out in the Examination Hall of answers supplied by external sources is expressly forbidden.

All Examiners have been instructed to mark down very severely, answers which are substantially the same as those received from other candidates.

Such answers are unlikely to contribute to a pass grade.

Answers must be candidates' own work during the examination.

2 *The June 1991 Examination Case*

Morton Packaging plc

Examination paper

DIPLOMA IN MARKETING

(12) Marketing Management (Analysis and Decision)

Tuesday 18th June 1991 **Time: 14.00 — 17.00**

3 hours duration

This paper requires you to make a practical and reasoned evaluation of the problems and opportunities you have identified from the previously circulated case material. From your analysis you are required to prepare a report in accordance with the situation below. Graphing sheets and ledger analysis paper are available from the invigilators, together with continuation sheets if required. These must be identified by your candidate number and fastened in the prescribed fashion within the back cover of your answer book for collection at the end of the examinations.
READ THE QUESTIONS CAREFULLY AND ANSWER THE ACTUAL QUESTIONS AS SPECIFIED CHECK THE MARK ALLOCATION TO QUESTIONS AND ALLOCATE YOUR TIME ACCORDINGLY. CANDIDATES MUST ATTEMPT ALL PARTS. CANDIDATES SHOULD ADOPT REPORT FORMAT. THOSE WHO DO NOT WILL BE PENALISED.

MARKETING MANAGEMENT
(Analysis & Decision)

Morton Packaging Plc

1 State three major marketing opportunities open to Morton Packaging in the single European market of 1993. For each opportunity examine critically how the company is positioned to exploit these opportunities in terms of its current strengths and weaknesses. **(30 Marks)**

2 For one of the marketing opportunities selected, outline the procedure to be adopted to achieve effective European market penetration over the next five years. State clearly the human resource and financial implications that would need to be considered. **(40 Marks)**

3 Using a time scale of five years, outline the steps to be taken and the internal procedures to be adopted to enable the company to achieve improved levels of marketing orientation. **(30 Marks)**

Morton Packaging Plc

CANDIDATES' BRIEF

In your capacity as the new Marketing Director of Morton Packaging you have a clear brief to report to the Managing Director on longer term marketing strategy.

There are also a number of shorter-term matters requiring your attention.

In putting forward your proposals it is necessary to be aware that other projects will be competing for scarce resources both at company and group level.

Following your initial assessment you will be required to report your findings at the time of the examination and be required to make clear recommendations for future action.

This case material is based upon experience with actual companies. Alterations in the information given and in the real data have been made to preserve confidence.

Copies may be obtained from the Chartered Institute of Marketing, Moor Hall, Cookham, Maidenhead, Berks. SL6 9QH

Morton Packaging Plc

Morton Packaging is now part of a large group (Calway International PLC) operating internationally, having expanded rapidly from relatively modest beginnings, as a small independent packaging company in the South of England. Profitable expansion can be traced back to the late 60's when this small packaging company with the name of Boxit acquired Japanese machinery. This enabled them to offer cardboard carton buying customers the service of plastic strapping to add greater strength, security and ease of handling during transit.

The original intention had been to move into packing services in addition to supplying packaging products. However, it was soon realised that a greater potential existed for supplying customers with the strapping and the applicators, since most customers already did their own packing and preferred to do so. Applicators enabled customers to apply plastic strapping around cartons and seal in a way that provided greater security and ease of handling.

Once this potential was realised, Boxit negotiated sole UK rights with the Japanese suppliers, both for the machinery to produce the plastic strapping and for the much smaller hand-held applicators. Boxit also recruited Sales Engineers capable of identifying potential users and uses of this new packaging concept.

Within a few years as more and more industries were added to their client base, Boxit expanded to many times its previous turnover and in 1974 was taken over by a Group renowned for its technical innovation and leadership. In the meantime Boxit had withdrawn from the highly competitive market of cardboard cartons in order to concentrate on strapping, applicators and associated products.

On taking over Boxit the Group (Calway International) re-named it as Morton Packaging and immediately found a new application for Morton's strapping process in its building division when, for the first time, the potential for more easily handling large quantities of housebricks by this method was discovered.

Other divisions within the Calway International Group including the ceramics division and the printing division, were soon trading with this new acquisition.

The Group's tradition of technical innovation and service was maintained with Morton Packaging who added other related products such as adhesive tapes and stretchwrap to their portfolio, to maintain effective growth.

Within the last few years, Morton Packaging have devoted R&D resources to the idea of enhancing the appearance of their strapping and tapes in recognition of the increasing importance of corporate identity to many of their client companies as well as to Morton Packaging itself and the Group. Morton Packaging have, as a result of this initiative, secured a lead in the "own label" ribbon and bows market sector but this only accounts for about 5 per cent of total company turnover at present. Although both the Group and Morton Packaging were looking financially sound on the accounts for 1990/91, the Group's Consultants were counselling caution and were particularly concerned about the competition for Morton Packaging escalating considerably from 1992 as a result of the European "free market" changes. They feel that whilst the Group's technological supremacy mission has served them well to date, too little emphasis has been placed on marketing. Morton Packaging therefore appointed Mike Watson, as their first Marketing Director (a qualified person with industrial experience) who was placed in post in April 1991.

The fastest growing sector of the business is what Morton Packaging refers to as "Easy Access Systems" containing two primary products. The first of these the company calls "Ziptape". This is a pressure-sensitive self adhesive tear-tape applied to cardboard which is used to manufacture cartons for foodstuffs, detergents, canned and bottled products and many other products. Such cartons can be neatly split into shelf merchandisers in supermarkets without fear of damaging the goods inside as may be the case if a sharp tool was to be used to cut the carton. Standard tape widths are from 3mm to 10mm, in three thicknesses and with different breaking strengths to suit different types of case or carton. "Ziptape" has been on the market for well over twenty years.

The second product in the "Easy Access System" sector of the business is a more recent product the company calls "Tearaway". "Tearaway" is a pressure-sensitive, self adhesive, easy opening tear-strip for overwrapped packaging. Morton Packaging claims that it outperforms most conventional tear strips in consumer appeal, versatility and cost-effectiveness. Promotional offers, statutory information and other messages can be printed onto Tearaway in any language and it is available in a wide range of colours, in widths from 2mm to 6mm. The minimum tape width for a printed design is 3mm which is narrower than is the case for most other conventional tear-tapes. Other consumer benefits claimed as a result of the ease-of-use in opening packages are "no spillage, no wastage, no resorting to scissors, knives, teeth or finger nails" which therefore contributes to brand loyalty amongst consumers. In conjunction with today's packaging films and end-seals, Tearaway also provides tamper evidence, assuring consumers of security of pack contents and hygiene standards.

As with the strapping system, applicators for Ziptape form part of the Company's product range but account for very little of the turnover — about one per cent. It is possible however, that one major contract for a large manufacturer of consumer goods might account for up to £100,000 of machines, but this would be a one-off purchase at the beginning of a long term arrangement.

Calway International has recently been through a major divestment programme, shedding businesses that represented approximately 50% of the 1990 turnover, whilst retaining the most profitable businesses in the group.

This has provided a reserve of cash, ready to support the strong growth of the continuing businesses with appropriate acquisitions where such acquisitions can be fully justified. Indeed, arrangements were about to be finalised for the purchase by Morton Packaging of a nearby strapping manufacturer for a sum approaching £7.0 million. The decision whether or not to go ahead with the purchase of Morton Packaging's West German distributor, Alexis Brauns of Frankfurt has yet to be taken.

The Group have also allocated £2m for investment for developing Morton Packaging in 1992 with further funding to follow subject to profitability.

The possible takeover of Brauns was a suggestion that had recently been put to Morton Packaging's Managing Director Chris Burgage, prompted by two factors. Firstly the forthcoming Single European Market provided a catalyst for the company, to see the European customers as an extension of its "home" market rather than as "foreign" customers.

The second factor was more opportunistic. Brauns had been Morton Packaging's German distributor since 1972 and relied on them for more than

70% of its turnover. Brauns' Sales Director, who was already semi-retired had expressed a willingness to provide introductions to his key customer contacts for Morton Packaging if they were to take over the business but showed some reluctance to do so for Brauns' current owners. Morton Packaging's sales had already taken a dip in Germany in 1989/90, although they had picked up again in 1990/91 and have risen again very substantially in the last few months. Tearaway sales accounted for over 40% of the 1990/91 turnover. About 45% of Tearaway sales in Germany in 1988/89 were to a subsidiary of a major cigarette manufacturer which also purchased the product in the UK, Belgium, Holland, Africa and potentially in the USA (overall, 20% of total company revenue came from four cigarette manufacturers).

Litigation was always a possibility when getting involved in buying out an agent but, then again, if Morton Packaging did not take Brauns over, the market was sufficiently vulnerable to need alternative channels to be created at some extra cost anyway. The decision in either case seemed likely to be rather fraught with difficulties.

Exports represented approximately 16% of Morton Packaging's revenue in the financial year ending 31 March 1991. Almost all of these exports came from the "Easy Access Systems" sector of the business and 53% of exports went to European Community countries. In the 1991/92 financial year an estimated £8.75 million from an expected revenue of £43 million would be exported. Whereas in Germany the distributor, Brauns, who had originally handled Ziptape (which is primarily sold into the cardboard industry) took easily to selling Tearaway into a very different market, the French distributor for Ziptape had not responded well to the new product. It seemed that it was probably too committed to the cardboard industry and not easily able to make the transition to new and different sales of Tearaway. This agent's main supplier, however, was a German manufacturer of packaging film for whom it expended perhaps a disproportionate share of its time and effort. Consequently sales of Tearaway in France were not very buoyant.

On the other hand it may have been just the difficult market situation in France which prevented major successes for Tearaway there. The French tobacco industry was controlled by a state monopoly which insisted on using one of Morton Packaging's competitors and the agent had no leverage to make the necessary breakthrough. It was clear that new market potential was needed to provide the main thrust for development in France.

A recent success for the German distributor had been to persuade a biscuit manufacturer to use Tearaway in its packaging, thus providing a real benefit to the consumer who was then able to more easily access the pack's contents without damaging them. In the UK, too, a supermarket chain had been persuaded of the benefits of using the Tearaway opening system on a number of its own-label products. The head office of this supermarket had indicated that they would be prepared to act as a "product champion" for Morton Packaging when dealing with its fast moving consumer goods (FMCG) suppliers over their future packaging decisions.

The potential for Tearaway in the FMCG market seemed, on the face of it, to be limitless given the consumer benefits available with its use. Quite a degree of persuasion seemed to be needed, plus substantial technical expertise but the key problem lay in identifying target companies.

As Mike Watson pointed out to his MD, Chris Burgage recently in an internal memorandum "The international nature of the FMCG business with its international brands, demands a professional and integrated supplier response from Morton Packaging."

To date, sales literature has been the responsibility of the Home and Export Sales Managers who have commissioned their needs through the Sales Office Manager who in turn works through a full-service Advertising Agency.

Morton Packaging have previously adopted a strong push policy which has worked extremely well in their industry to industry marketing role.

Morton Packaging also use exhibitions in the home market, the selection of which has largely been the province of the R&D Director in discussion with the Home Sales Manager.

Inserts of literature in trade magazines occur intermittently. From time to time editorial coverage has been received in technological journals of innovative developments by the company. The total size of the sales force has varied from 15 to 20 people in the last three years.

Individual Sales Engineers specialise in particular industries and operate nationally. They work on a salary plus expenses basis, individually negotiated. The salesforce are supported by a small "systems" project team drawn from R&D and Production, who assist customers in the installation, changeover and start- up phases.

Whilst the vast majority of business is conducted directly by direct delivery to customer companies, Morton Packaging have recently met orders from a small number of industrial and consumer goods distributors.

Selling costs amount to approximately 2 1/2 per cent of turnover with R&D accounting for a further 2 1/2 per cent. Marketing costs other than for selling, currently account for less than 1 per cent of turnover.

Morton Packaging have established market leadership with Tearaway and are particularly strong in the cigarette manufacturers' segment.

Buying behaviour varies considerably according to the type of product and market segment served. Plain cardboard cartons or "outers" segments tend to be dominated by paper and board manufacturers whose packaging interests negotiate contracts with user companies. This is in order to keep prices down by enabling the carton manufacturer to produce in bulk say a year's supply where the carton is of a non-standard size or composition. Sometimes the carton manufacturer will keep stock on call for the user company. Whilst the situation seems on the face of it to be a straight re-buy, in practice many Buyers seek competitive tenders on an annual basis and this market segment is highly competitive. Morton Packaging do not operate in this sector.

With regard to plastic strapping to add strength, security and ease of handling to cardboard outers the Production Manager (or sometimes the Distribution Manager) plays a more dominant role in the buying decision. Influencers include Union Safety Officers and Marketing personnel.

Product packaging on most goods (as opposed to carton outers) carries illustration and wording since in a self-service retail environment, packaging becomes "the silent salesman" and is crucial in the effort to gain favourable attention from the shopper. For this reason the Marketing Manager tends to be the decision taker and works closely with a full-service advertising agency or a design specialist on the concept and formulation of the packaging. Legal considerations and graphics play an increasingly important role in the decision process. Tags, labels, ties and now ribbons/tapes can add value to the product packaging, in particular market segments, as can ease of opening and re-closing devices.

In the world of packing and packaging, it is expected that aspects of service will become increasingly important as more large manufacturers adopt Total Quality Management, 'Just in time' policies and Relationship Marketing philosophies.

Appendix 1

Extracts from Calway International Plc's Annual Report & Statement 1991

"1990/91 has been a year of sweeping change for us. The Group has sold businesses which represented a considerable proportion of the 1990 turnover, substantially expanded its Building Products Division, moved its head office and embarked on many new projects."

Key Figures

	1991	1990
Turnover	£1289m	£1436m
Operating Profit	£140m	£143m
Profit before Taxation	£134m	£130m
Earnings per Share	33.5p	33.0p
Dividends per Ordinary Share – Paid and Proposed	16.0p	14.4p
Operating Margin	10.8%	9.9%
Debt to Equity	3.1%	30.5%

The net cash received from the disposals and acquisitions amounted to £168m and at 31 March 1991 net debt had been reduced to 3.1% of equity compared with 30.5% at the previous year's end.

Emphasis on Quality

An even greater emphasis is now being placed on the Total Quality Concept throughout the Group, including the introduction of new designs, new manufacturing and distribution systems and new management training and development programmes. The aim is to improve the quality of the business and therefore earnings, both from organic growth and from acquisitions. A series of customer care courses has been arranged for all personnel to take place in the 1991/92 financial year.

Appendix 2

Consolidated Balance Sheet as at 31 March 1991

	1991 (£1,000's)	1990 (£1,000's)
Fixed Assets		
Tangible Assets	216,346	301,092
Investments	27,694	19,926
	244,040	321,018
Current Assets		
Stocks	166,836	180,274
Debtors	191,428	271,124
Cash at Bank & in Hand	16,070	13,168
	374,334	464,476
Creditors (short-term) Amounts falling due within 1 year:		
Borrowings	6,570	5,768
Other	222,166	365,158
	228,736	370,926
Net Current Assets	145,598	93,640
Total Assets Less Current Liabilities	389,638	414,658
Creditors (long-term) Amounts falling due after more than 1 year:		
Borrowings	20,376	99,842
Other	2,292	4,816
Provisions for Liabilities and Charges:	10,510	6,482
	356,460	303,518
Capital and Reserves:		
Shareholders' funds	352,458	295,602
Minority interests	4,002	7,916
	356,460	303,518

Appendix 3

Group Turnover and Operating Profit

	1991 (£1,000's) Operating Turnover	1991 (£1,000's) Profit	1990 (£1,000's) Operating Turnover	1990 (£1,000's) Profit
By Class of Business:				
Building Products	296,702	35,128	213,090	21,344
Ceramics	290,510	43,656	252,532	38,746
Print & Packaging *	190,308	30,416	175,542	31,250
Property		27,706		17,674
Other Interests	50,918	4,038	47,040	864
Head Office		(8,282)		(7,670)
Associates Interest		(4,708)		(2,598)
Continuing Businesses	828,438	127,954	688,204	99,610
Discontinued Businesses	460,982	11,772	748,028	43,286
By Geographic Market				
European Community	1,145,286	116,422	1,305,060	126,626
Africa	41,600	9,390	40,986	6,338
Asia	13,156	2,736	–	574
Australasia	55,472	8,068	37,636	4,734
North America	33,906	3,110	52,550	4,624
	1,289,420	139,726	1,436,232	142,896

NOTE:

In order to present a more meaningful relationship between divisional turnover and operating profit, in the above analysis by class of business the Group's share of associate company turnover and profit before interest has been included within the relevant divisions, and the Groups' share of interest paid by those associate companies has been disclosed separately. The comparative figures for 1990 have been restated on the same basis.

* Morton Packaging contributed approximately 20% of the turnover and 30% of the operating profit for this class of business in 1991.

Appendix 4
Sheet 1 of 2

Tearway and Competitive Products

1) Tear Tape Systems

There are six types of tear tape systems and these are listed below:

- i) Hot Melt Adhesive
- ii) Heat Sealing
- iii) Hot Wax
- iv) Solvent
- v) G.D. Cross-Cut System
- vi) Pressure Sensitive Adhesive

i) Hot Melt Adhesive

Tear tape is fed under a temperature controlled heater. The heat partly melts the hot-melt coating. A guide roller presses the tear tape to the wrapping film.

ii) Heat Sealing

The sealants of the tear tape and of the wrapping material must be compatible.

A precision adjusted, temperature controlled heating shoe simultaneously melts the sealing layers of the wrapping material, thus effecting a strong bond. The length of the heated surface has to be matched to take-off speed of the wrapping material.

iii) Hot Wax

There are two ways of applying with wax:

- a) The wax is applied to the tear tape
- b) The wax is applied to the wrapping film

The tear tape and wrapping film are then joined together, sometimes with further heating subsequent to joining.

iv) Applying With Solvent

This involves the use of a lacquer-coated tear tape. Using an appropriate solvent, even dissimilar coatings can be bonded together.

Appendix 4
Sheet 2 of 2

The tear tape is fed to the packaging material over a felt wick soaked with solvent. Under slight pressure, the partly dissolved coating now combines with the overwrap coating. To accelerate the process, the wrapping material, with the tear tape already adhering to it, is passed along a heating unit so that excess solvent can evaporate more rapidly.

v) G.D. Cross-Cut System

The G.D. packing systems can be equipped with a patented device for the application of tear tape taken from a large reel, the width of which is equal to the cut-off length of the tear tape. This system does allow considerable materials savings but is only suitable for clear (or clear with coloured tabs) tear tapes. This tear tape would generally be applied using the hot wax system.

vi) Pressure Sensitive Self Adhesive

The adhesive coating is on one side of the tear tape itself. The tear tape is joined directly to the wrapping material under tension.

Competitor Costs

All competitors to Morton Packaging's pressure sensitive adhesive system are actually cheaper. If Morton Packaging's system is represented as an index cost of 100 the index of a heat sensitive product would be about 75, that of a wax product about 50 and a G.D. Cross-Cut product about 30. The application of tear tape is however a very small proportion of the cost of any packaging, which in turn is only a small part of the overall cost of a product. Morton Packaging applicators have the considerable advantage of being able to handle much longer runs of tape than their competitors.

To change to using Morton Packaging's Tearaway would also cost a customer around £6000 per production line for a "dispensing kit".

Tear Tape Suppliers

World wide there are many alternative suppliers of tear tape systems but few suppliers of self adhesive tapes.

Appendix 5
Sheet 1 of 2

Advantages of Tearaway

The following advantages of Tearaway are as those listed below by a major user:

1) It is easy to apply due to it being self-adhesive.
2) There is no need for hot wax, solvent or heating units, which means that there are better working conditions.
3) The set up time is reduced drastically owing to not having to wait for wax baths to heat up.
4) The packing line efficiency is increased by 2% when conversion to Tearaway takes place.
5) Bobbin changes are reduced from six times per shift to less than one when jumbo reels are introduced.
6) Production time lost due to web-breaks is eliminated, as previously tear tape was of BOPP not MOPP.*
7) The pack appearance is improved and unsightly wax marks eliminated.
8) Better consumer acceptance is achieved through a tear tape which works every time.
9) 100% adhesion to the film, leading to no jams in the cutting head.
10) Due to lengths available in jumbo reels, there are fewer stoppages resulting in fewer consequential problems.
11) The film used in Tearaway is MOPP which has a lower extension than BOPP, resulting in less herringboning on the finished pack.
12) The reels are supplied without flanges which means that no trapping and hence snapping of tear tape occurs.
13) Tearaway is less susceptible to claimant influence than ordinary tear tapes, especially cellulose.
14) As Tearaway is self adhesive, there is no need for solvent, wax or heat. Hence there is no odour and risk of splashes or burns.
15) As no wax is required, there is no need for topping up of wax baths or maintenance of wax pots, heaters and equipment located below the pot.

* Biaxially orientated polypropylene & monoaxially-orientated polypropylene

Appendix 5
Sheet 2 of 2

16) Due to Tearaway being self adhesive, there is no side ooze of adhesive onto the packet.

17) The adhesive nature of Tearaway means that bond retention is good under extreme conditions.

18) Longer lengths are available in self adhesive tapes than in ordinary tear tape.

19) The nature of the tear tape allows for fewer reject packets which saves time and costs.

20) Usage of Tearaway has resulted in reduced wrapping film wastage.

21) Metallised Tearaway does not have the tendency to curl of the ordinary metallic tear tape.

22) Compared with ordinary tear tape, there are far fewer quality rejects of tear tape reels.

23) Usage of large reels of Tearaway cost wise, is much more economical than the cross-cut G.D. system with respect to spares — a cost of £186,000pa had been quoted by a G.D. supplier for maintenance of this system compared with a fairly low total spares cost for Tearaway applicators.

Patent

The patent for Morton Packaging's Tearaway is based on the "novelty" of the means of applying the product onto a moving web of film and the sensing mechanism which enables the correct tension and speed to be maintained. Thus a patent infringement would occur if a customer were to use Morton Packaging's applicator with a competitor's tape.

Tear Tape Applicators

In order to dispense large reels of Tearaway, it is necessary to utilise a motorised applicator.

The applicator allows for:

1) Smooth dispensing of tear tape on high speed wrappers

2) Precise tension control and adjustment

3) Correct application of thin/narrow Tearaway

Appendix 6

Disadvantages of Tearaway

There are a few complaints of Tearaway — Morton Packaging's self adhesive tear tape. These are listed in a decreasing order of occurrence.

1) Faulty Winds

This problem shows itself in a variety of ways:

a) Tear tape snapping

This can occur due to a variety of reasons.

b) Lost ends

This occurs if the tape snaps or is cut, and the end cannot always be found, or if the tag is missing.

c) Reversal of tear tape

This generally occurs due to the tape twist (turnover) during winding. The problem does not usually become apparent until the tape is being unwound.

2) Build-up of Adhesive on rollers

This problem occurs upon unwinding of the tape. As the tape passes over the rollers, it traverses them. When the tape reaches the rims of the rollers it is believed that any excess adhesive on the edge of the tape is deposited by the rim. This adhesive deposit gradually builds up — eventually causing the tape to stick to the roller. This problem is easily remedied by regular cleaning of the rollers, during the maintenance programmes.

3) Missing Adhesive on Tear Tape

Occasionally a complaint arises due to lack of adhesive on parts of the tape. This can occur during the coating process at the edge of a roll film, when the reservoir of adhesive runs low, the centre of the reservoir only is filled, leaving the edges adhesive-free. This phenomenon only occurs over a short length of film.

Appendix 7
Sheet 1 of 2

Some Competitors of Morton Packaging

2 i) Wurstenbode

Wurstenbode are owned by Schmidt and are based in Germany. The bulk of their business is taken up by selling film to the packaging industry. They started by selling cellulose film but, due to changing trends, have turned over to orientated polypropylene.

2 ii) Hockenbrot

Hockenbrot are owned by Weiss. They have an office in the UK but their head office is in Germany.

Again, the bulk of the business has been films for a variety of packaging applications.

2 iii) Abtaff

Abtaff, based in Holland, manufacture a wide variety of products, e.g. single and double-sided adhesive tapes; coloured and transparent tape; reinforced tape; tearstrips and carton sealing machines.

They supply tear tapes in adhesive and non-adhesive forms.

2 iv) Grunner

Grunner is based in West Germany. Their main concern has been in films, but they have diversified into self-adhesive tapes and tear tapes.

2 v) Saunders

This company is an American corporation.

The tear tape system is predominantly hot melt, but can be applied by a hot wax method. The textile wound bobbins are available in 30,000 metre lengths.

2 vi) ABC

ABC is an American corporation. The company advertises extensively and is mostly concerned with tear tapes and packaging tapes.

ABC offers a wide range of tear tapes, including self-adhesive tear tapes under the ABC Tape trade name. They compete on Ziptape i.e. heavier duty segment.

Appendix 7
Sheet 2 of 2

2 vii) Champion Tape

Champion Tape is part of the Eiko Corporation of America. The tear tape that is offered is made of polyester film with a hot melt coating. It is sold under the trade name of Champion Tear Tape and is offered in a variety of designs.

2 vii) Lewis Ltd

This company is part of the Sabuto Group and is based in London, England. It offers a wide range of tear tapes in cellulose, polypropylene and polyester. The tear tapes would be applied by hot wax application.

2 ix) Ply Packings Ltd

Ply Packings Ltd is based in Manchester, England. It is owned 51% by Browns and 49% by Tough Timbers Ltd. Browns is, in turn, a wholly owned subsidiary of a Group. It only offers uncoated tear tape.

2 x) Pulton Tape Industries

Is a privately owned company with offices in Canada, and the USA.

The company was established in 1978.

The pressure sensitive tape supplied by PT Industries is based on a polyester film (probably biaxially orientated).

Pulton Tape have full facilities for coating, printing, slitting and winding. They supply both self-adhesive and ordinary tear tapes.

Appendix 8

Brauns

Braun's have been a distributor for Morton Packaging since 1972.

Sales of Ziptape and Tearaway to Brauns have been as shown below:

Year	Ziptape (£1,000's)	Tearaway (£1,000's)
1985/86	516.6	—
1986/87	610.0	—
1987/88	709.8	129.5
1988/89	733.6	274.0
1989/90	588.8	346.2
1990/91	623.8	*478.2

* approx 1/3 tobacco, 2/3 non-tobacco

The drop in sales in 89/90 coincided with a change of ownership.

Braun's also act as agents for Morton Packaging in Switzerland and Austria (turnover not shown above).

Ziptape Market Shares; Germany

Ziptape currently accounts for around 20% of the market in Germany. The leading competitor accounts for nearly 40% of the market and there are two other important suppliers.

Current Sales Staff

By acquiring Brauns, Morton Packaging would gain 6 sales staff and the office, all for a purchase price expected to be less than £180,000.

Appendix 9

Morton Packaging Organisation

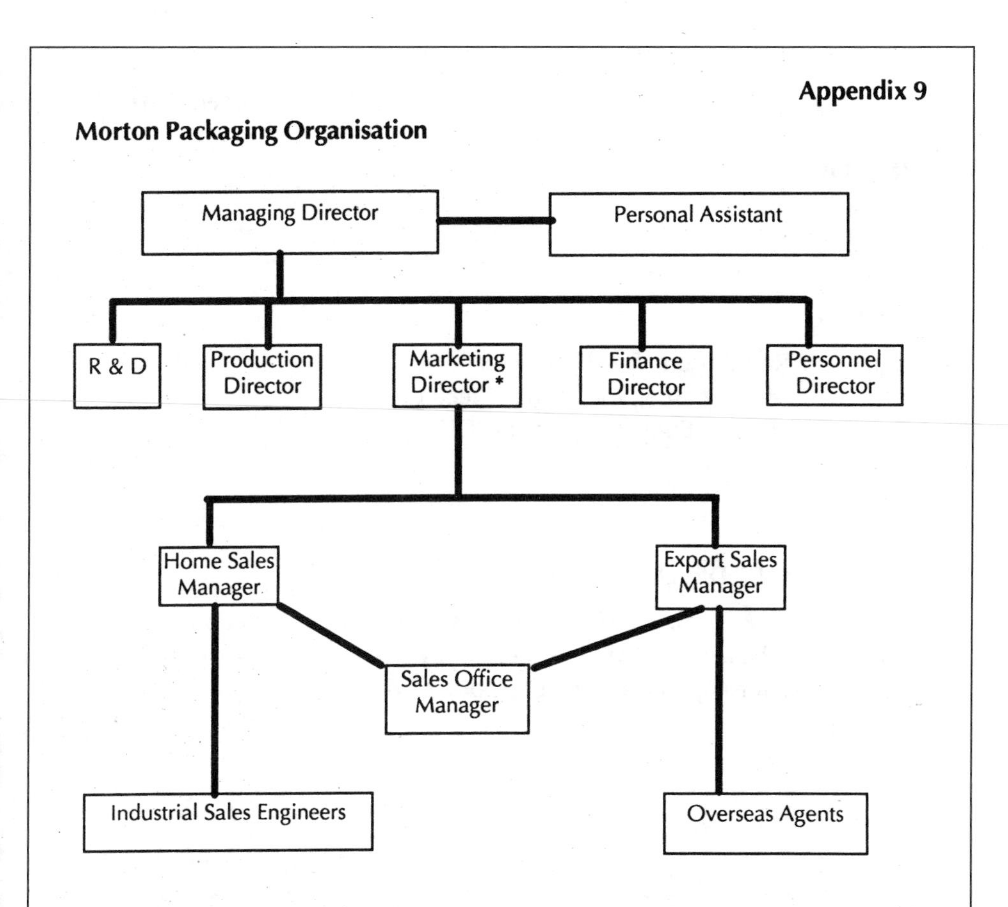

NB The three Sales Managers previously reported to a Commercial Manager who has now retired.

* New post with effect from 5.4.91. The new Marketing Director is Michael Watson B.Sc. M.CIM, with a degree in mechanical engineering and fluency in German and French, plus a little Spanish. His previous position was European Development Manager for a UK machine tool company.

Appendix 10

Marketing

MEMO

From: Rad Wilson, R & D Director 11 June 91
To: Mike Watson, Marketing Director
cc Chris Burgage, Managing Director

NEW PRODUCT DEVELOPMENTS

A number of interesting new developments are nearing completion and I think it might be a good idea if we met shortly to talk over which of these look most promising from a marketing point of view.

Appendix 11

MEMO

To: Marketing Director 3 June 91

From: Home Sales Manager

MARKETING PRESENTATIONS

Our Sales Engineers have reported several instances recently where prospective customers (particularly those in consumer goods) are asking for own label and/or exclusive deals.

We have also received a request from Fast Moving Consumables Ltd for a formal marketing presentation early next month.

Could we please meet urgently with regard to these issues.

Appendix 12

MEMO

From: Managing Director 10 June 91

To: Export Sales Manager
cc Marketing Director

EUROPE AND 1992

We have attended many seminars organised by the Department of Trade and Industry (UK) etc and received many reports, yet we appear to have achieved very little in the way of real progress on this issue.

Can you please report to the Marketing Director with an action schedule within the next 4 weeks.

Appendix 13

MEMO

From: Chris Burgage 10 June 1991

To: Mike Watson

MARKETING PLANNING

Now that you have settled in, I would like to hear from you no later than 31 July regarding the major tasks for which your post was designed and which we discussed during our various selection interviews.

We will also need to discuss resources and your proposals should clearly indicate these.

Should you wish to submit anything else for consideration by the forthcoming Board meeting please let me know.

Appendix 14

Morton Packaging's Product Range

1 Stretchwrap and associated machinery
2 Strapping and associated machinery
3 Ribbons and bows
4 Self adhesive tapes
 4.1 Ziptape
 4.2 Tearaway
 4.3 Others
5 Applicators
 5.1 Hand-held
 5.2 Semi automatic
 5.3 Fully automatic

Pricing is currently on a cost-plus basis. The Group's commitment to technological advantage dictates a substantial mark up on direct costs.

Examiners' report

General comments

With yet a further surge in the number sitting this Examination, some decline in overall standards was perhaps to be expected.

Despite all the strictures given in these reports, candidates' briefs and tutors guidance notes over the years, examinees are still making the same three basic mistakes:

(i) Poor time management
(ii) Failure to answer the questions set
(iii) Lack of report format.

In response to course tutors' requests and without wishing to appear over-dogmatic, the following constructive advice is offered:

(i) Poor time management

This is not simply a matter of failing to allocate time to each question in the proportion indicated on the examination paper. Candidates are also failing to apportion time to different parts of a question in a logical and professional way. Such strong signals of a lack of planning ability are hardly conducive to granting a pass on a paper testing marketing management. Examinees are strongly recommended to plan the structure of all their answers before starting to write. At least 20 minutes' thinking and planning time is needed and a further 10 minutes for thoroughly checking and correcting each answer. Thus a 3-question paper with 30, 40 and 30 marks should receive 180 less 30 = 150 minutes of actual writing time in the proportions 45, 60 and 45 minutes. If Question 2 was concerned with environmental factors and this candidate was using the PEST approach then about 15 minutes writing on each of the four parts would be appropriate. If a sub-structure of 3 items per part was adopted then about 5 minutes writing on each item would apply. Better still to maintain a spatial as well as a temporal control so that if it takes a candidate 10 minutes to write a page legibly, then 6 pages for the complete answer – 1.5 pages per part and 0.5 page per item would apply.

(ii) Failure to answer the questions set

A disturbing amount of candidates just do not answer the questions and thus cannot possibly be passed. Some examinees actually start their answers with 'Before answering the question set I would just like to . . .' thereby telling the examiner that what follows is irrelevant. Many candidates do not start receiving marks until they have written 2 or 3 pages which is when they get down to actually answering the question set.

Lengthy introductions and summaries (which merely repeat points made earlier and cannot therefore receive further marks) are inappropriate in a paper of this level.

Unfortunately a growing number of candidates are simply copying out pre-prepared answers irrespective of their relevance to the question asked. Such practices are clearly doomed to failure.

(iii) Lack of report format

A high proportion of candidates appear to have no idea of what constitutes report format and submit over-wordy, rambling essays without headings or structures leaving the examiner to determine what parts apply to which aspects of the question.

Such an approach simply confirms a lack of marketing management ability.

Taking the earlier example of a question on environmental factors, report format would involve a structure involving main and sub-headings in the manner indicated below:

1 **Political factors**
  1.1 Government policies ....
  1.2 Sub-heading ....
  1.3 Sub-heading ....
2 **Main heading**
  2.1 Sub-heading ....
  2.2 Sub-heading ....
  2.3 Sub-heading ....

The structure might continue through 4 main headings each with 3 sub-headings (to 4.3.). The dotted lines above indicate explanations amounting to about half a page each.

While mere listings are not acceptable in a paper of this standard, explanations should be abbreviated to a business report mode. For example instead of writing:

'My first choice would be the German market and within this the tobacco industry and I would start with a full evaluation of the market followed by research into buying behaviour and the marketing mix. Conditional upon the results of this evaluation and research being satisfactory I would then buy Brauns. The resource implications of the evaluation of the market and the subsequent research would be who is going to do this and at what cost. Buying Brauns would also involve a capital cost and the use of management time . . . .'

(Total = 90 words, Time to write = 5 minutes)

The answer might be more appropriately expressed as:

1 **Choice Number 1 = Germany**
  Subsegment = tobacco industry
  1.1 Procedures
    (a) Evaluate market

(b) Research buying behaviour and required marketing mix
(c) Buy Brauns subject to (a) and (b) above
1.2 Resource implications
(a) Staff time and costs (Est £2K)
(b) Brief MR agency, staff time and costs (Est £6K)
(c) Capital cost (£180K), management time (Est £5K)
(Total = c. 40 words, Time to write = 3 minutes)

Report format is clearer, quicker and conveys more information than the essay style. Not only is it more efficient from the writer's standpoint, but it also saves the more expensive time of senior management readers. More points can be also made in the time saved, so as to gain higher marks.

Candidates need only write one lead page indicating to whom the report is addressed, from whom it emanates, date and contents (main headings only). There is no need to start each question off with a lead page or indeed to detail not only the sub-headings but the page numbers applying.

Finally candidates are reminded that only material submitted on official CIM examination script papers (or charts on graph paper supplied by the invigilator) can be marked and that examination question numbers need to be entered on script covers as instructed.

Question 1

The major problem on this question arose from candidates selecting opportunities which were vague or unfocused such as 'to increase sales' with no reference to specific countries, products, segments or which overlapped such as '(1) to penetrate the German market' and '(2) to purchase Brauns'. Such poor choices caused difficulties in answering the second part of the question. Some answers gave opportunities for countries outside the European market.

Many examinees submitted general pre-prepared SWOT analyses rather than specific strengths and weaknesses for each opportunity. Quite a large number of candidates justified their choice of opportunities rather than examining them critically against weaknesses as well as strengths.

Since it is standard practice to pre-prepare a SWOT analysis, it is clear that far too many candidates failed to think this through selectively in the examination room itself and relied on straight regurgitation rather than understanding and manipulating their analyses as required.

Question 2

The major cause of failure on this question was the submission of general pre-prepared marketing plans without reference to one of the marketing opportunities evaluated in Question 1.

Candidates were generally stronger on the outline procedural plan than they were on human and particularly financial resource implications (despite strong signals that this area will be increasingly tested in this examination paper). On this latter point, it is still worrying that many aspiring marketing managers appear to be totally unable or unwilling to discuss the financial aspects of their marketing decisions. In some cases those that did simply stated for example that 'it would cost a lot of money' or gave an overall estimate of costs seemingly plucked out of the air. At the other extreme a few candidates simply wrote down every financial ratio they could think of and/or submitted pre-prepared cashflow statements and balance sheets without reference to the procedural plan outlined.

Many candidates did not give any indication of time scales for implementation, nor details of responsibilities, staffing etc.

As the major question on the paper there was a lot to cover but few adopted the time saving device of a chart format.

Question 3

The answers to this question often distinguished the pass from the fail candidate. It had been expected that most examinees would have relished this question but a surprisingly large proportion just did not understand the term 'marketing orientation' and of those that did, many were unaware of how to achieve it. This understanding is basic for marketing management to be effective and the subject is well documented in the literature. Clearly candidates are failing to do adequate reading. Many candidates wrongly interpreted the question as an extension to Question 2 and wrote out a pre-prepared marketing plan which differed little from that already advanced.

The good candidates had recognised that organisational change was needed in Morton Packaging in order to exploit new marketing opportunities in Europe. They also understood that cultural change and company wide training was required in order to create a corporate environment where a true marketing orientation could flourish.

Regrettably, relatively few candidates adequately scheduled their proposals over a five year period and even fewer indicated appropriate budgets and/or control mechanisms.

3 *The December 1991 Examination Case*

Brewsters Ltd

Examination paper

Diploma in Marketing

(12) Marketing Management (Analysis & Decision)

Tuesday 10th December 1991 **Time: 14.00-17.00**
3 hours duration

This paper requires you to make a practical and reasoned evaluation of the problems and opportunities you have identified from the previously circulated case material. From your analysis you are required to prepare a report in accordance with the situation below. Graphing sheets and ledger analysis paper are available from the invigilators, together with continuation sheets if required. These must be identified by your candidate number and fastened in the prescribed fashion with the back cover of your answer book for collection at the end of the examinations.

READ THE QUESTIONS CAREFULLY AND ANSWER THE ACTUAL QUESTIONS AS SPECIFIED. CHECK THE MARK ALLOCATION TO QUESTIONS AND ALLOCATE YOUR TIME ACCORDINGLY. CANDIDATES MUST ATTEMPT ALL PARTS. CANDIDATES SHOULD ADOPT REPORT FORMAT, THOSE WHO DO NOT WILL BE PENALISED. CANDIDATES WHO SUBMIT IDENTICAL ANSWERS TO THOSE OF OTHER CANDIDATES IN A GROUP, WILL BE PENALISED.

Market Analysis

(Analysis & Decision)

Brewsters Limited

1. Specify and justify the research needed to explore potential markets and to determine effective methods of market entry in order for Brewsters Limited to adopt an improved strategic marketing position in Europe.

(30 marks)

2. Detail and schedule the specific actions required to establish the marketing and financial viability of the launch of Brewsters' conceptual new branded products aimed at the wider European market.

(40 marks)

3. Taking into account changes in the marketing environment, state clearly the steps needed to achieve a more professional selling and sales management strategy for the UK market.

(30 marks)

Brewsters Ltd

Candidates' Brief

In your capacity as David Downing the Marketing Director of Brewsters Ltd for the past six years, you have a clear brief to develop longer term marketing strategy in a wider European context.

A number of external uncontrollable factors as described in the case are affecting the brewing industry sufficiently for you to need to re-think your strategic marketing plans.

In putting forward your proposals it is necessary to be aware that other projects will be competing for scarce resources both at company and group level.

Following your initial assessment you will be required to make clear recommendations for future action.

This case material is based upon experience with actual companies. Alterations in the information given and in the real data have been made to preserve confidence. Candidates are strictly instructed not to contact companies in this industry.

Copies may be obtained from the Chartered Institute of Marketing, Moor Hall, Cookham, Maidenhead, Berks, SL6 9QH.

Brewsters Ltd

Brewsters Ltd represents the beer brewing interests of a large Group (Leighlow Leisure plc).

The Leighlow Group describes itself as a UK company with businesses involved in the production and distribution of drinks; the ownership and franchising of pubs, hotels and restaurants; the manufacture, distribution and servicing of amusement machines and the operation of a diverse range of leisure facilities.

Its mission is one of creating value for shareholders, customers and employees by supplying products and services of high quality in all its businesses. It also conducts its operations with a high regard for the interests of the general public and the environment.

Like most large brewers, Brewsters Ltd own the freehold of several thousand pubs and hotels but is being obliged by the Monopolies and Mergers Commission (MMC) to dispose of a proportion of these.

About a third of all UK pubs are known as "tied" houses because they are managed by brewery staff or independently tenanted but obliged to sell the brewers brands - See Appendix 1. However, in 1988 the Office of Fair Trading in the UK asked the MMC to investigate the brewing industry on the grounds that consumer choice was being unfairly restricted by this system and prices were unnecessarily high. At that time tenanted pubs made up about 33,000 of the 82,000 pubs and bars in the UK. Tenants pay a rent to the brewer on a leasehold arrangement and take a margin on all goods and services sold including drinks, food and takings from pool tables, fruit machines, juke boxes etc. Whilst rents were charged below commercial rates tenants were reasonably happy with this arrangement but in recent years brewers were also charging tenants up to 40% more for a barrel of beer than some licencees in the "free" trade, (those owning their own pubs and bars and therefore not tied to a brewery) taking advantage of the captive market.

The 1973 Fair Trading Act defines monopoly in two ways. A "scale monopoly" is where a company takes 25% or more of any market. However, the largest brewer claimed only 21%. What the MMC examined therefore was the possibility of a "complex monopoly" which exists where companies which together command 25% or more or a market act in a way which prevents, restricts or destroys competition.

In 1989 the MMC declared its findings that a complex monopoly existed and made the following recommendations:

- No brewer to own more than 2000 on-licenced premises including pubs and restaurants.
- Tied tenants to be allowed to sell "guest" draught beers and beers brewed by companies other than the pub's owners.

- Tied tenants also to be free to buy low alcohol beers, wines, spirits, cider and soft drinks from the most competitive suppliers.
- No new loan ties, which oblige owners of so-called "free houses" to sell only one brewer's products. (It was common for brewers to offer low interest loans, provided owners agreed to stock their drinks).
- Protection and security of tenure for tied tenants under the Landlord and Tenant Act.
- Brewers to publish and adhere to wholesale price lists.

The above recommendations are to be put into effect by March 1992 and will have considerable implications for the strategic marketing plans of all brewers.

The introduction of guest beers would, for example, allow strong regional beer brand brewers to manoeuvre themselves onto the bars of the major national brewers' pubs. It is felt that some brewers might decide to opt out of brewing in favour of transforming their pubs into retail outlets offering a wide variety of choice (where high proportions of their profits are derived from retailing). The City Press also considers that other brewers might dispose of their pubs altogether to concentrate on brewing and that foreign brewers might seize the opportunity to buy into the UK market. Yet further possibilities are that pubs will be bought by their licencees (tenants) or perhaps by groups of licencees in management buyouts. Some licencees might buy several pubs. Regional brewers whose estates are currently below the 2000 limit might also be tempted into buying.

Legal changes are only one of a number of environmental factors affecting the brewing industry over the last decade.

Reports indicate that social change is radically altering British drinking habits.

The 1980's greatly increased the internationalisation of world consumer markets (lager brands being a notable example). UK consumers have become more discerning and more cosmopolitan in their outlook. As a result, former core products in the drinks market such as stout and whisky have given ground to more 'exciting' items (often imported) such as light spirits, wines, mineral waters, lagers and fruit juices.

Other trends are:

- A move away from alcoholic towards soft drinks
- A tendency towards "healthy" drinks.
- A preference for lighter, less alcoholic drinks rather than the heavier, stronger types.
- Increased market share of the off-licence (shops and supermarkets) over the on-trade (pubs and bars) resulting from more drinking at home.

- Drinks once seen as the preserve of particular sections of society are now being consumed by all members of society.
- Demographic changes including a smaller proportion of young people and people generally living longer are also having effects on brewers' markets.

These factors combined with the advent of 1992 (the freeing of markets within the European Community) and the current UK economic climate are causing Brewsters' Marketing Director David Downing much concern. He is already foreseeing the need for a professional salesforce (perhaps with special account executives) as a result of greatly increased competition in the future. Up to the present Brewsters have been in the happy position of being able to tell their tied trade what they should stock and so have not felt the need for a truly professional salesforce as such. The sales force's role has been more to maintain and develop existing business rather than seek new outlets. External trade has tended to be negotiated by the Brand or Product Group Managers (through Sales Administration Managers) whether for the home market or abroad. Exports are effected either direct or through distributors according to the nature of the product (draught beer in barrels or bottled/canned), the size and nature of the outlets (pubs/bars or retail shops) and the logistics involved. An export division is operated by the Group to handle the physical distribution aspects of all its companies.

The product portfolio is particularly in need of constant review in light of all the changes referred to above.

Quality circles were recently extended to include white collar office staff (as opposed to blue collar brewery production workers, as formerly) as part of a total quality management programme.

Following brainstorming sessions by these quality circles some novel ideas have emerged from the office staff which are worthy of further consideration despite the somewhat piecemeal and amateurish nature of the outline marketing plans submitted (appendices 2, 3 and 4).

David Downing, inspired by the notion of developing "Continental" brands from scratch, rather than endeavouring to internationalise UK brands, has received authority from the Managing Director to form a project team derived from all functions to investigate the viability of this notion using the three brainstormed ideas as prospective new products for Europe 1992.

The question of branding raises a number of issues such as whether to produce beer under private or own label as well as under the brewer's brands. In the latter case a brewer may use its corporate name as a manufacturer's brand but then use sub-brands to attack particular market segments.

When attacking overseas markets, brewers have to decide whether to use standard formulations for their beer brands or to adapt these to suit individual market tastes. Unlike the US, where beer is the same in most states, European beers in particular areas can be quite different. In Europe lager beers predominate.

Some companies prefer to position brands within niche markets such as those for really strong beers or those with a low alcohol content.

The final outcome of the debate on the extent to which European homogeneity takes preference over national distinctions may in time come to mirror the present UK situation where there are both national brands (mainly lagers) and also regional brands catering usually for a particular market segment.

Other complications in Europe occur with regard to packaging and green issues. Whilst cans predominate in the UK take home market, returnable bottles form the main medium in mainland Europe, strengthening the position of local brewers due to the need to have cost effective re-cycling networks.

Advertising restrictions vary. France has banned the advertising of alcohol on television whilst the Spanish have doubled their T.V. rates for alcohol advertisements. The position in the UK with regard to advertising is largely governed by a code of practice as indicated in Appendix 5.

For the British brewer the key to the market is felt to be the distribution system. The major options for foreign brewers seeking to enter a beer market would be:

i. direct export using local wholesalers.

ii. joint ventures with local companies, possibly involving cross shareholding or the setting up of a new company. A variation on this theme is an alliance.

iii. licencing where the product is attractive but the brewer lacks the means to distribute it.

iv. acquisition - although this can be difficult given the way some continental companies are structured.

Included in the area of product strategy are the concepts of company, brand and product brand life cycles in addition to that of the product life cycle. Some brands appear to have a built-in obsolescence and so the strategy needs to take this possibility into account. "Cash Cows, Rising Stars, Question Marks and Dogs", can be identified but at a brand level rather than a product level.

Nevertheless, despite these considerable problems David Downing is convinced that opportunities for developing strong European brands exists for Brewsters and is determined to fully investigate these.

Appendices

1. Brewers ownership of tied houses
2. Quality Circle Department A - Charmonix du Monde
3. Quality circle Department B - Vronsky or Minsk
4. Quality Circle Department C - Effré
5. Code of Advertising practice - alcoholic drinks
6. Brewsters - Ratio Analysis
7. Sales Analysis
8. Market Data
9. Extract from recent article on the price of beer
10. Marketing and Sales Organisation charts

Appendix 1

Brewers Ownership Of Tied Houses In The UK

Brewer	% of Beer Market	Tied Pubs Independently Tenanted	Tied Pubs Managed by Brewery Staff
1	21	4642	2545
2	13	4600	2300
3	13	3655	1509
4	13	5000	1500
5	10	1400	850
6	9	4600	400

Source - Trade (1988)

Pub And Restaurant Ownership In The UK

Brewer	No.	No. To Be Divested
1	7300	5300
2	6600	4600
3	6100	4100
4	6500	4500
5	2300	300
6	5100	3100
Total	33900	21900

Source - MMC (1989)

Appendix 2

Quality Circle Department A

Product Concept - "Charmonix Du Monde"

A low alcohol sparkling wine mixed with a fruit juice in a range of flavours including peach, pineapple, kiwi and blackcurrant. Presentation would be in distinctive glass bottles with a cocktail image and of individual long drink size. Major market segment seen as wealthier 25 to 40 year olds aspiring to sophistication. Positioning - the fashionable drink of the '90's.

Justification

i) the general move away from alcohol drinks towards soft drinks

ii) increased preference for "healthy" drinks

iii) trend towards light, less alcoholic drinks (as opposed to strong and heavy)

iv) increasing success of off-licence retailing as more people drink at home

v) greater consumption of mineral water and fruit juices

viii) global warming resulting in greater demand for refreshing drinks

ix) opportunities for a European brand aimed at "sophisticates"

Appendix 3

Quality Circle Department B

Product Concept - "Vronsky or Minsk"

A strong high quality, refreshing lager drink with an appealing flavour capable of becoming an acquired taste. Distinctively packaged in a black 300ml bottle with a red star shaped label (most of the competitive brands are 275ml) to reinforce the image of robustness, vigour and solidity and enhance on-shelf impact.

Positioning is seen as a mix of both humour and seriousness demanding a response from the consumer. Copy platforms based on statements such as "This is the beer that came in from the cold" and "What kept the Russians warm during the cold war?" Name Vronsky or Minsk depending on the outcome of further MR.

Justification

i) the market size was 5 million barrels for draught and premium lager in 1990

ii) the bottled lager market is of the order of 360 million units p.a.

iii) our target market size for the Russian theme premium lager would be 20 million units of 300ml glass bottles

iv) environmental considerations indicate that a preference for a glass bottle exits. An EC beverage directive giving global recycling/refilling targets within 5 years seems likely. Germany and Denmark have already implemented legislation to promote recycling. 35% of consumers consider drink cans an environmental issue

v) the premium lager market segment has grown by 72% since 1985 and is characterised by many brand names occupying relatively small market shares

vi) we need something distinctive with an international appeal in order to counteract current trends and competition

vii) the concept would proact with current political climates whilst at the same time remain flexible in its interpretation, over time

Appendix 4

Quality Circle Department C

Product Concept - "Effré"

Effré was chosen as a more inviting alternative to other well known carbonated mineral waters which nevertheless would benefit from a favourable attitude towards a French name for a water product. It is felt Effré reflects an image of quality, sophistication and naturalness. The bottle will be made of glass in a long circular shape with a gold metal sealed screw-type replaceable cap and frosted to give it the "cool" appearance. The formulation would be carbonated water (drawn from local sources) available with a hint of flavour, packaged in both a small size - 375ml (for pub consumption) and a litre (for hotels and restaurants). In both cases this capacity is deliberately slightly larger than competitors to give Effré a value edge without degrading the image. Effré would be launched initially unflavoured, with flavoured versions rolling out and riding on the back of the initial publicity.

Justification

i) the idea of developing an alcoholic drink was rejected on the basis of a static beer market scenario combined with the perceived public interest moving away from alcoholic drinks due to increasing severity of the drink-drive laws throughout Europe

ii) a non alcoholic drink would be good for Brewsters' image

iii) Brewsters is sited in an area renowned for its water springs

iv) within the soft drinks market, sales of bottled water grew by 70% in 1988-89

v) hotter summers

vi) increased concern over water quality in the UK and Europe

viii) consumers more discerning and cosmopolitan with increased interest in "healthy" drinks

Appendix 5
Sheet 1 of 3

Code of Practice
Advertising For Alcoholic Drinks

Introduction

1.1 Moderate drinking is widely enjoyed and helps to make social occasions cheerful and pleasant.

1.2 The Alcoholic Drinks Industry, with others, is aware that a small, but significant minority cause harm to themselves and others through misuse of alcohol. They share the concern about this social problem, the causes of which are complex and varied. There is no evidence connecting such misuse with the advertising of alcoholic drinks.

1.3 The industry is concerned that its advertisements should not exploit the immature, the young, the socially insecure, or those with physical, mental or social incapacity. The industry accepts that its advertising should be socially responsible and should not encourage excessive consumption.

1.4 The industry believes that it is proper for advertisements for alcoholic drinks:

1. to indicate that they give pleasure to many, are of high quality and are widely enjoyed in all classes of society;
2. to seek to persuade people to change brands and/or types of drinks;
3. to provide information on products;
4. to employ such accepted techniques of advertising practice as are employed by other product groups and not inconsistent with detailed rules.

Implementation and Interpretation

2.1 The industry has therefore proposed the following rules for inclusion in the British Code of Advertising Practice. The CAP Committee has accepted this proposal and the Advertising Standards Authority has agreed to supervise the implementation of the rules.

Appendix 5
Sheet 2 of 3

2.2 The rules are to be interpreted in the light of the considerations set out in paragraphs 1.1 to 1.4 above. So far as the scope and general interpretation of the rules are concerned, the provisions of the British Code of Advertising Practice apply, as they do to those aspects of advertisements for drink not covered by the rules.

2.3 "Drink", for the purposed of this Appendix, is to be understood as referring to alcoholic beverages and their consumption.

Rules

Young People

3.1 Advertisements should not be directed at young people or in any way encourage them to start drinking. Anyone shown drinking must appear to be over 21. Children should not be depicted in advertisements except where it would be useful for them to appear (e.g. in family scenes or in background crowds) but they shoud never be drinking alcoholic beverages, nor should it be implied that they are.

Challenge

3.2 Advertisements should not be based on a dare, nor impute any failing to those who do not accept the challenge of a particular drink.

Health

3.3 Advertisements should not emphasise the stimulant, sedative or tranquillising effects of any drink, or imply that it can improve physical performance. However, references to the refreshing attributes of a drink are permissible.

Strength

3.4 Advertisements should not give the general impression of being inducements to prefer a drink because of its higher alcohol content or intoxicating effect. Factual information for the guidance of drinkers about such alcoholic strength may, however, be included.

Social Success

3.5 Advertisements may emphasise the pleasures of companionship and social communication associated with the consumption of alcoholic drinks, but it should never be implied that drinking is necessary to social or business success or distinction, nor that those who do not drink are less likely to be acceptable or successful than those who do.

Advertisements should neither claim nor suggest, or make the drinker more attractive to the opposite sex.

Drinking and Machinery

3.6 Advertisements should not associate drink with driving or dangerous machinery. Specific warnings of the dangers of drinking in these circumstances may, however, be used.

Excessive drinking

3.7 Advertisements should not encourage or appear to condone over-indulgence. Repeated buying of large rounds should not be implied.

Appendix 6

Brewsters Ratio Analysis

Profitability

	87	**88**	**89**	**90**	**91**
Return on Capital %	12.9	13.8	14.8	15.2	15.7
Return on Assets %	9.9	10.9	11.3	11.7	11.9
Profit margin %	11.4	12.0	13.1	13.9	14.8
Efficiency Ratios					
Asset utilisation	87.5	90.9	86.2	88.1	87.9
Sales/fixed assets	1.2	1.3	1.2	1.2	1.2
Turnover/stocks ratio	11.7	12.2	13.2	13.8	14.2
Credit period extended (days)	29.0	27.0	23.0	25.0	28.0
Liquidity ratio	0.8	0.9	0.8	0.8	0.8
Creditor/Debtor ratio	0.8	0.7	0.7	0.7	0.8
Quick ratio	0.5	0.5	0.5	0.6	0.6
Financing Ratio					
Equity gearing ratio	0.7	0.6	0.6	0.7	0.7
Borrowing ratio	7.7	9.1	12.9	13.8	13.9
Employee Ratios	**£**	**£**	**£**	**£**	**£**
Average remuneration	5839	5940	6479	7062	7782
Sales per employee	40498	44011	44776	45701	52556
Profit per employee	4600	5292	5869	6227	6630
Capital employed per employee	35569	38459	39606	40552	41099

Appendix 7

Sales Analysis

Index

	87	88	89	90	91
Group Turnover	100	118	137	149	165
Brewster Turnover	100	120	140	145	160

Segmental Sales Analysis (percentages)

	90	91
Brewing	29	30
Pub Retailing	21	22
Hotels & Restaurants	15	11
Leisure	20	18
Soft Drinks	9	9
Other	6	10

	Internal Sales %		External Sales %	
	90	91	90	91
Brewing	38	39	62	61
Pub Retailing	-	-	100	100
Hotels & Restaurants	-	-	100	100
Leisure	2	3	98	97
Soft Drinks	8	15	92	85

% Group Turnover	90	91
UK	86	91
Rest of Europe	5	5
USA	8	3
Rest of World	1	1

Appendix 8
Sheet 1 of 6

Market Data - (Sources = Industry and Internal Estimates)

% of consumer expenditure at constant 1980 prices

Alcoholic Drinks	**1980**	**1986**	**1992** (Est.)
Beer	45.7	38.1	33.0
Spirits	23.3	20.4	18.0
Wines, cider & perry	16.4	21.0	26.0
	85.4	79.5	77.0
Soft Drinks			
Carbonates	10.4	15.1	15.0
Concentrates	2.0	1.8	2.0
Fruit juices & mineral water	2.4	4.6	6.0
	14.8	21.5	23.0

International Comparisons 1984
(Consumption Per Head Per Year)

Beer (Pints)	
West Germany	255
East Germany	250
Czechoslovakia	247
Denmark	236
Belgium	220
UK	194

Appendix 8
Sheet 2 of 6

International Comparisons 1984
(Consumption Per Head Per Year)

Wine (Litres)

Portugal	84
France	82
Italy	80
Argentina	66
Switzerland	50
UK	11

40% Spirits (litres)

Hungary	13
East Germany	12
Poland	11
Czechoslovakia	8
USSR	8
UK	4

Carbonates (litres)

West Germany	66
Belgium	62
Netherlands	58
Spain	55
UK	46
Italy	30
France	20

Appendix 8
Sheet 3 of 6

International Comparisons 1984
(Consumption Per Head Per Year)

Bottled Water (litres)	**1984**	**1992 (Est.)**
France	72	74
Belgium	54	55
Italy	54	55
Germany	53	58
Spain	20	26
Netherlands	9	10
UK	2	8

Combined Market Shares of 4 Largest Brewers In Each Country (1988)

Country	**% Share**
Japan	99
Australia	98
Canada	95
Netherlands	95
France	92
Denmark	90
UK	60

Source: Financial Times

Notes:

Overseas trade in beer is not heavy. Most countries have their own native industry. Only Holland is significant in Europe with a third of its output exported. British ales tend to be sought as specialist beers in a number of countries but little British lager is exported. Many British lagers are, in any case, imitations of foreign beers. Imports of beer to the UK in 1988 were 7% of total consumption whilst exports were 2%.

Appendix 8
Sheet 4 of 6

UK Exports Of Beer by Country of Destination (1988)

USA	36
Eire	23
Belgium	13
Italy	6
Others	22
Total	100%

Average No. of Brands Per Pub/Bar (1989)

Country	**Draught**	**Packaged**	**Total**
UK	6.5	9.8	16.3
W. Germany	2.2	1.7	3.9
France	1.9	4.7	6.6
Denmark	0.6	8.5	9.1
Ireland	8.5	9.2	17.7

Appendix 8
Sheet 5 of 6

World Drinking Trends (Litres of Pure Alcohol Consumed Per Head Per Year)

	Country	1987	1988	1989	1992 (Est.)
1.	France	13.0	13.4	13.4	13.5
2.	Luxembourg	12.1	12.0	12.5	12.8
3.	Spain	12.7	11.9	12.0	12.5
4.	E Germany	10.8	11.0	11.1	12.0
5.	Switzerland	11.0	11.0	10.9	11.0
6.	Hungary	10.7	10.5	10.7	11.0
7.	W Germany	10.6	10.4	10.4	10.0
8.	Portugal	10.9	9.9	10.4	10.6
9.	Austria	10.1	10.1	10.3	10.3
10.	Belgium	10.7	10.0	9.9	10.0
11.	Denmark	9.6	9.7	9.6	9.6
12.	Italy	11.0	9.9	9.5	10.0
13.	Bulgaria	8.9	9.1	9.3	9.8
14.	Czechoslovakia	8.6	8.5	8.7	9.2
15.	Australia	8.5	8.3	8.5	8.7
16.	Netherlands	8.3	7.9	8.3	8.3
17.	Romania	7.8	7.7	7.9	8.0
18.	New Zealand	8.4	7.7	7.8	7.8
19.	Canada	7.8	7.3	NA	7.5
20	Finland	7.1	7.6	7.6	7.6
21	United Kingdom	7.5	7.6	7.6	7.5
22.	USA	7.6	7.5	7.5	7.5
23	Argentina	8.9	8.0	7.1	7.2
24.	Cyprus	6.3	6.7	7.0	7.0
25.	Poland	7.2	7.1	7.0	7.3

Appendix 8
Sheet 6 of 6

Advertising Beer in the UK in 1989

Lagers received twice as much expenditure as other beers and 40% of the expenditure on others was on low/non alcohol types. Total advertising expenditure was estimated at £102m, 90% of which was on T.V.

Lager Brand	£m on advertising (Est.)
Carlsberg	8.5
Carling Black Label	6.3
Heineken	3.7
Castlemaine XXXX	3.4
Fosters	4.2
Pils	3.1
Labatts	2.9
Miller Lite	2.3
Tennants Extra	4.6
Lowenbrau	1.9

In the UK c.73% of beer consumed is in draught form and 27% packaged. Low/non alcohol beer has c.1.5% of the total market split 0.4% draught; 1.1% packaged. Lager accounts for 51% of consumption of all beers.

Appendix 9
Sheet 1 of 2

Extract from Newspaper Article June 91

Brewing giants pumped up the price of a pint by 10p yesterday.

And it puts the final froth on a mind-blowing 1,150 per cent increase in ale costs over the last 20 years.

Now a survey has revealed that, even when inflation is taken into account, beer has rocketed way ahead of other items.

In 1971, the year we went decimal, you could sup your favourite tipple for 12p a pint - now the average price is a whopping £1.50.

In contrast to beer, bread has gone up just 500 per cent and butter 217 per cent.

The rise will affect big-selling brands like Fosters, Carlsberg, Budweiser, John Smiths, Manns and Samuel Websters. Other big breweries are expected to follow.

In the South, lager is likely to soar to £1.60 a pint and bitter to £1.48 while in the North and the Midlands the cost will be around £1.35 and £1.20.

The cheapest pint in Britain is from Manchester brewer Joseph Holt. Their mild sells for a mere 79p a pint and bitter for 84p.

Courage last night defended their increase. "Our prices are still competitive when compared to other breweries" a spokesman said.

But furious Labour Consumer Affairs spokesman Nigel Griffiths is demanding an urgent government inquiry.

He said "I'll be referring this to the Director General of the Office of Fair Trading for him to investigate".

Profit

Last night beer drinkers slammed the rise. The Campaign for Real Ale's Iain Loe said "Brewers should stop being so greedy. I don't know how they can justify it."

Taxes swallow almost one third of the cash which drinkers spend on their pint.

But our breakdown of exactly where the money goes shows the brewer stands to make a tidy profit.

Appendix 9
Sheet 2 of 2

Landlords fear the latest round of price rises could force them to call time on their hard-pressed businesses.

Tenants of brewery-owned pubs have already been hit by crushing rent increases and the economic slump.

A spokesman for their union, the National Licenced Victuallers' Association, stated: "This couldn't be more unwelcome. The budget added up to 10p on a pint and now this. The price just keeps going up and up. It's crippling us."

"It won't be long before you see the 2.00 pint."

The £1.50 Pint: This is how cash breaks down

V.A.T.	**22P**
Excise Duty	**23p**
Raw Materials	**3p**
Production & Distribution	**21p**
Advertising	**3**
Pub Costs (Landlord's salary, heating, maintenance etc)	**57p**
Profit	**21P**

Where The Money Goes

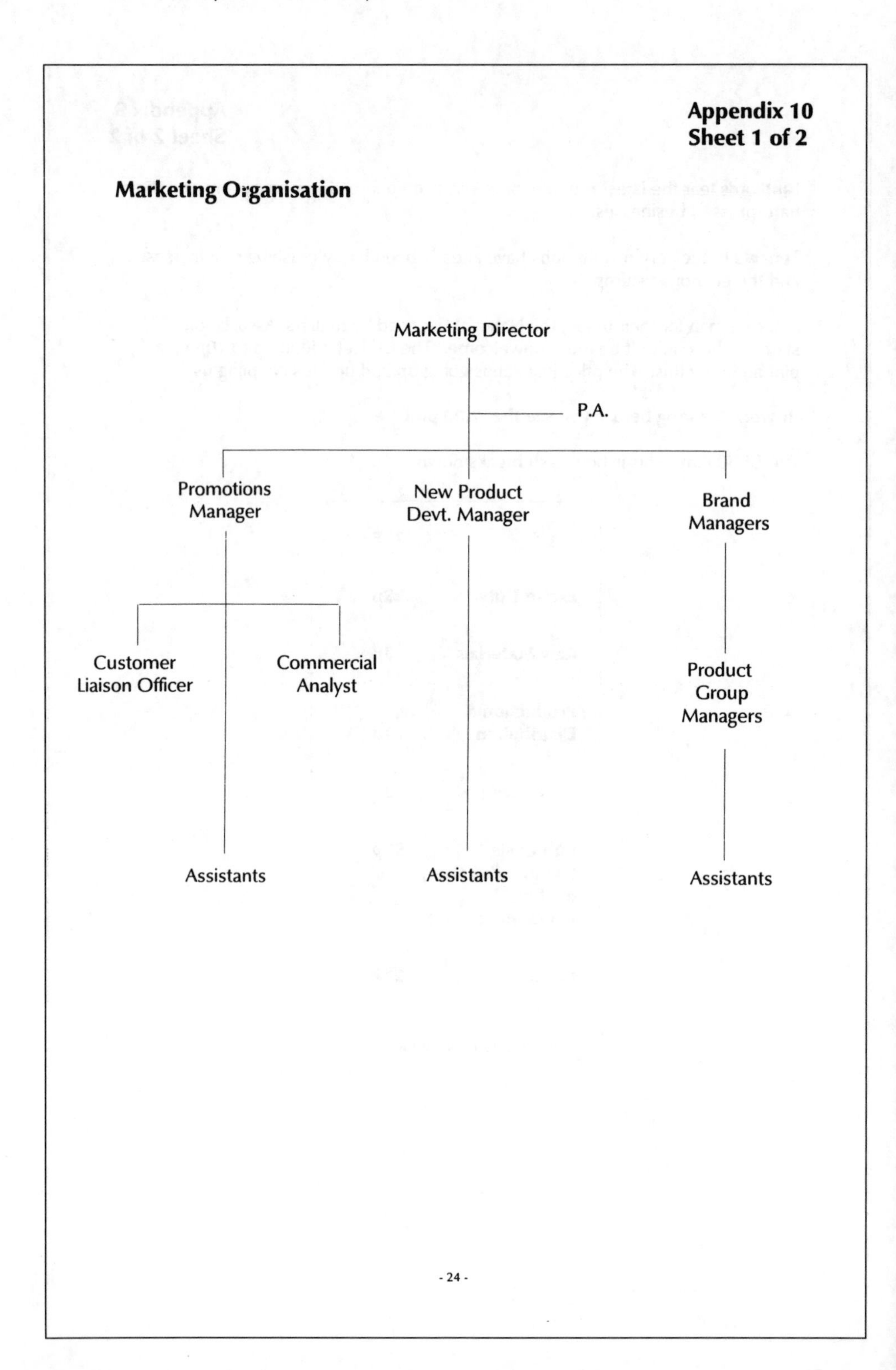
Appendix 10
Sheet 1 of 2
Marketing Organisation
Marketing Director
P.A.
Promotions Manager
New Product Devt. Manager
Brand Managers
Customer Liaison Officer
Commercial Analyst
Product Group Managers
Assistants
Assistants
Assistants
- 24 -

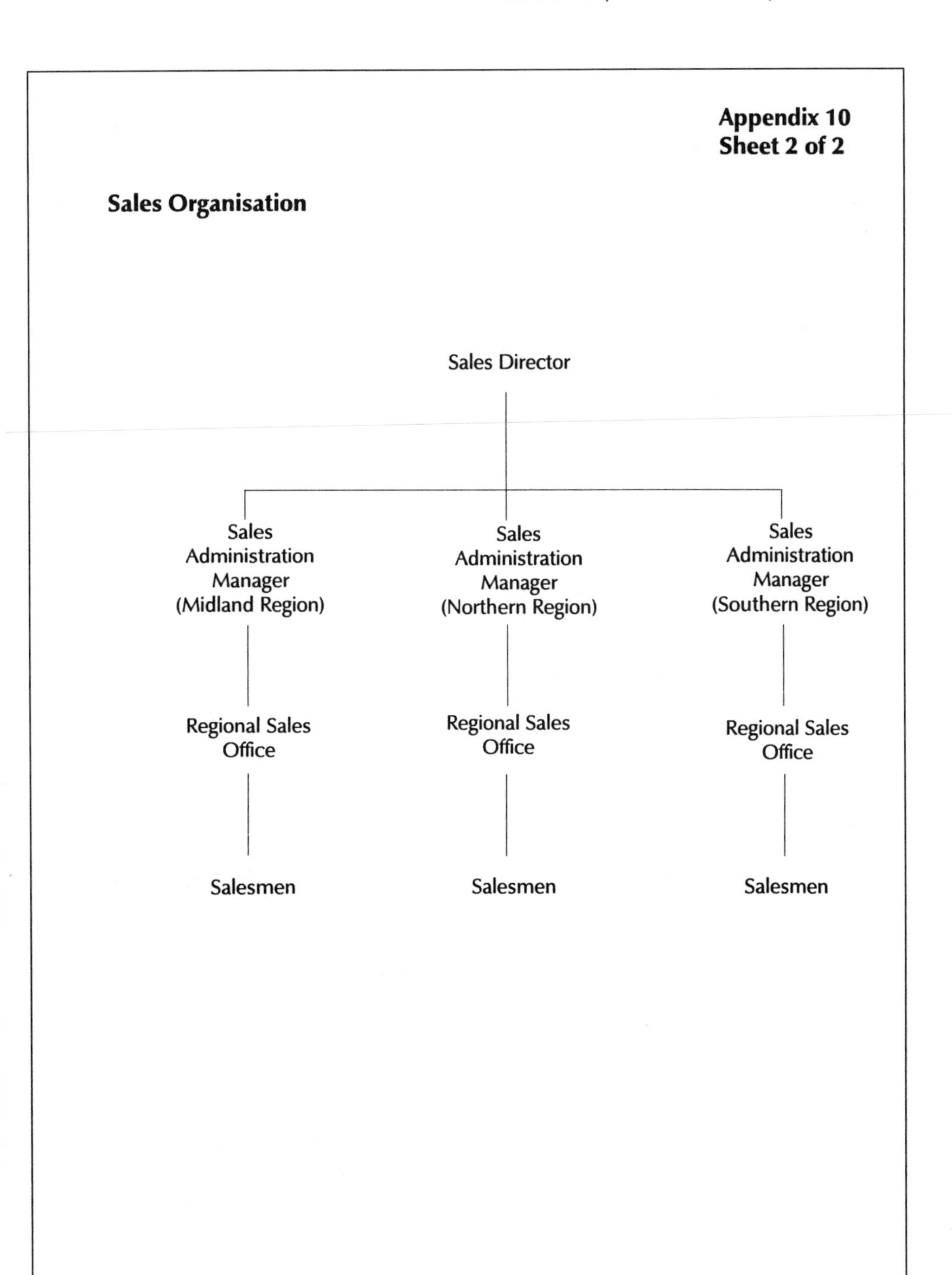
Appendix 10
Sheet 2 of 2
Sales Organisation
Sales Director
Sales Administration Manager (Midland Region)
Sales Administration Manager (Northern Region)
Sales Administration Manager (Southern Region)
Regional Sales Office
Regional Sales Office
Regional Sales Office
Salesmen
Salesmen
Salesmen
- 25 -

Examiners' report

General comments

The worldwide pass rate showed a slight improvement over the previous year's December sitting, which is encouraging bearing in mind the increase in numbers attempting this paper.

This improvement in the pass rate was largely due to increases in the proportions of candidates who:

(a) Adopted report format as instructed
(b) Applied exam techniques to answer all 3 questions adequately and to allocate time properly between questions
(c) Presented answers in a better standard of layout, structure and visual presentation.

However, too many candidates are still ignoring the actual questions set and adopting the 'write all you know' technique or presenting ill-fitting pre-prepared answers, identically worded to others in the group.

Overseas candidates in particular tend to spend far too much time on presenting detailed pre-prepared content pages, followed by over-lengthy lists of pre-prepared objectives and assumptions. The answers to each question then start with extensive introductions and finish with mangement summaries so that far too little time is devoted to the actual question asked. The result is usually answers which are far too superficial to pass.

Another practice which is causing some concern is that of taking assumptions too far and contriving by this means to considerably alter the questions in an attempt to bring these into line with pre-prepared answers. Such deliberately evasive techniques cannot result in a pass mark. It would seem that the weaker candidates will do anything to avoid answering the actual questions set.

With the above concerns in mind it is worth repeating some of the constructive advice given in previous examiners' reports:

'It is clearly stated in the Tutor's Guidance Notes for this subject that candidates are expected to think and make decisions in the examination room and that pre-prepared analysis on its own, however well done, will be insufficient to pass. Candidates must therefore develop the ability to use their analysis *selectively* according to the specific questions set. Essentially this would entail some practice on an *individual* basis in adapting and extending analyses, so as to achieve a more flexible approach to the examination. Some *tuition centres* appear to be gambling on pre-prepared group analyses fitting the questions actually set, which they rarely will. In any case, this approach is entirely contrary to the intent and spirit of the subject, which is to develop individual marketing management ability to a professional standard.

'Candidates must also refrain from including overly detailed reference to textbook material, a knowledge of which is being tested in other Diploma papers. The subject of Analysis and Decision is testing the *application* of this knowledge to a practical situation and answers *must be case-specific* rather than general treatises, in order to pass.'

Question 1

While some candidates demonstrated an excellent grasp of marketing research, others were unable to distinguish between the information needed to explore potential markets and that required to determine effective methods of market entry. Too few candidates attempted to justify the research specified. A four part answer was needed (specification and justification of research required on potential markets and market entry methods). While frameworks for these exist in the recommended reading for the Diploma, answers needed to be case-specific i.e. related to the formulation of an improved strategic position for Brewsters in Europe.

Weaker candidates also failed to structure their research and presented rambling essays. Some candidates insisted on simply describing the information that Brewsters already had, as given in the case study.

Question 2

Answers to this, the major question, were generally disappointing. Too many candidates failed to appreciate that the three proposed new products were still in the concept stage and therefore action was needed to develop actual products and put these through the appropriate screening processes to ascertain both their marketing and financial viability. Assumptions that these products were fully developed, had been thoroughly test-marketed and had already enjoyed a successful national launch in the UK were inappropriate. All three concepts were in fact variations on the theme of a potential pan-European brand so that separate treatments with regard to broad actions were unnecessary.

A three-part answer was required namely marketing actions, financial actions and their scheduling (in a timed and logical sequence). Unfortunately the vast majority limited their answers on financial viability to giving pre-prepared marketing plan costs. Candidates really do need to show a better appreciation of the financial implications involved in a potential major new product launch in overseas markets. This essentially means extending their horizons beyond marketing costs to total cost, capital required, projected returns on capital employed and pay-back periods, as a minimum. An assessment of financial risks is also appropriate with particular regard to fluctuations in exchange rates, foreign banking and legal restrictions etc. Marketing candidates needed to demonstrate their understanding that corporate objectives dictate that their proposed developments will be compared with other perhaps safer, quicker and more profitable opportunities.

Question 3

It had been hoped that this question would have been foreseen by all those candidates who had conducted a thorough analysis of the case. Clearly selling and sales management is still being under-valued. Candidates who thought that all that was required was organisational change were failed. This in itself would achieve nothing if the existing salesforce remained untrained in modern selling techniques. The essential problem was that the salesforce were unprofessional order-takers and that in the new marketing environment they would be required to sell against competitors' salesforces. Some answers actually stated that the entire existing salesforce would have to be replaced, rather than assessing individual potential and training needs, and only replacing people when necessary.

A typical answer listed the changes in the marketing environment but made no attempt to link these to specific changes in the salesforce and its management. A hope that timescales and cost indications would accompany answers to this question proved over-optimistic. It appears that most examinees are happy to make proposals without any consideration of cost or implementation. Where organisational changes are recommended it is expected that suitable charts will be submitted in illustration, particularly when changes are being made in stages.

4 The June 1992 Examination Case

Euro Airport Ltd (EAL)

Examination paper

Diploma in Marketing

(12) Marketing Management (Analysis and Decision)

Tuesday 16th June 1992 **Time: 14.00 — 17.00**

3 hours duration

This paper requires you to make a practical and reasoned evaluation of the problems and opportunities you have identified from the previously circulated case material. From your analysis you are required to prepare a report in accordance with the situation below. Graphing sheets and ledger analysis paper are available from the invigilators, together with continuation sheets if required. These must be identified by your candidate number and fastened in the prescribed fashion within the back cover of your answer book for collection at the end of the examinations.

READ THE QUESTIONS CAREFULLY AND ANSWER THE ACTUAL QUESTIONS AS SPECIFIED. CHECK THE MARK ALLOCATION TO QUESTIONS AND ALLOCATE YOUR TIME ACCORDINGLY. CANDIDATES MUST ATTEMPT ALL PARTS. CANDIDATES SHOULD ADOPT REPORT FORMAT. THOSE WHO DO NOT WILL BE PENALISED.

EURO AIRPORT LIMITED

Question 1

Detail your long-term proposals to counteract the potential loss of duty free revenue, by the strategy of increasing sales of non duty free goods and services at the airport site. In making your proposals, you should pay due regard to the most important financial indicators by which the airport's commercial performance is currently measured, plus any non financial performance standards which you may additionally suggest.

40 marks

Question 2

Suggest and justify changes in the current organisation structure and specify a set of internal marketing initiatives which might lead to a more unified approach (between operations and commercial divisions) to the marketing of the airport as a whole, to both passengers and airlines.

30 marks

Question 3

Submit reasoned approaches which might create a more favourable and informed opinion within the local community, towards the airport's development plans for a new terminal and other possible future expansions.

30 marks

EURO AIRPORT LIMITED (EAL)

Candidates' Brief

You are Irma Bergmann the recently appointed New Business Development Manager reporting to the Commercial Director of Euro Airport Limited. This is a new position created largely by the threat of the loss of duty free sales. Also an inherent part of the justification for this appointment is however, a need for completely fresh thinking at a time of rapid change in the EC environment. EAL are wanting particularly to create a unified approach to the marketing of the airport as a whole and all applicants for vacant management positions within both the Commercial and Operations divisions are being judged with this requirement in mind.

You therefore have considerable scope for development of your role in the longer term. You are young, talented and ambitious.

In putting forward your proposals it is necessary to be aware that other projects will be competing for scarce resources both at company and group level.

Following your initial assessment you will be required to make clear recommendations for future action.

This case material is based upon experience with actual companies. Alterations in the information given and in the real data have been made to preserve confidence. Candidates are strictly instructed not to contact companies in this industry.

Copies may be obtained from the Chartered Institute of Marketing, Moor Hall, Cookham, Maidenhead, Berks, SL6 9QH.

EURO AIRPORT LIMITED (EAL)

Euro Airport Ltd (EAL) is a large airport situated in Europe which hosts most of the major airlines in the world. Although EAL owns substantial assets in the form of land and buildings only a small proportion of these are actually used by the millions of passengers who arrive and depart from the airport each year and whose expenditure at the airport constitutes a major proportion of its revenue. EAL is part of a group of related holdings but operates autonomously as a separate SBU (Strategic Business Unit).

The airport normally operates 24 hours every day and has over 25,000 employees including aircrews, air traffic controllers, security staff, cleaners, catering staff, baggage handlers, shop assistants and the management/clerical support staff.

EAL sees itself not only as an airport but also as a substantial retail shopping centre which incorporates shops, bars, restaurants and banks, most of which operate on a concession basis. This is an arrangement whereby a retailer is allowed to establish an outlet at the airport in return for a rent plus a percentage of the outlet's turnover. This large retail operation is extremely successful and the profits generated contribute considerably towards the very high costs of maintaining the runways and terminal buildings.

Like most airports, EAL is expanding in its effort to cope with the long term increase in demand for air travel by both the business and leisure segments and for airfreight services. However, expansion is constrained by environmental pressures. EAL has to conform to stringent safety standards and has to ensure that building developments blend naturally into the surrounding landscape insofar as possible. The containment of noise is another very difficult problem. These factors have given rise to what has become known as the "not in my back yard" syndrome. Any attempts to extend runaways or to increase the number of flights are strongly resisted by consumer protest groups which are particularly vociferous in the immediate vicinity of the airport.

The smooth operation of the airport is also interrupted by events outside its immediate control in the form of government interventions and industrial actions, not only in the home country but in countries throughout the world. However, undesirable though these hold-ups may be in causing customer dissatisfaction, they can actually result in more sales at the airport's retail outlets.

EAL is highly conscious of its responsibilities not only to its customers but to the community at large and seeks to be pro-active towards the increasing sensitivity of the environmental factors and within these, the "green" issues, particularly those of conservation and anti-pollution. Very high levels of skills in forward planning, technological and environmental forecasting are needed in order to anticipate the nature and strengths of these uncontrollable variables several years ahead.

Particularly as a result of a commitment to quality, EAL has sought to establish a competitive advantage through the medium of design. This attempt to sustain a distinctive competence extends not only to buildings and landscapes but to all systems concerned with handling internal and external customers. More recently EAL has embarked on policies involving the concept of "relationship marketing". This concept in essence recognises the importance of building up long-term relationships with its customers, other people in the DMU (Decision Making Unit), with suppliers and with other publics such as local government, in a partnership type of approach.

A serious threat to EAL's future viability is the decision of the European Community Finance Ministers to take action to ban the practice of offering goods "duty free". These lower priced goods are a major attraction for passengers shopping at airports and revenue from sales of duty free goods contribute a considerable proportion of EAL's turnover and profits.

EAL is therefore actively identifying and considering alternative ways in which this potential loss in revenue and profit might be alleviated such as moving into the hotel business, joint ventures with other airports and developing non duty free sales.

Other opportunities for profitable development are felt to emanate from Eastern Europe's political changes and possible integration with providers of other transport services.

With these and other potential opportunities in mind EAL have recently created the position of New Business Development Manager reporting to the Commercial Director. Irma Bergmann, a former Merchandising Director of a prosperous chain of supermarkets operating nationally and internationally is to undertake this role with effect from 1 May 1992. Irma has a degree in European Business Studies, the CIM Diploma and is fluent in German, French and English.

Apart from her considerable expertise in buying and selling instore goods, Irma was consulted regularly with regard to new store sites and competitor acquisitions by her former company. Irma has already made a start on a marketing audit as part of her Business Development Plan and found her freedom to develop business limited by a number of factors including;

1. Customer perceptions of airports as being expensive places in which to shop or to eat and drink
2. Limited shopping time
3. Limited space for retail development

4 Some conflict between commercial and operational interests

5 Bad publicity regarding airports over-exploiting a captive market

6 Difficulties in positioning caused not only by the proliferation of concessions, but also by the international nature of the airport's passengers

7 Changes in customer profiles eg. the increasing proportion of Japanese in both business and leisure segments

8 Bureaucracy - number of groups/departments to consult

9 Traffic congestion in the vicinity of the airport and difficulties in parking

10 Increases in security restrictions

Irma also feels the need for new types of marketing research data in order to more effectively identify new product/service opportunities and new market segments/niches. She has been used to regularly receiving sophisticated data from retail audits, consumer panels, electronic point of sale systems, geodemographic surveys etc. in her former position. This national and international data has not been seen as particularly relevant to EAL's retail concessions (concessionaires) in their limited geographical position, dealing with a diverse range of customers. However, Irma remains reasonably confident that some of the critical success factors relevant to her former business apply also to EAL and that she can make a considerable contribution to profitability in her new role.

She has been made aware by the Commercial Director that the most important indicators by which airport's commercial performance is measured are:

- Sales turnover
- Sales per passenger

- Revenue
- Revenue per passenger
- Sales per square metre
- Revenue per square metre
- Profit
- Return on investment

There is of course a difference between the total value of sales made through the concessionaires and the revenue received by EAL. This revenue is only a share of retail sales made by the retail concession, plus a rent.

Airlines pay to use EAL's facilities to operate flights to and from the airport and for each departing passenger. These airline and passenger charges make up approximately 35 per cent of total airport revenue, with commercial activities from retail concessions and other income making up the remaining 65 per cent.

Airline passengers do therefore provide two sources of revenue for EAL. Firstly an airport charge for each departing passenger (paid by the airline) and secondly that from goods and services purchased whilst at the airport.

A further source of revenue comes from expenditure made by people visiting the airport to meet or to bring passengers or for other purposes.

Market Segmentation

Passengers

Passengers segment into many categories but the major ones are:

- Business / Leisure

- Domestic / Foreign
- Starting point / End destination
- Standard / Transfer

A transfer passenger is someone who arrives from another airport and transfers flights at the airport, for example, taking a local airport flight to EAL for transfer onto a long-haul flight to America. Although it varies, transfer passengers can have more time to spend in the terminal but may have already bought duty free goods at their local airport or on their local flight. Transfer passengers can make up as much as 30 per cent of total traffic although this proportion is slowly decreasing as more regional airports lay on longer-haul flights. However, EAL are finding that airside transfers (passengers arriving by air and staying in the duty free area as opposed to landside transfers who arrive by coach and taxis and have to go through Passport Control to get to the duty free area) are spending more per head on duty free items than either landside transfers or standard, non-transfer passengers.

There are trends towards increasing proportions of leisure passengers, long haul passengers and female passengers.

Marketing Research

Marketing research is regularly conducted to monitor passenger profiles and satisfaction levels with all operational aspects.

Competition

Competition is seen as emanating from two main areas:

Alternative forms of transportation
ie. car, coach, rail, boat

- Other airports, both domestic and international

In addition the Commercial Sector must compete:

- for the passengers' time against;
    * check-in procedures
    * security procedures
    * airlines' embarking procedures

- for the passengers' spend against
    * airlines' in-flight sales
    * High Street shops (indirectly)

Promotion

Promotion is carried out by EAL, by concessionaires and by makers of products sold on the airport. This takes many forms, including;

On Airport
- Illuminated signs
- Posters
- Trolleys
- Leaflets to arriving and departing passengers
- Staff incentive campaigns
- Shop sales promotion
- Merchandising
- Staff discounts
- Point of sale displays

Off Airport	-	Railway posters
	-	National newspapers
	-	Hotels
	-	Radio
	-	In the High Street branches of shops who have concessions at the airport
Regular Airport Users Club	-	To create 'brand loyalty' amongst regular travellers

With regard to the element of place, airports can be stressful and confusing for some passengers, and this can be aggravated by security measures, congestion and delays. All these can affect the moods of the passengers and their consequent inclination towards or against shopping or spending money. As far as possible therefore, attempts are made to make the commercial environments attractive, calm, spacious and logical.

Pricing policies are such that EAL guarantees any products/services bought at the airport are of equal or comparable price to their equivalent on the High Street. Exceptions include Duty/Tax free goods on which a specified saving is guaranteed and the "Bureau de Change" where exchange rates are within one per cent of the rates of a specified major bank.

The organisation of an airport as large as EAL is necessarily complex and tensions often arise between staff in the Operations sections and those in the Commercial sector. Some of these tensions can be seen to arise from a basic conflict of interests. The main objective of the Commercial division is to satisfy customers needs for retail goods and services, during the time they are in the airport. The operations division's main objective is by contrast, to process passengers safely and efficiently from arrival at the airport, to the timely departure of their flight. Any activities which get in the way of this process can be regarded by operations personnel as counter-productive, causing problems. Passengers tempted to linger in the airport's duty free shops might for example arrive late at their departure "gate" and extra baggage means extra weight and storage. Operations personnel do not always appreciate that the purpose of generating income from commercial activities is to invest this in developing the airport generally. Both operations and commercial divisions need to learn that marketing the airport as a whole both to passengers and to airlines is a key element of the airport's mission.

LIST OF APPENDICES

			PAGES
Appendix 1	-	services provided by the airport for its customers	12, 13
Appendix 2	-	product/service range - share of income - share of space	14
Appendix 3	-	domestic and international terminals, passenger profiles	15, 16
Appendix 4	-	commercial facilities, domestic and international terminals	17
Appendix 5	-	performance analysis - external and internal factors	18
Appendix 6	-	marketing research activities	19
Appendix 7	-	SWOT analysis	20, 21
Appendix 8	-	characteristics of main European airports	22
Appendix 9	-	ranking of charges for typical aircraft types - main European airports	23
Appendix 10	-	memo from Commercial Director to New Business Development Manager	24
Appendix 11	-	extracts from newspaper articles/letters	25
Appendix 12	-	memo from Commercial Director to New Business Development Manager	26
Appendix 13	-	organisation charts	27 to 33
Appendix 14	-	financial accounts	34 to 36

LIST OF APPENDICES

Appendix 15	-	memo from Commercial Director to New Business Development Manager	37
Appendix 16	-	memo from Public Relations Director to New Business Development Manager	38
Appendix 17	-	survey of airport shoppers and their buying behaviour	39, 40

APPENDIX ONE
Sheet 1 of 2

SERVICES PROVIDED BY THE AIRPORT FOR ITS CUSTOMERS

Airline Operators

- are provided with an internationally known airport with access to the centre of a large city in Europe, which attracts both tourists and business people. Many people want to fly there and the airline will therefore gain business because of this.
- Use of modern facilities, offices, baggage handling machines etc
- Engineering and maintenance facilities
- Check-In desk and ticket office space
- Fuel and filling up facilities
- Hanger space
- Runway time
- Inflight catering facilities
- Use of staff leisure facilities
- Strict security
- Strict safety regulations and controls
- An environment which will keep passengers informed and occupied

APPENDIX ONE
Sheet 2 of 2

Airline Passengers

- Regular flights enabling them to choose the one most convenient for them
- Direct flights to over 100 destinations worldwide
- Safety and security
- Well trained staff
- Efficient passenger information service
- Porters, luggage trolleys
- Free transfer buses
- Information desks
- Facilities for the disabled
- Cleanliness
- Shopping facilities
- Catering outlets

Concessionnaires

- Provided with a large number of potential customers
- Space in the terminals
- Support from EAL Commercial Department

APPENDIX TWO

PRODUCT/SERVICE RANGE - SHARES OF EAL REVENUE AND SPACE

PRODUCT/SERVICE	SHARE OF REVENUE (%)	SHARE OF TERMINAL SPACE (%) (inc store rooms, kitchens etc)
Duty/Tax Free Shops	50.5	25.9
Catering	5.3	53.1
Banking/Bureau de Change	5.8	3.0
Car Rental	3.0	0.8
Hotel Reservations	0.6	0.2
Payphones	0.6	1.3
Insurance	0.2	0.3
Bookshops	5.7	8.3
Specialist Shops	3.5	6.0
Advertising	5.2	-
Car Parks	19.4	-
Sundry	0.2	1.1

APPENDIX THREE
Sheet 1 of 2

TERMINAL PASSENGERS - DIFFERENCES BETWEEN DOMESTIC AND INTERNATIONAL TERMINALS

	DOMESTIC TERMINAL	INTERNATIONAL TERMINAL
PASSENGER TYPE		
Domestic Business	43.5%	27.4%
Domestic Leisure	28.8%	20.7%
Foreign Business	12.4%	26.9%
Foreign Leisure	15.3%	25.0%
AGE		
Less than 18	1.2%	1.4%
18 - 24	9.9%	10.1%
25 - 34	29.1%	27.4%
35 - 44	27.2%	27.4%
45 - 54	19.3%	20.6%
55 - 64	9.6%	9.4%
65+	3.7%	3.7%
SEX		
Male	69.6%	69.9%
Female	30.4%	30.1%
SOCIO ECONOMIC GROUP (Based on British JICNARS classifications)		
AB	56.0%	60.8%
C1	29.9%	30.3%
C2	10.0%	6.5%
DE	4.1%	2.4%

APPENDIX THREE
Sheet 2 of 2

PERMANENT RESIDENCE IN LAST 12 MONTHS	DOMESTIC TERMINAL	INTERNATIONAL TERMINAL
Domestic	72.3%	48.0%
Rest of EC	11.9%	24.1%
Rest of Europe	1.9%	10.6%
North America	7.5%	8.5%
Africa	1.8%	2.5%
Middle/Far East	2.3%	3.9%
Rest of the World	2.3%	2.4%

APPENDIX FOUR

COMMERCIAL FACILITIES AT EAL

Domestic Terminal

Bookshops
Clothes shops
Sports shops
Chemist
Music shop
Perfume shop
Fashion jewellers
Cosmetics shop
Waiter service restaurant
Self service restaurant
Bar
Small catering outlets
Car rental desks
Hotel reservations desks
Telephones
Amusement machines
Fax machines
Advertising sites

- posters
- special displays

International Terminal

Bookshops
Clothes shops
Fashion shops
Chemist
Music shop
Luxury food shop
Toy shop
Luxury jewellers
Shoe shop
Novelty shop
Cosmetics shop
Duty and Tax Free shop
Catering outlets
Waiter service restaurant
Self service restaurant
Fast food restaurant
Bar
Small catering outlets
Car rental desks
Hotel reservations desks
Bureau de Change
Telephones
Amusement machines
Fax machines
Advertising sites

- posters
- special displays

APPENDIX FIVE

PERFORMANCE ANALYSIS

Performance can only by analysed by taking into consideration the following:

External factors

- Inflation
- Growth in consumer expenditure
- Performance of overseas economies
- Growth in passenger numbers
- Exchange rate changes
- Changes in proportion of international passengers
- Changes in taxation
- Changes in passenger type
- Competition
- Global changes in consumer tastes
- Airline performance
- Air Traffic Control delays
- Absolute ie. actual prices received
- Price relative to alternative suppliers
- Propensity to spend
- Foreign approval procedures (bureaucratic delays)

Internal Factors

- Concessionaires performances
- Major redevelopment of terminals
- Promotional activities
- Changes in shop design and layout
- Contractual changes
- Introduction of new product lines
- Space allocated to commercial activities
- Congestion in terminals and in individual shops
- Terminal operational policies
- Design
- Staff training and motivation

APPENDIX SIX

MARKETING RESEARCH

Marketing Research is regularly carried out to provide information on:-

- Passenger profiles
- Attitudes towards shopping
- Domestic and foreign lifestyles
- Behaviourial studies
- Airport facilities
- Duty free purchasing motivations
- Price / value for money perceptions
- Characteristics of specific nationalities eg. Japanese
- Awareness and credibility of advertising campaigns
- Consumer needs and attitudes towards catering
- User profiles for specific outlets

APPENDIX SEVEN
Sheet 1 of 2

SWOT Analysis (incomplete)

STRENGTHS

- Growth market
- Captive market
- Big High Street names/branding
- High demand for commercial space
- High commercial growth
- Many high income passengers
- Customers can be easily identified, classified and targeted
- Flexible - can change to meet changing consumer needs
- Policy to give good customer service and value for money
- Centralised commercial function
- Control over concessionnaires
- Specialist operators
- Financial support from parent company
- Profitability
- Increasing retail expertise
- Well known
- Good access links

WEAKNESSES

- Image of airports as expensive
- Limited time for shopping
    - security measures
    - length of check in procedures
    - congestion
- Limited space for commercial development
- Location of commercial facilities restricted by operational considerations
- Duty/Tax Free purchases limited due to import allowances
- Organisation not commercially orientated
- Staff not in a single location
- Insufficient development land
- High building cost
- Bureaucracy - number of groups to consult
- Current ban on some night flights

APPENDIX SEVEN
Sheet 2 of 2

OPPORTUNITIES

- Market growth
- Passengers increasing
  - frequency
  - more leisure
  - more long haul
- New technology
  - more information on customers, shopping trends
- Arrivals Duty Free shopping
- Proposed new terminal
  - commercial given equal priority at design stage
- EC harmonisation - new commercial opportunities
- Potentially strong brand name
- Additional capacity
- Transfer passengers

THREATS

- Exchange rates eg. a weak dollar can result in fewer Americans travelling to Europe
- More congestion
  - additional security measures
  - size of aircraft increasing
- Increase in cost of travel
  - may limit spending at airport
- Competition from airlines
  - duty free goods
- Regulatory bodies
  - Monopoly
  - EC
  - Legal
  - Government
  - Airports Authorities
  - Customs and Excise
- Economic recession
- Terrorism
- Vulnerability to media
- Decline in cigarette/tobacco market
  - advertising restrictions
  - health considerations
- Competition - regional and European Airports
- Traffic congestion - on routes to the airport

21

APPENDIX EIGHT

Some characteristics of Main European Airports

	Airport A*	Airport B	Airport C	Airport D	Airport E
Within 10 miles of city centre	no	yes	yes	yes	no
Near a major tourist attraction	yes	no	yes	no	yes
Near a major business centre	yes	yes	no	yes	yes
Uncongested access routes	no	yes	yes	yes	no
Good passenger facilities	yes	yes	yes	no	yes
Relatively low risk from terrorism	no	no	yes	yes	no
Over 100 destinations	yes	yes	no	no	yes
Plans for major expansion/development	yes	yes	yes	no	yes
Active marketing of airport	no	no	yes	no	no

* Airport A = EAL

APPENDIX NINE

Ranking of Charges for Typical Aircraft Types - Main European Airports

DESTINATION	Long Haul Route	Medium Haul Route	Short Haul Route
Airport B	1	1	1
Airport E	2	2	3
Airport D	3	5	5
Airport A*	4	4	2
Airport C	5	3	4

1 = Most expensive
5 = Least expensive

* Airport A = EAL

APPENDIX TEN

MEMORANDUM

May 11, 92

From Commercial Director

To New Business Development Manager

This is simply to confirm our meeting last week when I asked you to become involved in the retail services for our new terminal for which we are expecting planning permission shortly.

I have enclosed drawings and other details of the proposed layout for this new terminal together with those of our existing terminals and would be interested to know:

a) What you think of these proposals
b) Whether you think we should make any changes

You will also have to get involved with discussions with concessionaires to agree fine details in due course.

It is quite some time since we looked at our competitors in any detail and I would like you to conduct a survey of our major competitor airports, to confirm our relative strengths and weaknesses but more importantly to observe which elements of their retail mix appear to be doing well and to assess whether we have anything to learn from them.

Please feel free to call in for discussion as necessary before our next formal monthly management meeting.

P.S. Our P.R. people want to do a feature on you for external publicity purposes as well as our in-house magazine. Could you please contact Mrs Norma Bernhardt on this one.

24

APPENDIX ELEVEN

Extracts from newspaper articles and letters during November 91

"EUROPE CLOSES DOOR ON DUTY FREE SHOPS"

European Community Finance Ministers agreed last night to abolish duty free shopping within the community by July 1, 1999.

The total turnover of duty free goods within the E.C. is estimated at £1.5 billion per year.

Britain has the E.C.'s biggest duty free industry with shops at airports and on ferries accounting for c£1.0 billion annual turnover.

Sir, Whatever Herr Peter Gundthardt may say it is not simply the British who spend heavily on duty free drink and tobacco. Few people of any nationality can resist a bargain, witness the queues of passengers at the Dubai duty-free shops in the small hours in order to save a little money on a bottle of Scotch or French Brandy. Scandinavians throng the duty-free shops at Mediterranean airports. Abolishing duty-free goods within the EC will boost the takings of Cointrin airport (Geneva) at the expense of Satolas (Lyons): Zurich and Salzburg will benefit at the expense of Munich. Above all Morocco, Bulgaria, Turkey and Tunisia will flourish to the detriment of the EC summer holiday destinations. Yours, Henri Le Coin

Evidence was uncovered this week that a concerted and co-ordinated effort is being made by lobbyists in Europe against further expansion in the number or size of airports. Environmentalists are planning to put pressure on the European Parliament against such expansions, on the grounds of destroying the green belt, polluting the atmosphere, creating more noise and exposing local communities to more danger from crashes and traffic congestion. Local communities are being urged to protest to their local political representatives on this issue.

APPENDIX TWELVE

MEMORANDUM

May 21, 92

From: Commercial Director

To: New Business Development Manager

As you know the immediacy of the threat with regard to the abolishment of duty free shopping within the EC has lessened with the announcement of July 1st, 1999 deadline.

However, we had hitherto nurtured hopes that total abolition might not occur. In this sense our longer term strategic position has worsened.

We now definitely need new ideas on how to replace our duty free sales by other, at least equally profitable, business within existing space/buy time constraints. Since some of these ideas may require several years before they can be brought in practice, we need to start the process now rather than postpone it.

I would suggest that you take action to generate some viable ideas against the more obvious criteria, which can then be screened in a more sophisticated manner. I would ideally like to have your ideas for our next strategic review on June 30th.

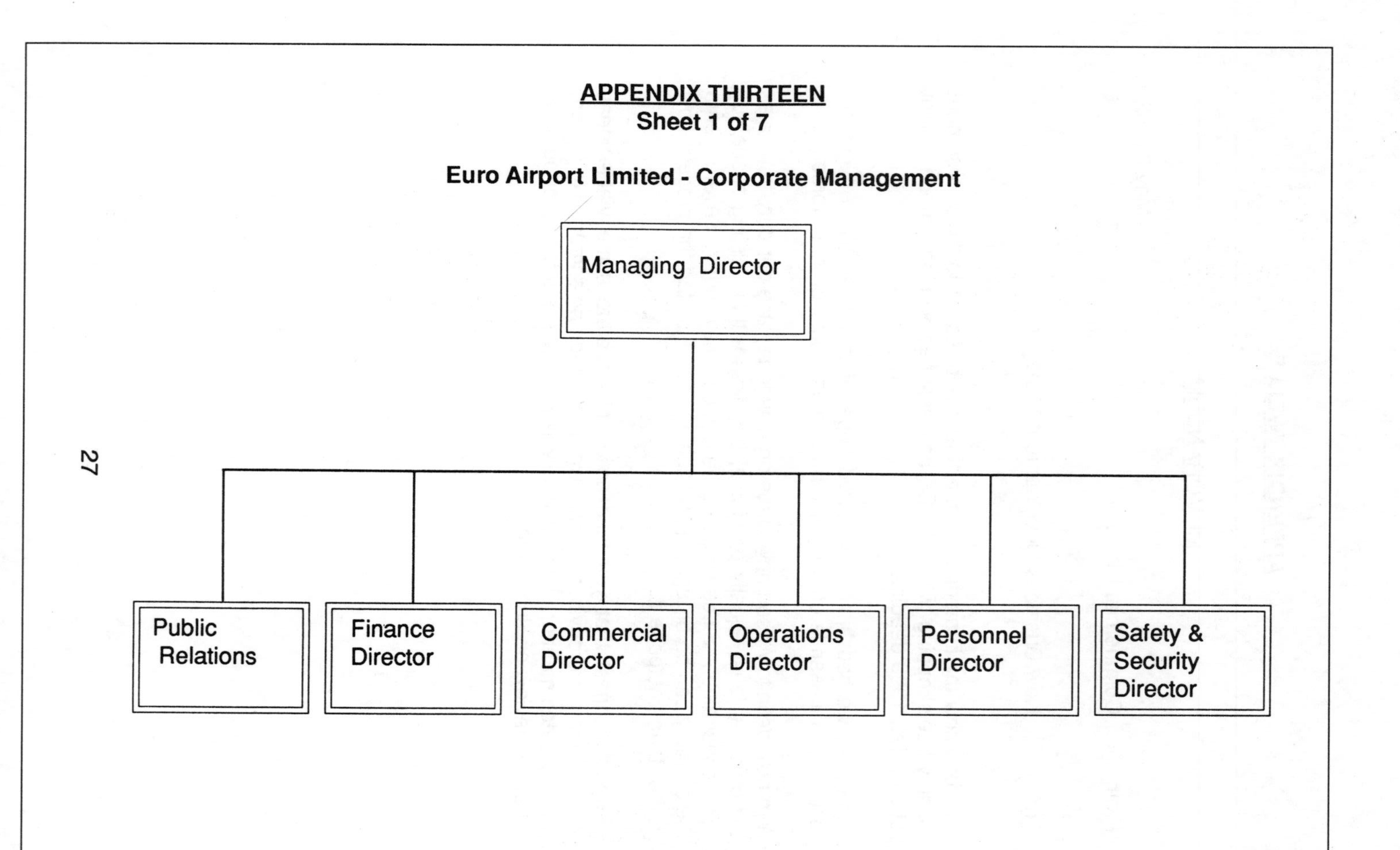
APPENDIX THIRTEEN
Sheet 1 of 7
Euro Airport Limited - Corporate Management
Managing Director
Public Relations
Finance Director
Commercial Director
Operations Director
Personnel Director
Safety & Security Director

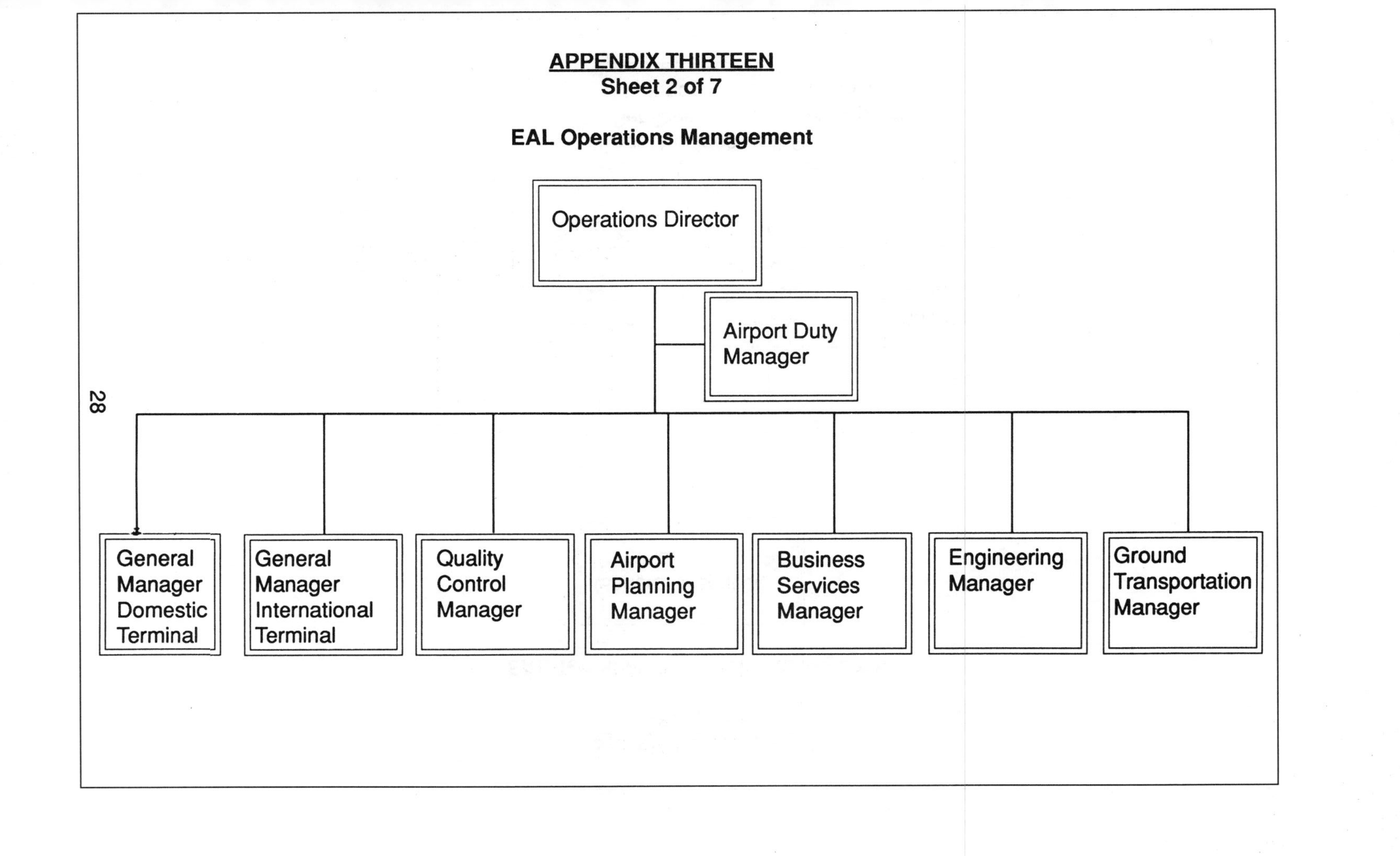
APPENDIX THIRTEEN
Sheet 2 of 7
EAL Operations Management
Operations Director
Airport Duty Manager
General Manager Domestic Terminal
General Manager International Terminal
Quality Control Manager
Airport Planning Manager
Business Services Manager
Engineering Manager
Ground Transportation Manager

APPENDIX THIRTEEN
Sheet 3 of 7

EAL Terminal Operations Management

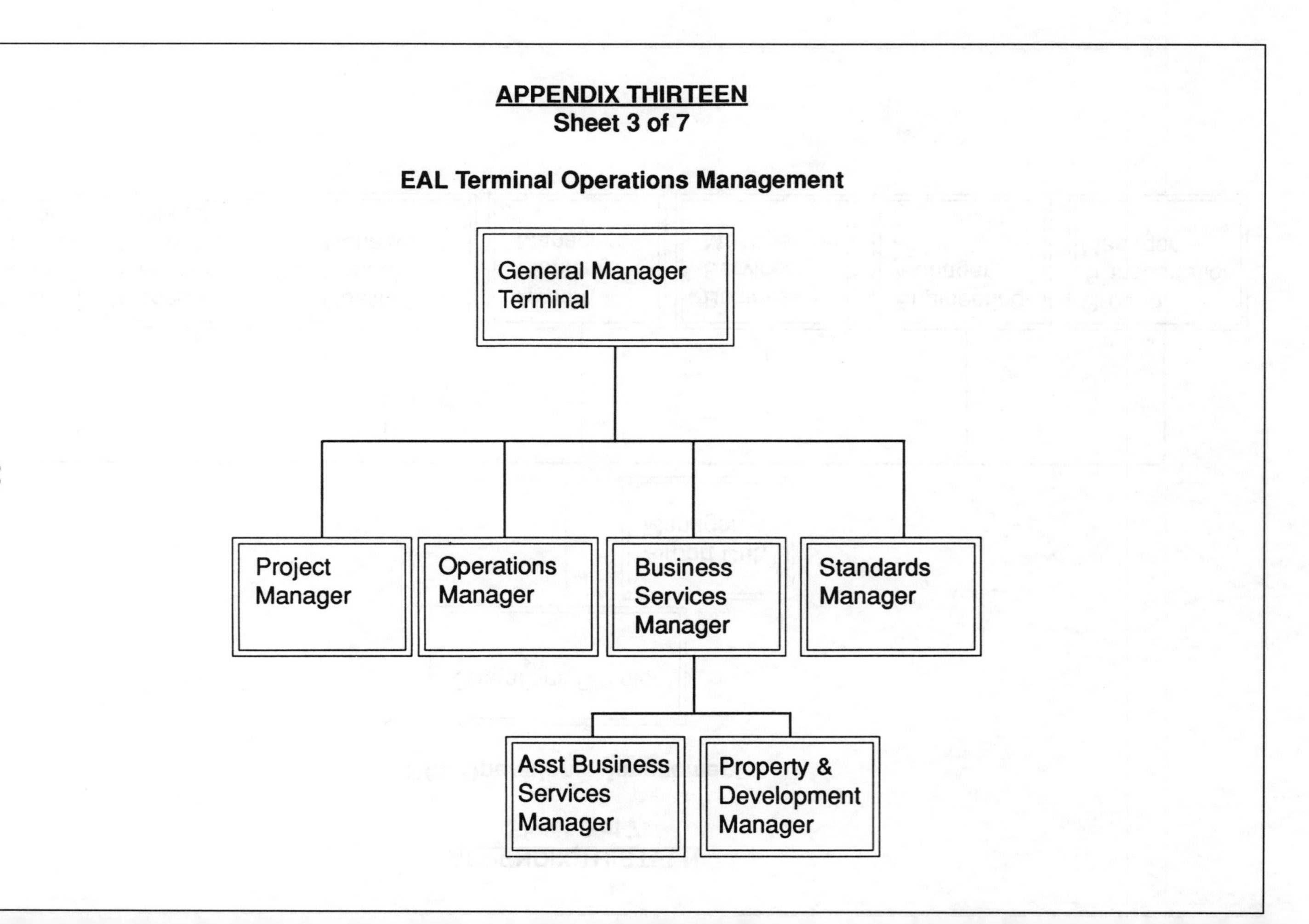

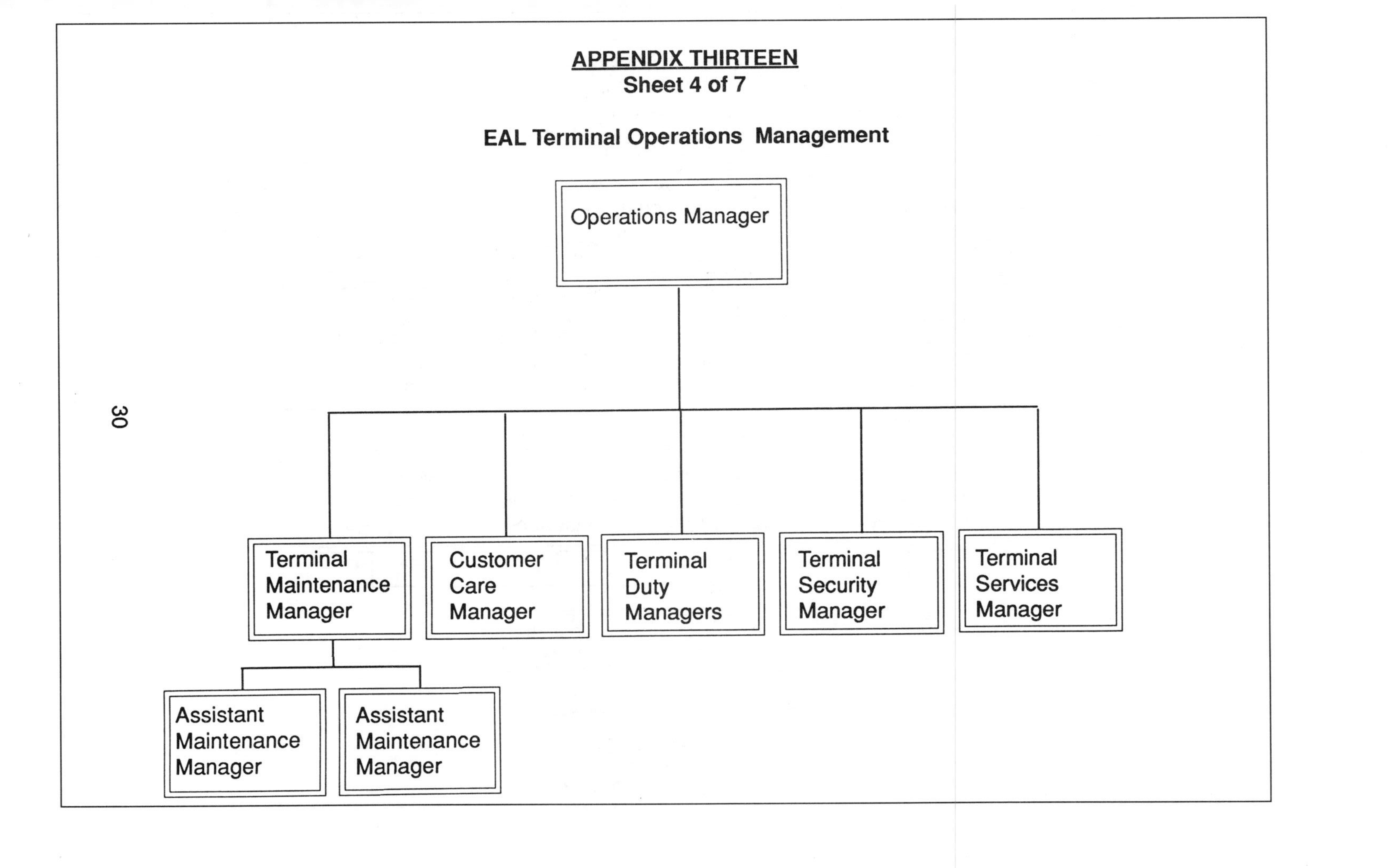
APPENDIX THIRTEEN
Sheet 4 of 7
EAL Terminal Operations Management
Operations Manager
Terminal Maintenance Manager
Customer Care Manager
Terminal Duty Managers
Terminal Security Manager
Terminal Services Manager
Assistant Maintenance Manager
Assistant Maintenance Manager
30

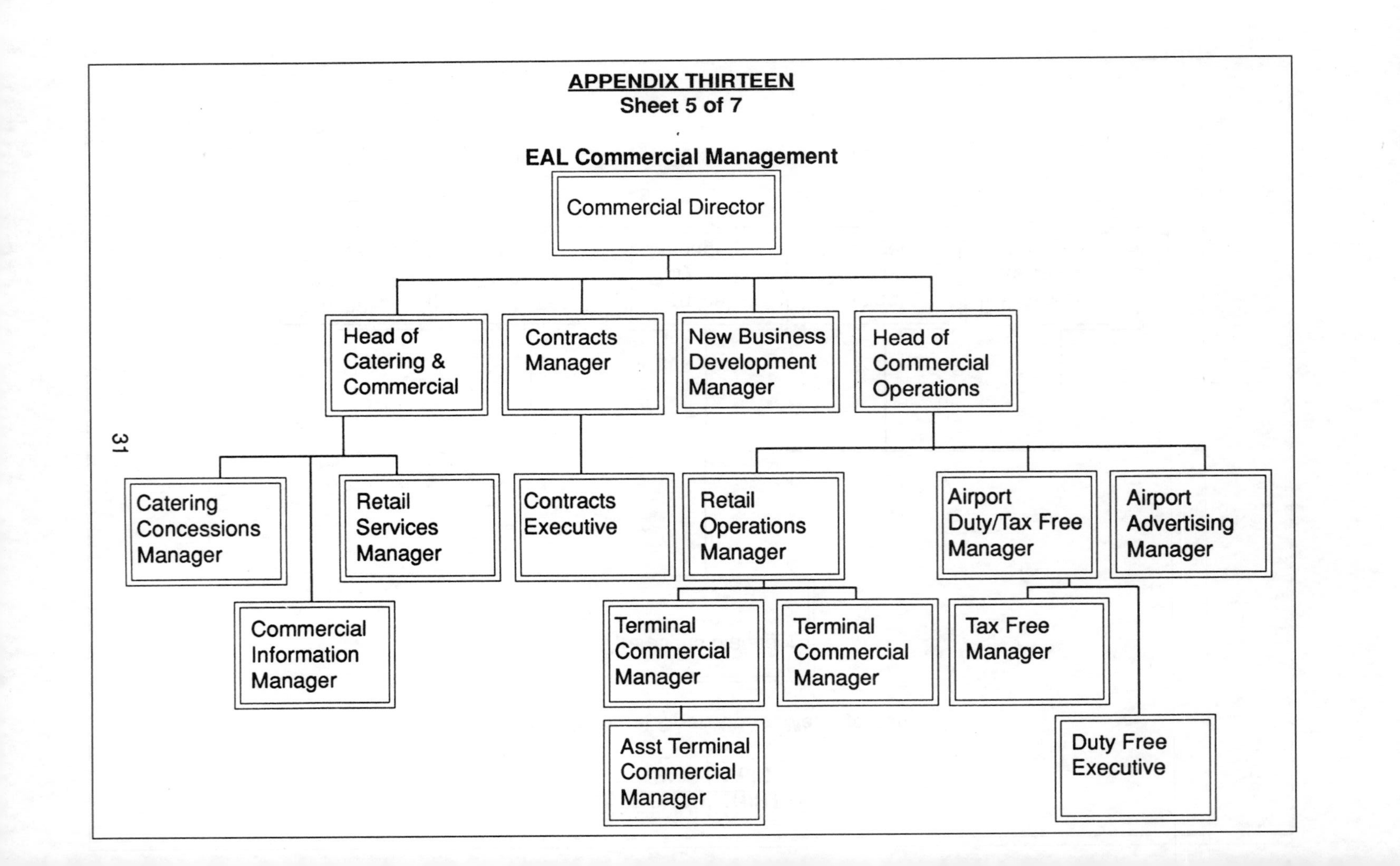
APPENDIX THIRTEEN
Sheet 5 of 7
EAL Commercial Management
Commercial Director
Head of Catering & Commercial
Contracts Manager
New Business Development Manager
Head of Commercial Operations
Catering Concessions Manager
Commercial Information Manager
Retail Services Manager
Contracts Executive
Retail Operations Manager
Airport Duty/Tax Free Manager
Airport Advertising Manager
Terminal Commercial Manager
Terminal Commercial Manager
Asst Terminal Commercial Manager
Tax Free Manager
Duty Free Executive

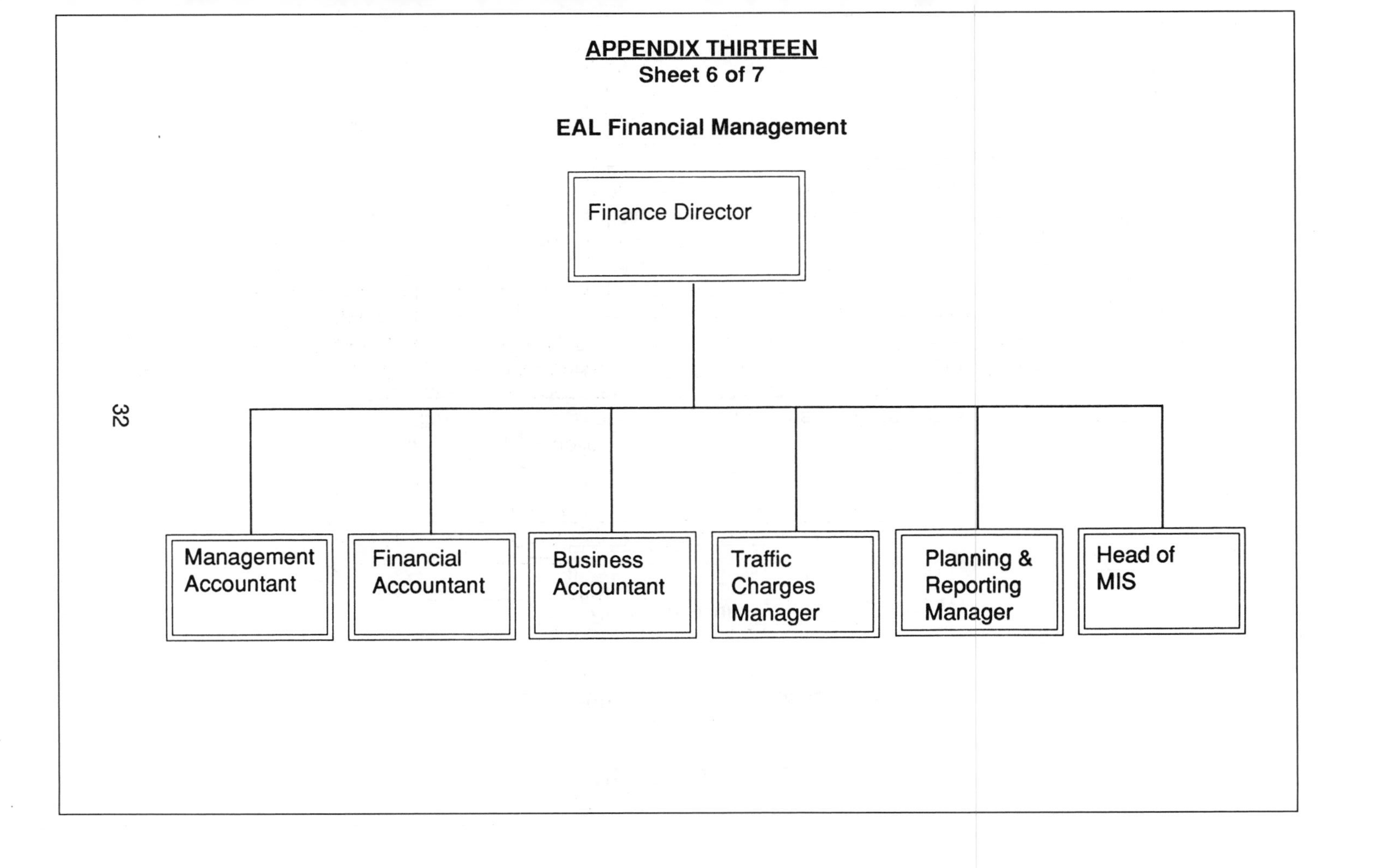
APPENDIX THIRTEEN
Sheet 6 of 7
EAL Financial Management
Finance Director
Management Accountant
Financial Accountant
Business Accountant
Traffic Charges Manager
Planning & Reporting Manager
Head of MIS

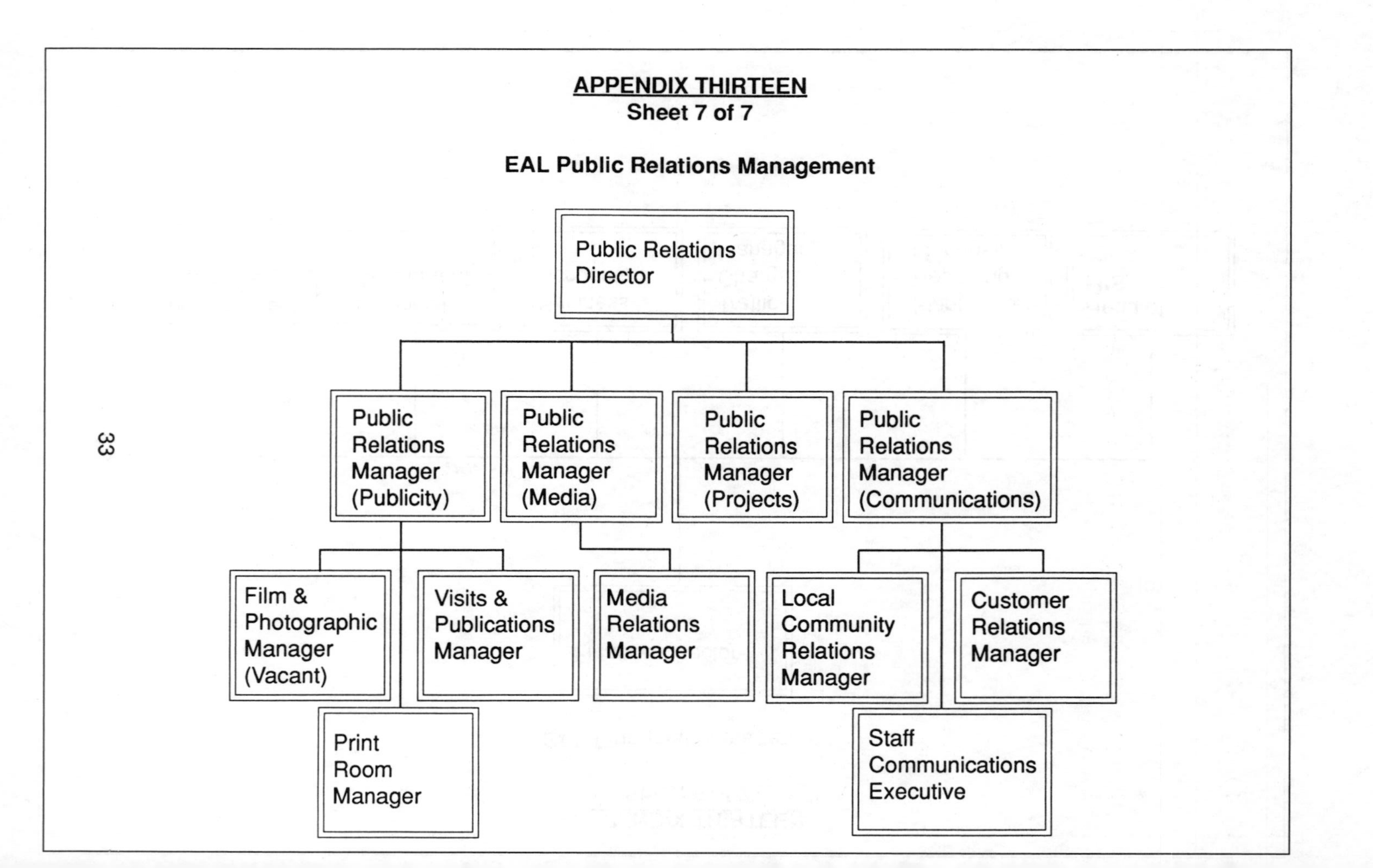
APPENDIX THIRTEEN
Sheet 7 of 7
EAL Public Relations Management
Public Relations Director
Public Relations Manager (Publicity)
Public Relations Manager (Media)
Public Relations Manager (Projects)
Public Relations Manager (Communications)
Film & Photographic Manager (Vacant)
Visits & Publications Manager
Print Room Manager
Media Relations Manager
Local Community Relations Manager
Customer Relations Manager
Staff Communications Executive

APPENDIX FOURTEEN
Sheet 1 of 3

PROFIT AND LOSS ACCOUNT (consolidated)
Year ended 31 March

	1992 £m	1991 £m	1990 £m	1989 £m
Revenue	220.3	199.5	171.95	154.3
Operating Costs	129.65	124.35	134.50	114.2
Operating Profit	90.65	75.15	37.45	40.1
Interest receivable	6.15	8.8	8.50	7.25
Profit on ordinary activities before taxation	96.8	83.95	45.95	47.35
Tax on profit on ordinary activities current year tax charge	33.4	3.25	20.50	22.10
Profit for the financial year	63.4	80.7	25.45	25.25
Dividends	-	(87.3)	(50.55)	(31.00)
Transfer from general reserve	-	6.6	25.10	5.75
Retained profit *	63.4	-	-	-

* In 1992 the directors did not recommend the payment of a dividend and the retained profit was transferred to reserves.

APPENDIX FOURTEEN
Sheet 2 of 3

EAL CONSOLIDATED BALANCE SHEET
(As at 31 March)

	1992 £m	1991 £m	1990 £m	1989 £m
Fixed assets				
Tangible assets	653.15	667.85	562.25	387.2
Current assets				
Debtors	72.6	70.7	53.45	67.65
Creditors: amounts falling due within one year				
- Trade	34.1	67.5	44.5	58.3
- other	32.55	32.65	20.65	19.0
Net current assets/(liabilities)	5.95	(29.45)	(11.7)	(9.65)
Total assets less current liabilities	659.1	638.4	550.55	377.55
Creditors: amounts falling due after more than one year	13.3	12.4	12.3	12.3
Net Assets	645.8	626.0	538.25	365.25
Capital and reserves				
Called up share capital	190.1	190.1	190.1	190.1
Revaluation reserve	386.35	429.95	335.6	137.50
General reserve	5.95	5.95	12.55	37.65
Retained profit	63.4	-	-	-
Shareholders funds	645.8	626.0	538.25	365.25

35

APPENDIX FOURTEEN
Sheet 3 of 3

SOURCE AND USE OF FUNDS STATEMENT (consolidated)
for the year ended 31 March

	1992 £m	1991 £m	1990 £m	1989 £m
Source of funds				
Profit for the financial year	96.8	83.95	45.95	47.35
Items not involving the movement of funds:				
Depreciation	19.25	19.35	45.5	29.05
Loss on disposal of fixed assets	1.35	0.25	0.75	0.80
Funds generated by operations	117.4	103.55	92.2	77.2
Proceeds from disposal of fixed assets	0.15	0.15	0.3	0.3
	117.55	103.7	92.5	77.5
Use of funds				
Purchase of fixed assets	49.65	31.00	23.5	20.75
Dividends paid	32.6	57.95	47.3	31.00
Tax paid	3.25	20.5	22.1	8.45
	85.5	109.45	92.9	60.2
Movements in working capital				
Increase in debtors	1.9	17.25	(14.2)	21.75
Decrease in trade creditors	33.4	(23.00)	13.8	(4.45)
	35.3	(5.75)	(0.4)	17.30
	117.55	103.7	92.5	77.5

36

APPENDIX FIFTEEN

MEMORANDUM

May 28,92

From: Commercial Director

To: New Business Development Manager

Subject: Space Management

Further to memo dated May 21, as you are aware, one of the severe limiting factors to our commercial development is lack of space. In order to find ways of overcoming this problem, I would like you to head a Working Party, specifically designed to look at ways of ensuring the most efficient possible use is made of the space available to us, thus maximising revenue.

In addition to this, I would particularly like you to consider the extra 1,000 square metres that have been made available to us in the International Terminal, and to consider new businesses that may be suitable.

Following the group's next meeting, I would like a report on the following;

1 Products/services that can be sold from or can operate from small outlets

2 Ideas for facilities that could be sponsored

3 Creative ideas for efficient use of space

4 Creative ideas for producing a high income per square metre

APPENDIX SIXTEEN

MEMORANDUM

May 31, 1992

From: Public Relations Director

To: New Business Development Manager

I understand from your chat with Norma Bernhardt that you have considerable experience of overcoming local community resistance to site development proposals, in your former position.

We are anticipating further strong protests from local political, environmental and consumer interest groups to our airport development plans and I would like to use your experience in drawing up some counter measures. I have spoken to your Commercial Director about this and he is quite amenable to your spending some time on this very important matter. Please ring my secretary to arrange an hour's preliminary discussion. Perhaps you could start by telling me how your former company tackled these sorts of problems.

APPENDIX SEVENTEEN
Page 1 of 2

SURVEY OF AIRPORT SHOPPERS AND THEIR BUYING BEHAVIOUR

Management Summary

* Over 90% of visitors expect shops and catering facilities at an airport

* About 80% rated duty-free shops in their three most important facilities needed at an airport

* Nearly 60% require self-service catering facilities

* Although some 80% of those questioned said they wanted financial services only a quarter of these had actually used them when available

* Airport shoppers are heavily weighted towards the higher social classes

* American and Middle/Far Eastern passengers, although occupying a relatively small proportion of total passengers, nevertheless spend very heavily in gift and personal item outlets

* Shoppers' profiles vary a great deal according to the nature of the concessionnaire. Some concessionnaires attract predominently female shoppers eg. cosmetics/perfumes, some attract more males eg. socks/ties and others have a predominance of younger shoppers.

APPENDIX SEVENTEEN
Page 2 of 2

* For all nationalities buying behaviour varies significantly according to whether the journey is outbound or homebound. Homebound overseas travellers spend much more heavily on gifts and duty free goods than outbound travellers.

* Generally speaking male shoppers are goal-orientated making planned purchases. Compared with females they buy rather than shop. Female shoppers are more inclined to look over all the merchandise and enjoy doing so when having the time.

* Stress reducing environments, logical layouts and clear signages have very positive effects on the amount of time and money spent on shopping in any locality, but particularly in airports. Fear of missing the flight and/or not hearing/seeing flight calls or alterations and confusion over gate locations - are all causes of stress which have negative effects on shopping behaviour.

Examiners' report

General comments

Overall, the pass rate was pleasingly higher than previous sittings. Students in all countries appear to have related well to the international airport setting and were able to make many creative suggestions within their answers.

A good case study should, given competent and thorough analysis, yield its key issues. These key issues should normally be the basis on which the examination questions are set, so as to preserve the integrity of the case. Most candidates (no doubt ably assisted by tutors) had not scrimped on their analysis and had therefore enjoyed their reward of some success in anticipating the likely question areas. Perhaps it should equally be pointed out that these questions were, nevertheless, highly demanding and will have occupied the minds of top marketing executives in the European airport market for some considerable time.

Unfortunately, however, standards varied between centres and within centres considerably, with some students clearly having conducted very little analysis, evidently hoping to be able to waffle their way through the paper.

Regrettably, far too many candidates are still submitting answers in inappropriate and unprofessional essay style, despite clear instructions calling for a more businesslike report format and warnings that not to adopt this format is courting failure. Some candidates also did not adopt the role stipulated in the candidate's brief, wrongly using statements such as 'What the New Business Development Manager should do' or 'Irma needs to'.

Papers from some centres failed to provide a single instance of costing or scheduling for any of the three answers given. This proliferates an impression of a lack of real management ability. Candidates wishing to be granted membership of the Chartered Institute of Marketing really must demonstrate their professionalism beyond the mere putting forward of ideas.

Candidates are again counselled to think clearly what the question is really about before writing out pre-prepared answers, the greater proportion of which are then irrelevant. A good method of ensuring the question is fully addressed is to identify its key words.

Distressingly, many candidates spend inordinate amounts of time on presenting overly-detailed contents pages, followed by over-lengthy lists of pre-prepared objectives and assumptions. Marks are not normally awarded for assumptions in themselves, especially those which are deliberately and unrealistically contrived to alter the questions so as to bring them into line with pre-prepared answers. Examinees should avoid extremely long lists of objectives which confuse rather than clarify the direction the company should take. Equally, candidates should not produce extensive introductions and summaries which gain no marks in themselves. All this timewasting only serves to convey the impression that the candidate is avoiding answering the actual question set. Even if this is untrue, the candidate then has too little time left to devote to the real question and is obliged to produce a superficial answer or listings which are unacceptable for a pass standard in this paper.

A relatively new practice has emerged at at least one centre whereby candidates attach appendices to their answers without referring the examiner to these in the text. The examiner therefore marks the question and has to remark upon finding the appendices. Worse still some candidates left blank pages inbetween their answers and the appendices, thereby running the risk of these being missed completely.

Question 1

Many candidates confined their answers solely to providing unstructured lists of proposals which, however good, were insufficient in themselves to secure a pass level.

It had been hoped that candidates would preface their proposals with some *quantified* and *time-scaled* objectives so as to provide an appropriate perspective. Also it had been expected that the majority of answers would be structured into strategy and tactics, using Ansoff and marketing mix (for services) headings.

Far too many candidates failed to propose any marketing research whatsoever. Some of the few that did went overboard and covered research and screening exclusively, failing to come up with any other proposals – hardly the right stance for a New Business Development *Manager* trying to make a name for herself in a new position.

While most candidates made some well-substantiated proposals, quite a number strayed outside the limitations of the airport site as directed in the question.

A surprising number of papers failed to allude to the most important financial indicators as asked, as well as to propose any non-financial performance indicators, as invited by the question. It was regrettable that some excellent creative thinking was spoiled by a general failure to answer the question fully.

Question 2

A refreshingly high proportion of candidates had appreciated that Irma's ability to develop new business to replace lost duty free sales would be constrained by the current organisation and that she might feel obliged to make some constructive *suggestions* for changes.

Quite a large number of students were also aware of the crucial role that internal marketing can play in service marketing and were able to suggest practical initiatives beyond the bland 'Put in TQM' approach.

Good candidates used simplified organisation charts to clarify their suggestions and indicated both timescales and costs. Poor candidates failed to justify changes and the worst seemed to think that creating a taskforce was the one miraculous solution to all problems. It needs to be emphasised that the mere appointment of a manager or the formation of a committee, in itself achieves nothing.

A number of students, mostly from overseas, suggested a matrix organisation or 'flattening' the current structure without any indication as to what they meant by this or indeed any real justification.

Question 3

Regrettably, some candidates saw the words 'development plans for a new terminal' within the question and immediately pitched enthusiastically into their pre-prepared answers without reference to the rest of the question which was really about PR.

Other candidates submitted PR or communications plans without a thought as to different target audiences and how they might have different motives requiring different approaches and messages.

Scripts incorporating plans which included even marginal references to timing, sequencing or costs were extremely rare. All future candidates are urged to include these aspects *as a matter of course*, bearing in mind they have four weeks lead-time to prepare for the examination.

Having made these constructive criticisms it has to be said that there were many really excellent answers to this question and tutors at most centres are to be congratulated on instilling a keen sense of environmental responsibility and awareness in their students. The understanding of environmental issues and the good grasp of the complexity of PR demonstrated by most candidates was very encouraging.

5 The December 1992 Examination Case

Regional Railways Central (RRC)

Examination paper

DIPLOMA IN MARKETING

(12) Marketing (Analysis and Decision)

Tuesday 15th December 1992 **Time: 14.00 — 17.00**

3 hours duration

This paper requires you to make a practical and reasoned evaluation of the problems and opportunities you have identified from the previously circulated case material. From your analysis you are required to prepare a report in accordance with the situation below. Graphing sheets and ledger analysis paper are available from the invigilators, together with continuation sheets if required. These must be identified by your candidate number and fastened in the prescribed fashion within the back cover of your answer book for collection at the end of the examinations.

READ THE QUESTIONS CAREFULLY AND ANSWER THE ACTUAL QUESTIONS AS SPECIFIED. CHECK THE MARK ALLOCATION TO QUESTIONS AND ALLOCATE YOUR TIME ACCORDINGLY. CANDIDATES MUST ATTEMPT ALL PARTS. CANDIDATES SHOULD ADOPT REPORT FORMAT. THOSE WHO DO NOT WILL BE PENALISED.

RRC - Examination Paper

Additional Information to be taken into account when answering the following questions

You have recently learned that the government is considering allowing the selling off of British Rail in a rather more piecemeal way than before. A relatively large number of 'lots' would be offered. A 'lot' would comprise any activity that can be clearly identified as a cost and profit centre. It is envisaged that such lots would include the compulsory purchase by the bidders of the freehold of land and buildings where available, together with stocks, work in progress and work in hand or under contract.

Whilst all lots would be auctioned at the same time, their actual handover to the successful bidder would be likely to occur at different times, according to the nature of the lot. However, all handovers would be made within 12 months of purchase.

A system of discounting would apply to encourage bids for 'packages' of lots i.e. the more lots bought, the higher the discount.

A set of government regulations to ensure the continuance of existing rail services at set quality and safety standards and within given price ranges would apply during the period of privatisation and for some time afterwards.

In your role as Brian Allen, the retained marketing consultant, you are required to report to your client, a prospective purchaser of RRC, upon the following:

Question 1 - (30 marks)

Outline the MAJOR marketing opportunities for profitable exploitation available to your client over the next five years, following the acquisition of RRC. For each opportunity given, indicate the financial implications and the major problems involved.

Question 2 - (30 marks)

Specify the information needed and the sources from which it might be obtained, to enable a medium to long-term marketing plan to be developed following RRC's acquisition by your client.

Question 3 - (40 marks)

Prepare an outline communications plan for internal and external use, to achieve the objectives of improving the perception of RRC by its customers/publics and of securing the support of RRC staff following the acquisition of RRC by your client. Your plan should include sequence, timings and approximate costs of the actions proposed.

REGIONAL RAILWAYS CENTRAL (RRC)

Candidates' Brief

You are Brian Allen a recently retired Marketing Manager with Regional Railways Central (RRC), who has now been retained as a consultant to advise a company interested in buying RRC if and when it eventually comes up for sale under the privatisation plans being considered by the present British government. Your client is particularly concerned to know which market opportunities are the most attractive from the viewpoint of future profitable growth and how to best exploit these opportunities, in the event of a decision to buy. Your client is also seeking your expertise with regard to identifying and solving the major problems or barriers against gaining a profitable return on the investment within a reasonable payback period. Your client is a Midlands based company operating a range of road transport services including freight and passenger services, with a high reputation for customer care.

Following your initial assessment you will be required to make clear recommendations for future action.

This case material is based upon experience with actual companies. Alterations in the information given and in the real data have been made to preserve confidentiality. Candidates are strictly instructed not to contact companies in this industry, and are to be aware that some additional information will be provided at the time of examination.

Copies may be obtained from the Chartered Institute of Marketing, Moor Hall, Cookham, Maidenhead, Berks, SL6 9QH

REGIONAL RAILWAYS CENTRAL

Regional Railways Central (RRC) is part of Regional Railways, which is part of British Rail. Regional Railways' decentralised management serves the rail transport needs of regional passengers in Great Britain (England, Wales and Scotland), excluding South-East England and the special inter-city services, which are separately managed by Network Southeast and InterCity respectively. These three organisations together form British Rail's national passenger railway run by the British Railways Board.

RRC serves an area of central England and central Wales running across the country from the East coast to the West coast. It is a separately managed cost centre. RRC runs urban, inter-urban and rural rail services throughout its area. It owns assets such as trains, tracks and stations. It has trading agreements with other sectors of British Rail to run services over their tracks.

Urban passenger services are those mainly concerned with taking passengers to and from work every day by rail from sub-urban districts to town and city centres and/or to other sub-urban districts where work exists. Sub-urban districts are those densely populated areas which surround a major town or city and can contain industrial as well as residential developments.

Inter-urban services link major towns and cities and provide for families and shoppers as well as business people. They should not be confused with InterCity services which concentrate on the provision of fast main line trains for business people wishing to travel non-stop from one city centre to another.

Rural services cover the more general needs of the smaller communities in the countryside, linking small towns and villages.

Different types of locomotives, carriages and lengths of trains are employed to suit the different types of services or market segments. Other elements of the marketing mix such as frequency of service, prices and promotion are also varied according to these different market segments.

RRC has its headquarters in Birmingham which retains responsibility for overall business planning and marketing strategy but devolves responsibility for day to day operations to geographically based District Managers located in Birmingham, Nottingham, Norwich and Shrewsbury.

RRC is striving to improve its profitability by developing services better suited to existing and potential new passengers and by creating a lasting image of quality/efficiency. In striving to achieve these aims however, RRC does of course have to work within the context of Regional Railways, which in turn has to work within the overall context of British Rail.

Regional Railways

Regional Railways has four other cost centres similar to RRC. These are North East, North West, South Wales and West, and ScotRail. In terms of route mileage and number of stations, Regional Railways is bigger than British Rail's other passenger business sectors of Network Southeast or InterCity and it employs about 37,500 staff. Total turnover is expected to be about £955 million for 1992 made up of an income from passenger fares of £305 million plus a revenue support in the form of grants from government and "Passenger Transport Executives" (PTE's) of around £650 million.

There are seven PTE's in Regional Railways' area of operation, which represent the interests of the Passenger Transport Authorities of the major cities of Birmingham, Sheffield, Manchester, Leeds, Liverpool, Newcastle upon Tyne and Glasgow.

Some 56% of Regional Railway's journeys are made within these PTE areas. The PTE's specify what they want in terms of train frequency, timings and pricing and then provide revenue support to Regional Railways towards the costs.

Apart from this financial support from the PTE's, Regional Railways also receive grants and assistance with capital investment from County Councils to fund new stations or to re-open freight lines to regular passenger services etc. Finally, national government contributes funding for socially necessary rail services which cannot fully recover their operating costs, in the form of the annual Public Service Obligation Grant (PSO). This PSO funding has however, progressively declined as efficiency has improved.

Since British Rail (in 1982) moved away from what was essentially a centralised control over a regional railways network, to the principle of organisation and control by business sectors (or Strategic Business Units), there have been ten years of considerable achievement within the three passenger transport business sectors. For Regional Railways perhaps the most notable element has been the near total replacement of the Regional Railways diesel fleet with a purpose built fleet of modern stock. In the nine years to the end of 1990, Regional Railways re-opened 106 miles of railway to passenger traffic and opened 122 new stations. There will be another 62 miles by 1994, with 54 more stations. The same nine years saw 100 miles of rail electrified and a further 105 miles will follow in the next five years. As Network South East and Regional Railways connected Stansted Airport to the national railway network in 1991, so Regional Railways will connect Manchester Airport, the North's principal international gateway, to the railway network in 1992. Passenger-train-miles increased by 15% over the period 1987-91, but it was nevertheless possible to reduce basic costs per loaded train by 25% and at Government's request to reduce the PSO grant by 22% in real terms between 1986 and 1990.

Perhaps the greatest problems still faced are a huge maintenance backlog, above all in respect of stations, and a need to modernise antiquated signalling. Regional Railways has 1497 stations, and on its 4600 miles of line there are no less than 612 signalboxes. Whilst Regional Railways has some of the most modern signalling in the country on its rural lines, and has some ultra-modern equipment, it has also inherited a vast number of very old signal boxes on what were once deemed secondary lines. Dealing with the problems these pose - both technical and in terms of containing signalling cost and road crossing costs - will be a major challenge.

Regional Railways' market is largely the commuter trade in urban areas during peak travel hours and those who are visiting friends and relatives in the inter-urban areas. For the urban business (run in partnership with the PTE's), marketing is essentially localised. The aim is however, to put over a common image of a consistent quality. The new Regional Railways corporate identity has been retained and adapted by the PTE's who use their own liveries within Central HQ guidelines. Detailed urban marketing is concerned with the creation of attractive packages. Many PTE's link their rail travel strategy with supplementary offers including buses, and such initiatives are strongly supported by Regional Railways HQ.

On the inter-urban routes the market is very similar to InterCity's. The customer-profile and journey distances are very much the same (with the difference that Regional Railways inter-urban services often also have a significant commuting role) so the overall marketing techniques of the two business sectors are not dissimilar. The two sectors do not think of themselves as being in competition and collaborate very closely with each other in many areas, so there are good grounds for avoiding possible confusion in the customer's mind and even for suggesting partnership. It will probably come as a surprise to some that InterCity trains actually serve more Regional Railways stations than there are InterCity stations and run over very substantial lengths of Regional Railways track. The fact that there are separate passenger business sectors does not mean there is no national railway. The rail customers perception is that of British Rail as a whole rather than one of three separate business entities.

No Regional Railways services cover their operating costs and the urban and rural services are certain to need continuing support. The rail business prefers the word' support' rather than 'subsidy'. It feels it has a valuable role to play in local transport networks and elected authorities have taken informed decisions to contribute towards the costs of services the community needs.

The current objectives for which the Government's grant is given, expire in March 1993 and require re-negotiation. Essentially they are those inherited from the Railways Act 1968: to maintain certain services. These were modified by a directive issued under the Railways Act 1974: to operate passenger services so as to provide a public service comparable with that then generally provided.

Simply to retain the status quo provides a rather uninspiring objective, and in the forthcoming re-negotiation Regional Railways would like to agree something much more positive, demonstrating clear justification for continuing income support. The business aims to present Government with a number of options setting out different levels of service at different costs.

The dominant issue now seems to have become the level of quality customers want rather than just a question of the lowest possible prices. The rail business has seen the very hostile reaction from the travelling public to notoriously unreliable services - people's aspirations are rising and their tolerance thresholds are falling. It is the view of the Regional Railways management that customers should enjoy a safe, efficient, and reliable railway service.

Now that there is clearly defined management responsibility for urban, inter-urban and rural services, this must bring benefits for the customer, whether the individual traveller or the local authority. This does however, need communicating to the target audiences.

The basic principle is geographical. Profit Centre Directors have total responsibility for all the resources employed in their part of the business. They have full authority to negotiate contracts, vary the utilisation of stock, improve the productivity of staff and produce the quality of service required. Having set up the contract, the Profit Centre Director must then deliver on it and negotiate any changes found necessary by either party. This direct line of communication represents a dramatic simplification of former patterns and eliminates the separation between negotiation and responsibility for delivery.

As on the other passenger sectors, the operating side has been separated from retail responsibilities. Retail covers everything from the telephone enquiry, through buying a ticket, up to the rail staff helping a passenger through the train door, and also the work of the conductor on the train itself. This allows the whole quality emphasis for the customer to be enhanced. If, for example, the conductor is a member of the retail staff rather than an operator, then his/her main duties are looking after customers throughout the journey - not just giving the driver the starting-signal at stations and then retreating to the brake-van. Obviously some retail staff have operating duties. Giving the right of way or winding points in an emergency are both clearly operating matters. But this must not disguise the fact that the normal duty of conductors and station staff is retail and the majority of their time will be spent directly looking after customers.

An example of the interface between retail and operations is punctuality, a vital aspect of quality. Station staff must always try to get trains out on time - which, as we have seen is an operational aspect of their mainly retail duties. The only way to purge out operational unreliability, including unpunctuality, is to identify all delays and assign them to their cause so that responsibility can be allocated. When a problem caused by slack station-working becomes apparent, it is the retail manager's job to tighten up the work of the staff. Thus there has to be close and effective co-operation between the operations side and the retail side. At the top of the structure is the Profit Centre Director, in whom all aspects of the railway, both operational and retail are united and who is answerable for total quality in the review that takes place before the annual budget for the profit-centre is agreed. The stress on quality is now paramount, and quality depends on everyone working together.

The urban railway promises to be Regional Railways' most exciting sphere of activity in the future. Congestion in towns and cities is now a major problem, especially at peak times, and the time has come when positive steps are needed to reduce it. The private car is the principal competitor for public transport - and very severe competition it is too! Growth in car-ownership and use, led to a fall in the public transport share of total passenger miles from 60% in the early 1950s to only 15%

by the late 1980s. Car ownership is forecast to grow further by the end of the century. The car provides not only a very high level of comfort but also a "seamless" journey. You get in at your own home, and you get out as close as possible to your destination - often actually at your destination if reserved parking has been provided. But given that the solutions of the last couple of decades to the growing congestion problems (measures to improve traffic-flows, provision of more parking-spaces, construction of new inter-urban linkroads, and so on), seem unlikely to be acceptable in the next decade to an electorate no longer willing to tolerate the loss of land and amenities that such answers involve, it appears as if the only possible ways forward are road pricing or improved public transport which does its best to match the car's indisputable convenience.

There are grounds for Regional Railways to think that the tide is now flowing in the direction of public transport. Because there has been an enormous change in local authorities' attitudes, accepting that pouring ever more money into roads is not the right thing to do and not what their voters want any more - some of the faults of no co-ordination between the various modes of public transport of the past, (like bus-stops well away from railway stations), are already beginning to disappear. Closer working arrangements with the local authorities can provide a much stronger role for the railways, and allow services to be offered of an attractiveness which neither railway or bus operators could produce on their own.

The railway is not really competing with the bus - or even the taxi. There is nothing to be gained from isolation: all the modes of public transport should join together in competition with the private car. Hence the importance of depicting the seamless journey: anything that shows that everything fits together must be good. There may only be a limited success in getting existing car-users out of their vehicles and on to public transport, but there is an enormous growth predicted for the numbers of cars. If even a part of this growth can be diverted to public transport, including Regional Railways, there is a huge potential market waiting to be tapped.

Rail can provide distinct, fast routes into the large cities offering something both positive and attractive to overcome the congestion, but its routes do not, on the whole, help for very short journeys.

However, the railway can be involved even with the short-trip transport needs. Much attention is focused on Light Rapid Transport (LRT) at the moment, for this has the great advantage of taking people from where they live to where they want to go, direct. However, speed considerations make LRT (a modern form of tram) inappropriate for longer-distance journeys and suggest the need for close working together with heavy rail for such travel.

British Rail

The dawn of the railway age in the UK was brought about by a number of small private companies which gradually expanded (with numerous takeovers and bankruptcies) until grouping in 1923 into the four mainline regionalised companies of London, Midland, Scottish; The Great Western Railway; Southern Railway; and the Great Eastern Railway.

By 1948 these were on the verge of collapse and a decision was taken by the Government to nationalise the whole railway system under the name of 'British Railways', controlled by the Railway Executive through five regions (London Midland; Western; Southern; Eastern; North Eastern and Scottish), with headquarters located in London, York and Glasgow.

The 1963 Transport Act merged the two Eastern Regions into one and abolished the Railway Executive replacing it with the British Rail Board.

In 1982 the regions based on geographical areas began to be replaced by business orientated organisations known as 'Sectors' including InterCity, Network South East, Provincial (now Regional Railways), Railfreight and Parcels. Ancillary activities such as shipping, road transport, hotels, catering and engineering were sold, and support activities such as maintenance, light rail, property etc. were converted into separately managed subsidiaries.

From April 1992, Parcels as a Sector was abolished and the last vestiges of a regional approach were replaced by a total asset owning business approach with each Sector responsible for all functions of Operations, Signalling, Engineering, Marketing, Retail, Personnel etc. The six Business Sectors are now InterCity, Network South East, Regional Railways, European Passenger Services, Railfreight and Telecommunications Limited which have real profit/loss responsibility and defined objectives co-ordinated by a much smaller headquarters (150 staff) known as the British Rail Board Holding Company, located in

London. The European Passenger Services Business Sector is responsible for the Channel Tunnel project.

The British Government is planning to sell off BR under its privatisation programme but the details of how best to do this are still undecided. Original ideas for privatising BR as a total entity appear to have been abandoned. Options under discussion include selling off the three primary sectors separately; retaining part of the business e.g. railway lines and selling off the remainder; and selling off the railway lines to a company which would maintain/extend these and lease their use to regional private companies operating rolling stock and providing passenger and freight services. Other options are likely to be proposed and evaluated before a final decision is made.

It is often argued that railways are environmentally friendly, especially in civilising our urban areas, and certainly the electric railway - the preferred option for urban services - is clean and quiet. However, the railway business itself would contend that there is little sense in simply claiming environmental benefits without putting these in strict economic terms. Everything has be shown to be financially beneficial to be environmentally 'sound. Decision-makers are not taken in by vague generalisations about the environment: unless the economic advantages can be truly demonstrated, they remain unimpressed.

Today this can be done quite effectively, for people are much more concerned about environmental issues than they were and the modern railway does have genuine and measurable benefits that a professional management can offer.

Looked at from a passenger point of view, services are provided for people by people. Inevitably the quality of the service is affected by the person who delivers it, be this a waiter, a porter or an enquiry office assistant. In the final analysis, excellence of passenger train carriage design, clean stations and frequent, punctual trains can all be marred by poor railway staff interfaces with customers.

The image of British Rail (as portrayed by the media) is not one of care for customers. The allegations are that in the past, (when the employee unions were extremely strong), the general public faced indifferent, surly or even downright rude attitudes from railway staff. No-one seemed to know or care which trains were going where, from what platform or at what time. Porters had long since ceased to carry cases even for the elderly or infirm. Trains ran late or were cancelled without reasons or apologies being given. Trains were dirty, unheated, draughty and noisy. Any announcements over the loudspeaker system were unintelligible.

Potential customers were put off by the nigh impossibility of getting through by telephone to the enquiry offices who seemed to be continuously engaged and closed to personal visits outside normal working hours - the very times when they were most likely to be wanted.

Whilst many improvements to stations, lines and trains have been made and/or have been planned for the future, a major problem is that of getting the idea of customer sovereignty unreservedly accepted by all staff and particularly those directly interfacing with the general public.

The railways not only have to change intrinsically but also to improve their image i.e. how they are perceived by their various publics. Although there is some fondness and nostalgia for the railways as they were, amongst older people - most media coverage is hostile. Until recently very little attention has been paid to the benefits of market segmentation.

RRC has opportunities to position itself favourably within the total railways spectrum and also within the market sub-segments. It is aware of these opportunities and planning to exploit them.

RRC's broad aims are, to be seen to be innovative in delivering 'the new railway' and within its target market, to be its customers' preferred choice of travel.

LIST OF APPENDICES

Regional Railways Central (RRC)

			Pages
Appendix 1	-	Organisation Charts	16
Appendix 2	-	Fact Sheets	18
Appendix 3	-	Objectives and Vision	22
Appendix 4	-	Budgets and Financial Performance Indicators	23

Regional Railways

Appendix 5	-	Organisation Chart	24
Appendix 6	-	Geographical Regions (profit centres)	25
Appendix 7	-	Comparisons with other Railway Business Sectors	26
Appendix 8	-	External pressures	27
Appendix 9	-	Pricing	28
Appendix 10	-	Marketing Research Findings	29
Appendix 11	-	Urban, Inter-urban and Rural Services	30
Appendix 12	-	Market Sub-segments and Customer Profiles	31
Appendix 13	-	Extracts from Proposed Advertising Campaign - inter-urban services	43

British Rail

Appendix 14	-	Organisation Chart	50
Appendix 15	-	Comparisons with other Countries	51
Appendix 16	-	Compendium of Press Articles	52

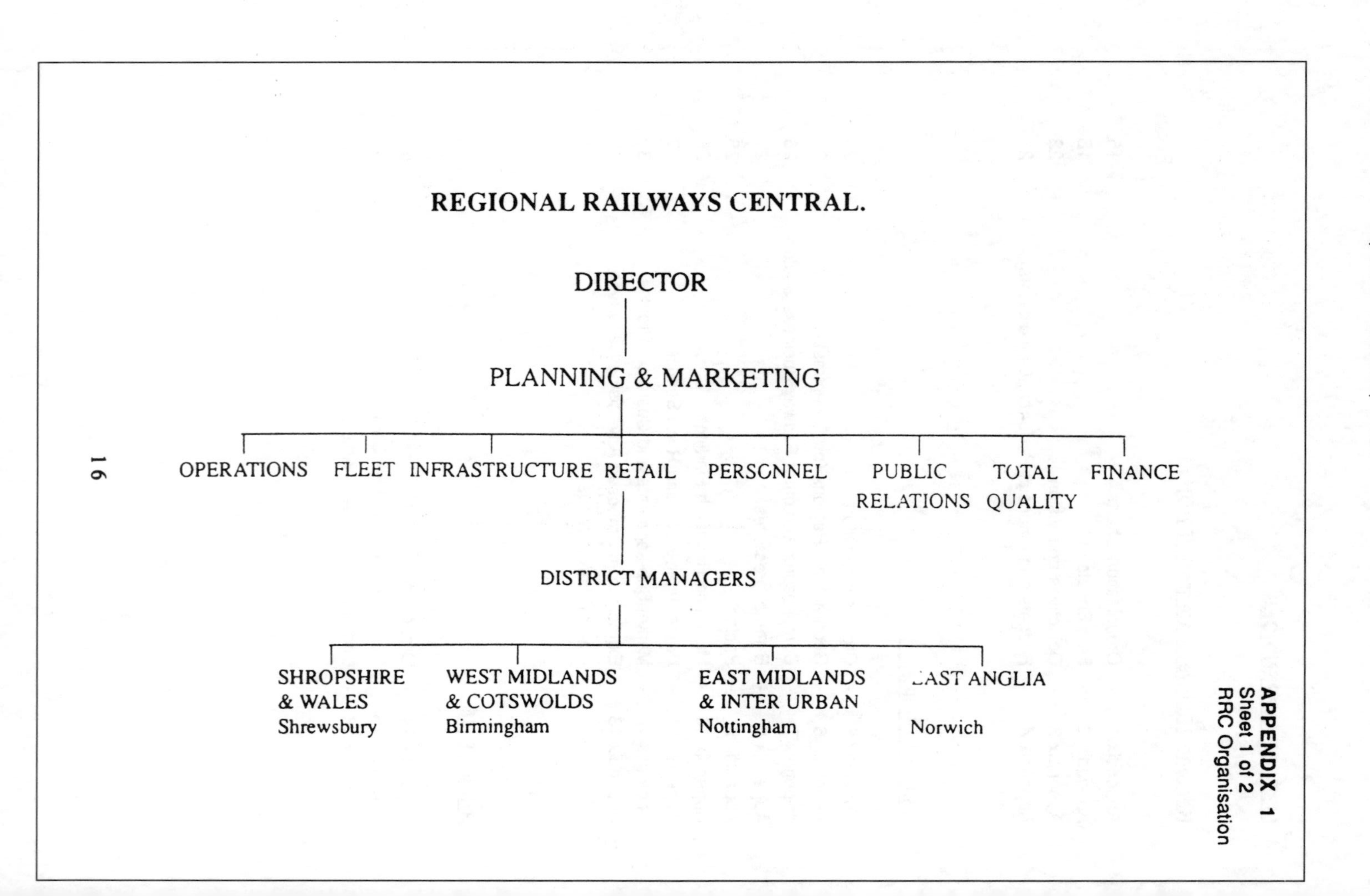

APPENDIX 1
Sheet 1 of 2
RRC Organisation
REGIONAL RAILWAYS CENTRAL.
DIRECTOR
PLANNING & MARKETING
OPERATIONS
FLEET
INFRASTRUCTURE
RETAIL
PERSCNNEL
PUBLIC RELATIONS
TOTAL QUALITY
FINANCE
DISTRICT MANAGERS
SHROPSHIRE & WALES
Shrewsbury
WEST MIDLANDS & COTSWOLDS
Birmingham
EAST MIDLANDS & INTER URBAN
Nottingham
EAST ANGLIA
Norwich
16

APPENDIX 1
Sheet 2 of 2
RRC Retail Organisation

DISTRICT RETAIL STAFF

↑

DISTRICT STATION MANAGER

↑

DISTRICT RETAIL MANAGER

↑

PROFIT CENTRE - RETAIL MANAGER

APPENDIX 2
Sheet 1 of 4
RRC Fact Sheet

FactSheet

Central

Regional Railways Central – a broad outline

REGIONAL RAILWAYS CENTRAL runs inter-urban, urban and rural services throughout Central England and Mid-Wales – the "Barmouth-Yarmouth Railway." It owns various assets such as trains, track and stations and employs staff in order to operate its services. It has trading agreements with other businesses of British Rail to run services over their tracks.

District Management

Regional Railways Central covers a large geographical area – from Pwllheli to Felixstowe in some 380 miles – nearly the distance from London to Edinburgh. The size has meant that Regional Railways Central has developed the concept of District Management in order to deliver the product, ie a safe, reliable and attractive train service, to local customers. District Managers are the "custodians of the product" and are based in Norwich, Nottingham, Birmingham and Shrewsbury. Their job is to co-ordinate the cross-functional management of operations, retail and infrastructure to ensure that strategies and day to day activities are developed and practiced in a co-ordinated fashion.

Continued

APPENDIX 2
Sheet 2 of 4
RRC Fact Sheet

Partnerships

Regional Railways Central runs many socially desirable but commercially unviable services in the English and Welsh counties under contract to the Government via the Public Service Obligation Grant. In the West Midlands, Regional Railways Central works very closely with the West Midlands Passenger Transport Executive – Centro. Centro specifies the level of service and contracts with Regional Railways for train service operations and investment in the local rail network. Outside the West Midlands Regional Railways Central works in partnership with local authorities and Government agencies in order to provide services people want to use.

Working together

Regional Railways Central, although a free standing business in its own right, could not operate without the active co-operation of other parts of the British Rail family. At a number of key locations Central's trains need to use the tracks of other Profit Centres whether they be InterCity, Network SouthEast, Regional Railways or Trainload Freight in order to provide a complete and comprehensive network. Agreements have been reached with these businesses so that Central's trains can make use of their track. Likewise other businesses have agreements with Central to use its tracks.

For example, Central has an agreement with InterCity to run local services on the route from Rugby to Wolverhampton whilst Trainload Freight and Railfreight Distribution run freight trains between Peterborough and Ipswich. By working together the various parts of British Rail provide a nationwide service for all its customers.

The quality of service given by Regional Railways Central to its customers is the most important task in hand. Everything, from running the trains to selling tickets, must delight the customer no matter whether they are travelling one mile or a thousand. Regional Railways is the fastest growing people carrying business in the country. It aims to stay that way.

Continued

APPENDIX 2
Sheet 3 of 4
RRC Fact Sheet

Personnel	
• Infrastructure	2600
• Operations	1770
• Retail	1650
• Fleet	520
• Personnel	260
• Planning and marketing	88
• Others	120
Trains Track and Infrastructure	
• Rolling stock - diesel vehicles	469
electric vehicles	56
• Stations	297
• Signal boxes	158
• Maintenance depots	2
• Traincrew depots	12
• Route miles	1121
• Trains per day	1460
• Level crossings	1300
• Bridges and culverts	6500
• Total length of tunnels	9 miles
• Passenger journeys per week	660,000
• Average journey (miles)	21.95
• County Councils within geographic boundary full or partially served	18
• Members of Parliament	97

APPENDIX 2
Sheet 4 of 4
RRC Fact Sheet

FactSheet

Central

Partnerships with Outside Bodies

REGIONAL RAILWAYS CENTRAL works in partnership with County Councils to provide services people want to use. In some instances County Councils support train services by means of grants whilst in others they assist with capital investment – funding new stations or helping to pay for improvements to existing ones.

There is, for instance, close liaison with Lincolnshire County Council and its associated District Councils ranging from regular meetings with the County Council to working groups with the Districts. Items of mutual interest are under discussion including the best way forward to enhance the railway network in the County.

In other areas Regional Railways Central is working closely with Leicestershire, Derbyshire, Nottinghamshire and Staffordshire to re-open freight lines to regular passenger services. These new services could not be considered if it were not for the financial input from the local authorities.

Some County Councils do, or have done in the past, provided revenue support for train services. Some services, for example, on the Redditch-Longbridge section of the Cross-City route are supported by Hereford and Worcester County Council. In East Anglia there is support for late evening services on some routes from both Norfolk and Suffolk County Councils.

In Mid-Wales the Development Board for Rural Wales together with all the local authorities along the Shrewsbury-Aberystwyth route have contributed towards its modernisation. Further financial contributions will allow the upgrading of the route to take place. This will enable Regional Railways to run faster, more regular services on this particular line.

APPENDIX 3
RRC Objectives and Vision

THE CENTRAL PROFIT CENTRE

OBJECTIVES:

- TO PLAN, IMPLEMENT AND MANAGE A COST EFFECTIVE RURAL, URBAN AND INTER - URBAN RAILWAY TO ACREED CONTRACTS.

- TO INCREASE AND SUSTAIN QUALITY THROUGHOUT THE PROFIT CENTRE TO MATCH THE EXPECTATIONS OF ALL OUR CUSTOMERS AND STAFF TO ENSURE REPEAT BUSINESS.

THE VISION:

- TO PLAN FOR SAFE, FREQUENT, RELIABLE, AND CLEAN TRAINS WITH A FRIENDLY, RELAXED, INFORMED, AND INFORMAL ON-TRAIN ENVIRONMENT.

- THEIR LEVEL OF PUNCTUALITY, CLEANLINESS, AND FARES WILL ENSURE THAT THE LEVEL OF NEW AND REPEAT BUSINESS GIVES A FIRM BASE FOR THE FUTURE.

- THAT WE REMAIN THE CONSUMER'S CHOICE FOR URBAN, RURAL AND INTER - URBAN JOURNEYS.

- THAT WE ARE PRO-ACTIVE IN OUR PLANNING, PROMOTION AND P.R AND THAT OUR CREDIBILITYAS A TEAM IS RECOGNISED AS PROFESSIONAL BY WITHIN AND WITHOUT OUR INDUSTRY.

- OUR SUCCESS WILL BE MEASURED BY THE EXTENT OF OUR REPEAT BUSINESS.

APPENDIX 4
RRC Revenue/Costs, Financial Performance Indicators and Marketing Budgets

4.1 Revenue and Costs

Source	Revenue Earnings (£000's)	Operating Costs (£000's)
Urban	38,400	88,000
Inter-urban	29,000	50,000
Rural	4,600	17,000
Miscellaneous	1,500	24,000
	----------	----------
TOTALS	**73,500**	**179,000**
PTE Support	19,000	
PSO Support	86,500	

NOTE: Revenue comes mainly from ticket receipts. Costs are incurred mainly by train services, staff, maintenance and infrastructure

4.2 Financial Performance Indicators

	1987	1988	1989	1990	1991
Receipts per train mile (£'s)	3.60	3.49	3.36	3.26	3.17
Total operating expenses per train mile (£'s)	9.63	9.10	8.66	8.78	9.37
Deficit per train mile (£'s)	6.03	5.61	5.30	5.52	6.20
PSO Grant per PSO supported passenger mile (pence)	27.30	24.54	19.14	19.78	18.58
PTE Grant per PTE supported passenger mile (pence)	8.74	8.37	7.42	8.12	9.20

Note: PSO = Government Grant
PTE = Grants from Passenger Transport Executive (urban areas)

4.3 Marketing Budgets (£000's)

Advertising	678
Information Services (timetables, notices etc)	395
Corporate Identity	127
Marketing Research - Advertising	40
Marketing Research - Pricing	60
Contingencies	50

TOTAL	1350

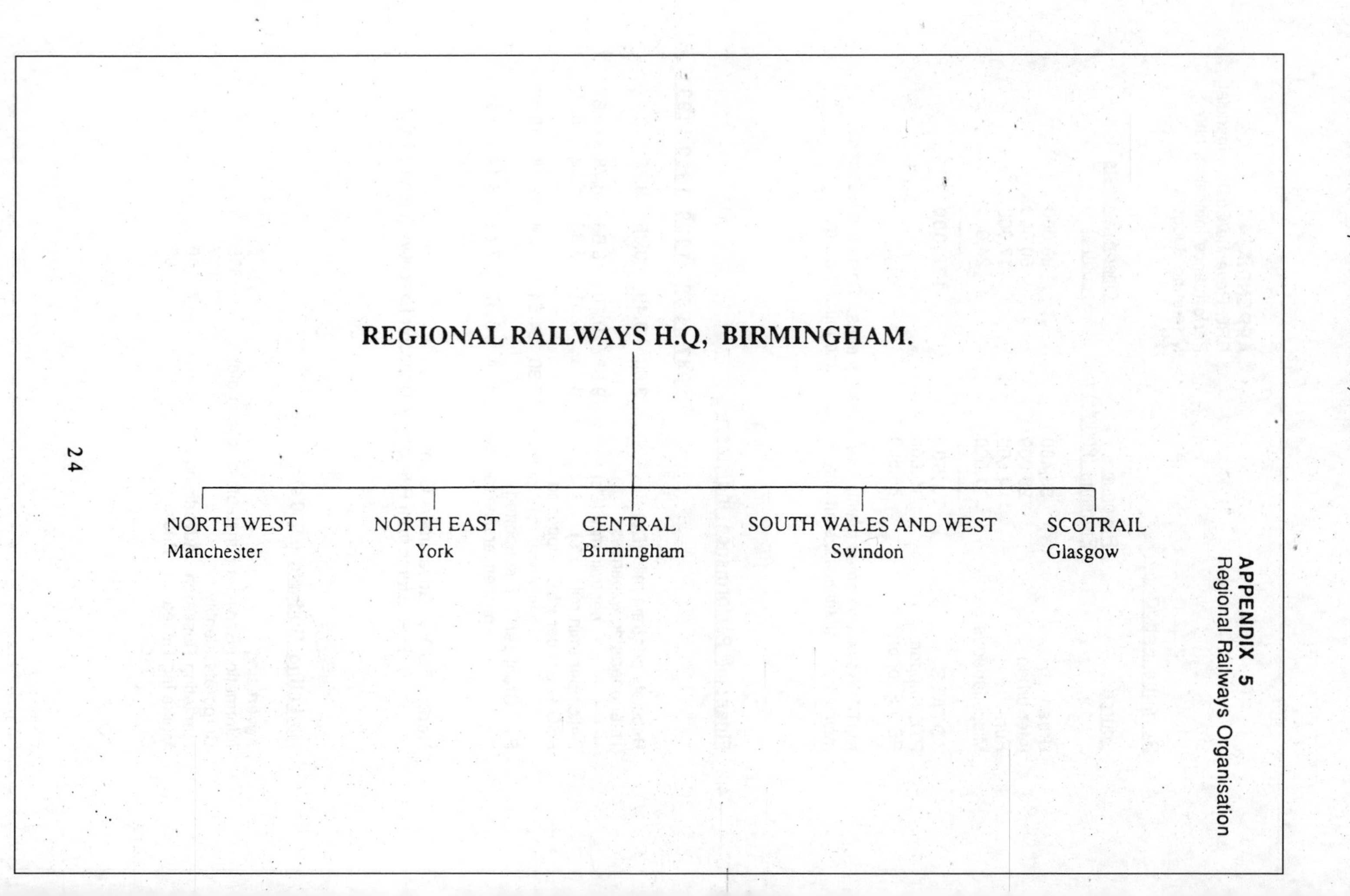
APPENDIX 5
Regional Railways Organisation
REGIONAL RAILWAYS H.Q, BIRMINGHAM.
NORTH WEST
Manchester
NORTH EAST
York
CENTRAL
Birmingham
SOUTH WALES AND WEST
Swindon
SCOTRAIL
Glasgow
24

APPENDIX 6
Regional Railways Profit Centres

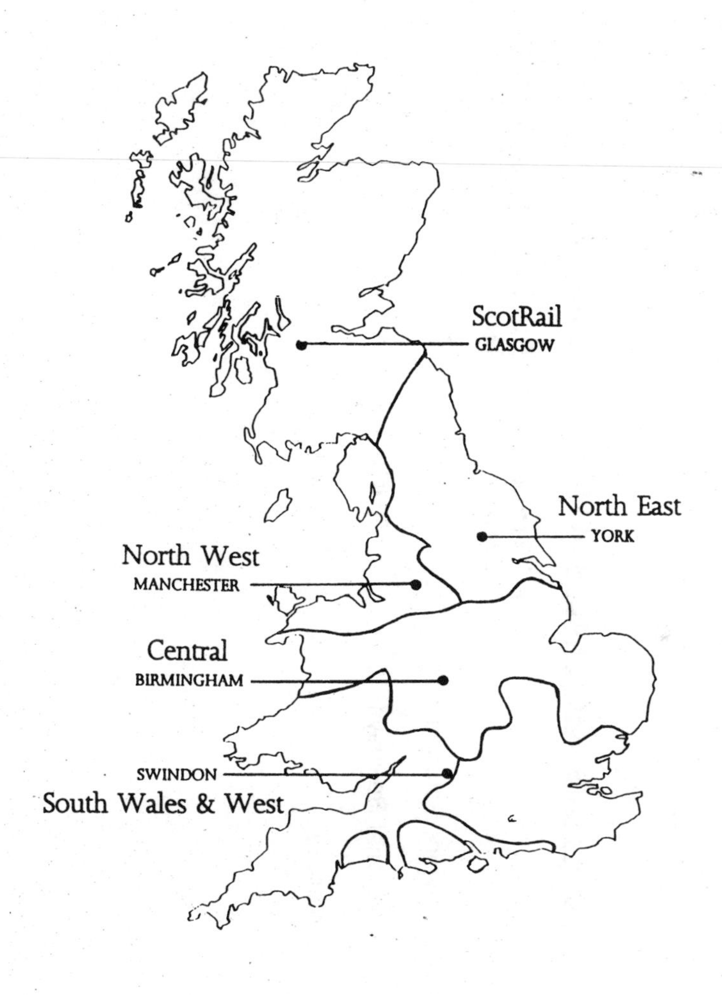

APPENDIX 7
Regional Railways Versus Other Railway Sectors

HOW DOES REGIONAL RAILWAYS MEASURE UP

	Train Mileage	**Route Mileage**	**Stations**
Network Southeast	40%	19%	38%
Regional Railways	38%	45%	59%
InterCity	22%	36%	3%

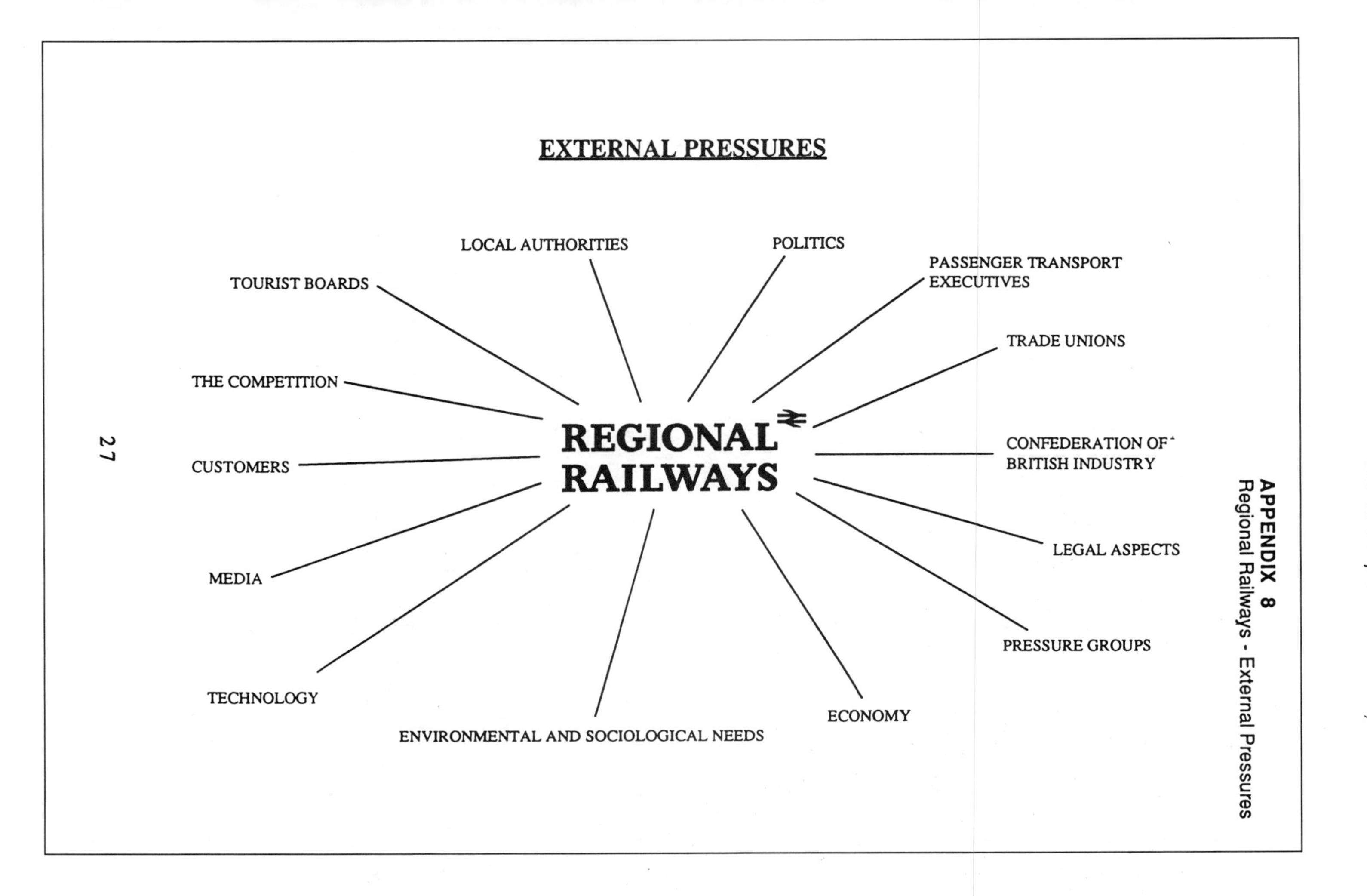
APPENDIX 8
Regional Railways - External Pressures
EXTERNAL PRESSURES
REGIONAL RAILWAYS
LOCAL AUTHORITIES
POLITICS
PASSENGER TRANSPORT EXECUTIVES
TOURIST BOARDS
TRADE UNIONS
THE COMPETITION
CONFEDERATION OF BRITISH INDUSTRY
CUSTOMERS
LEGAL ASPECTS
MEDIA
PRESSURE GROUPS
TECHNOLOGY
ECONOMY
ENVIRONMENTAL AND SOCIOLOGICAL NEEDS
27

APPENDIX 9
Regional Railways - Pricing

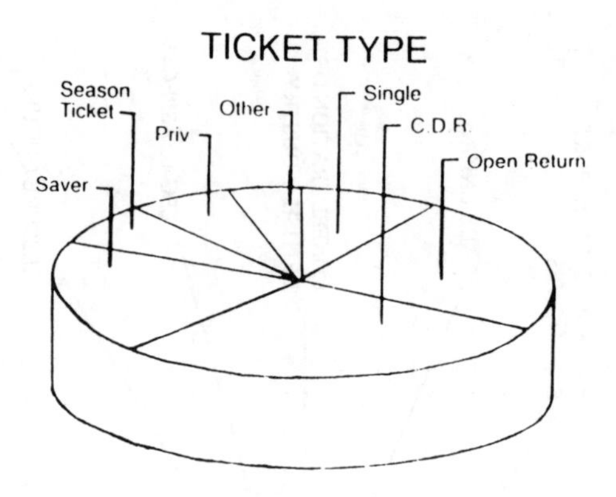

Key to Ticket Type

Saver/Supersaver	-	Off peak leisure ticket for longer distance (over 50 miles) journeys.
Season	-	Peak commuter ticket for regular (every weekday) journey.
Privilege	-	Staff discount rate tickets (75% off open return rates).
Other	-	Miscellaneous, Rover, Ranger etc. Off peak leisure tickets.
Single	-	Peak Business/Commuter ticket for individual one way journey.
Cheap Day Return	-	Off peak leisure ticket for shorter distance (less than 50 miles) journeys.
Open Returns	-	Peak Business/Commuter ticket for individual return journey.

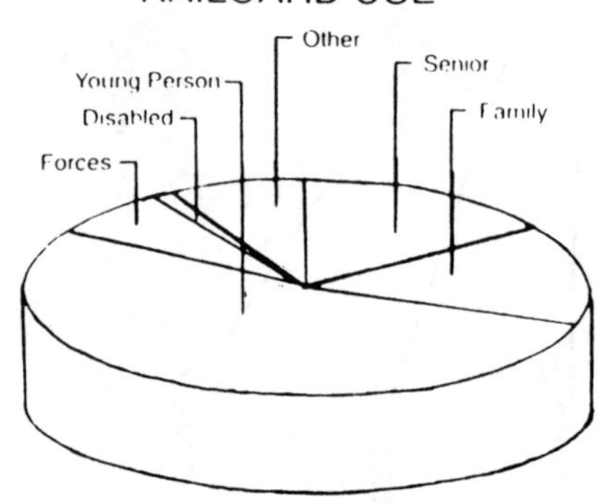

(Railcards account for 30% of all business)

Railcards

A railcard allows the holder to purchase off-peak tickets at substantially reduced prices. It is only available to people in the categories shown, such as students (young persons), senior citizens, armed forces personnel etc. The price of a railcard varies from approximately £15 to £20 per annum. Obviously it is particularly beneficial to people within the defined categories who make frequent rail journeys.

APPENDIX 10
Regional Railways - Marketing
Research Findings

WHAT THEY WANT AND HOW WE PERFORM

Table B shows how satisfied our customers are with our performance over a range of journey constituents by showing what percentage of them consider an item important and what percentage consider we are delivering what they want.

In some areas we are close to, or exceeding, expectations.

The areas where we still have most to do tend to be those that have traditionally been our weak spots; keeping trains, and especially toilets, clean; keeping customers informed about punctuality, especially, not except when, things go wrong; the price of the journey.

Management attention as well as staff effort, must be concentrated in these areas. Management must ensure that staff have the tools to do the job effectively, staff must then use them consistently and with pride.

On the issue of the cost of journey all staff will be pleased to know that Saver Prices, most relevant to a large element of our optional travel market segment, will not be raised during 1991, owing to the effect the recession has had on this business.

We have all made great strides in recent years, but we cannot afford to relax, we must redouble our efforts to improve still further.

Remember, as we improve the delivery of our product, so our customers' expectations rise.

Table B

Delivering to Customers Expectations

	Importance %	**Satisfaction** %
Information About Punctuality	88	71
Cleanliness of Toilets on trains	87	64
Ease of Finding a Seat	86	76
Cleanliness of Interiors of Vehicles	85	69
Cost of Journey	85	64
Seat Comfort	84	69
Journey Time	83	72
Helpfulness and Politeness of Staff	81	76
Luggage Space	76	65
Ease of Purchasing a Ticket	73	83
Catering Facilities	69	63
Station Facilities	64	70
Cleanliness of Exterior of Vehicles	56	63

APPENDIX 11
Regional Railways - Markets

Within the Urban Areas (URBAN)

In partnership with seven Passenger Transport Executives and enterprising county and regional councils, we take millions of people to and from work every day by rail.

Between Towns and Cities (INTER-URBAN)

Major towns and cities are linked using fast and frequent air-conditioned Class 158 trains on routes which cross the country, and provide convenient services for families, shoppers and people on business. The trains are equipped with facilities for nursing mothers and for people with disabilities, and every train has a BT telephone. With a top speed of 90mph and a catering trolley service to your seat, the Class 158 trains on the inter-urban routes offer the best Regional Railways service between major towns and cities.

In the Hinterlands (RURAL)

Regional Railways provides lifeline services on long rural routes. Responding to different community needs. Patterns o service vary according to the time of day. The Esk Valley and Cambrian Coast lines both have a key part in school transport, but can be quieter outside those times. In Cornwall, the service from Liskeard to the small port of Looe is a year round lifeline, but in summer it also acts as a 'park and ride' - an essential 'congestion-buster' for a seaside town with limited parking.

FARES INCOME

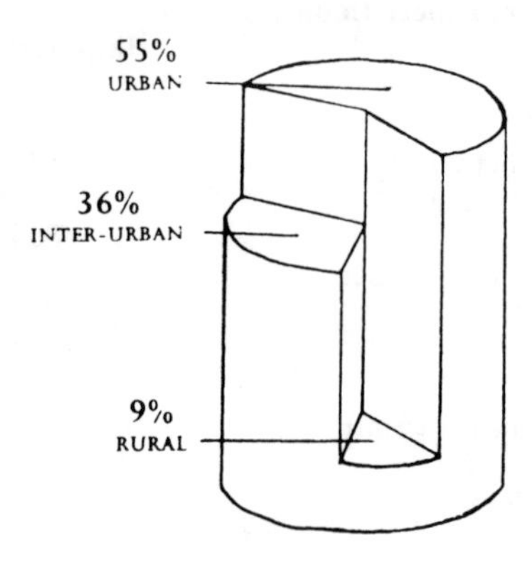

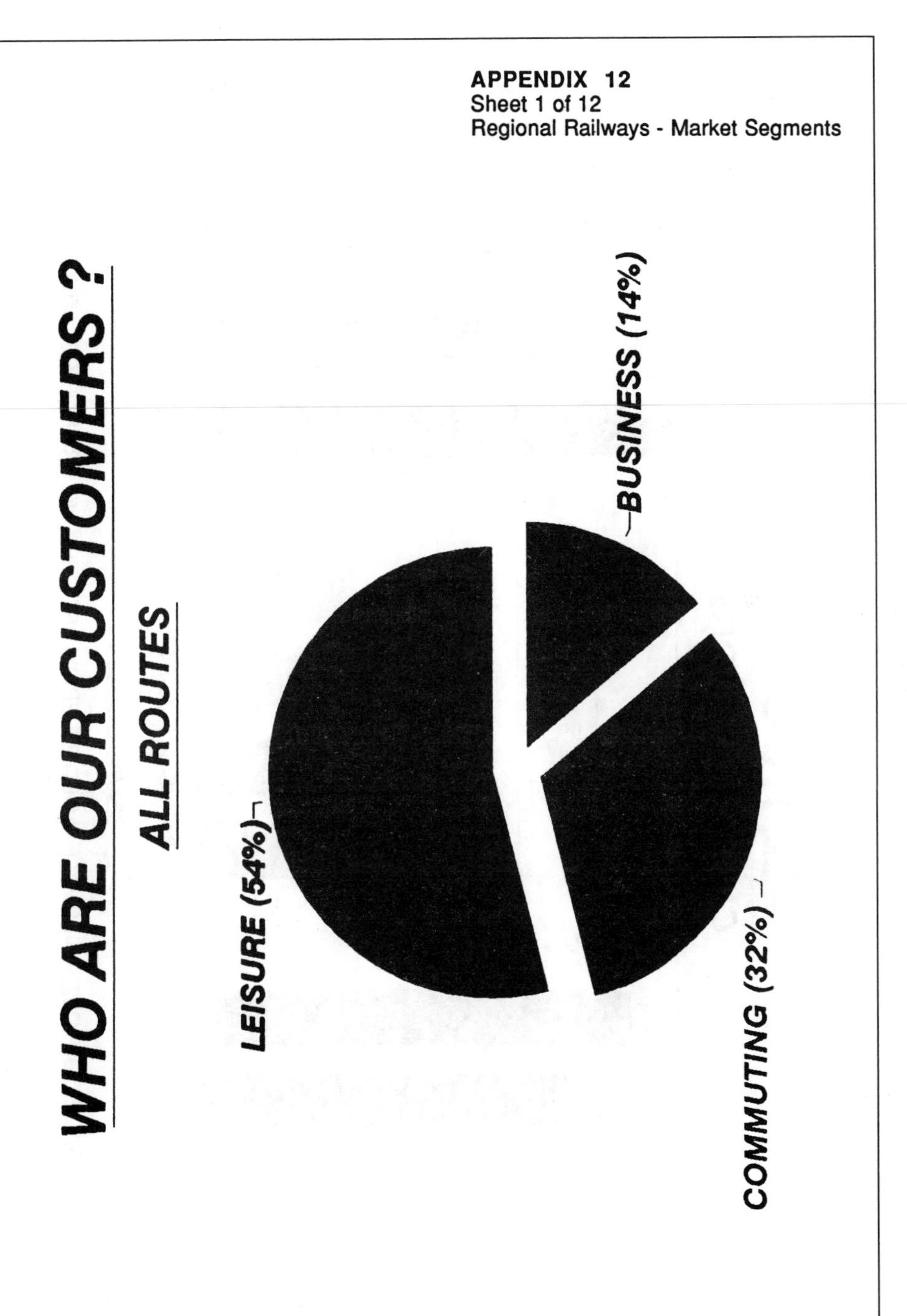
APPENDIX 12
Sheet 1 of 12
Regional Railways - Market Segments
WHO ARE OUR CUSTOMERS ?
ALL ROUTES
BUSINESS (14%)
LEISURE (54%)
COMMUTING (32%)
31

APPENDIX 12
Sheet 2 of 12
Regional Railways - Market Segments

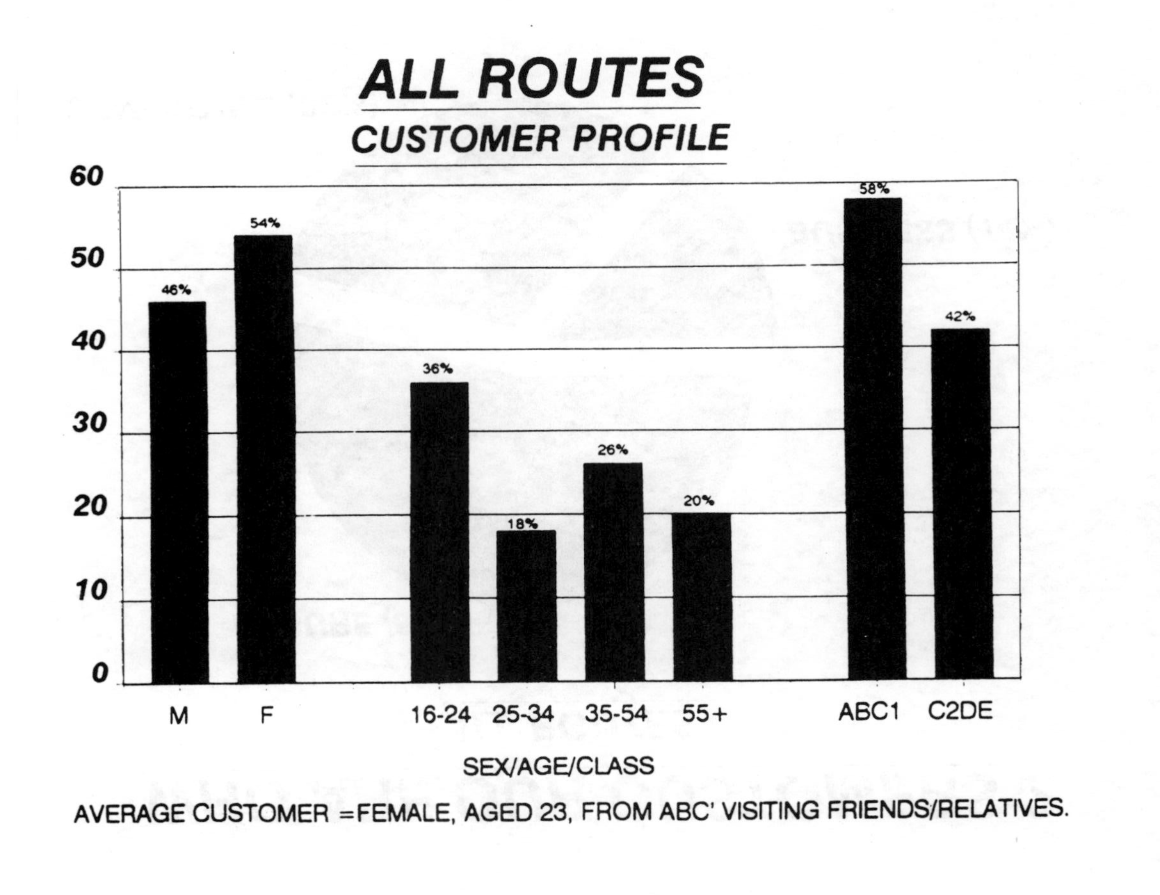

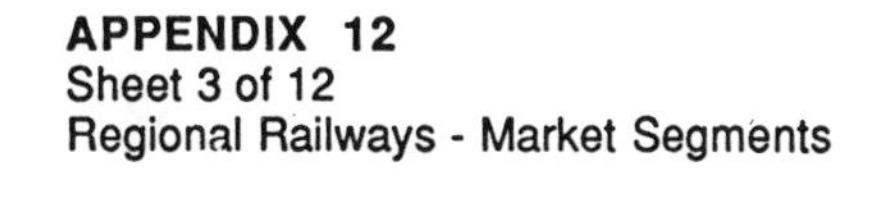
APPENDIX 12
Sheet 3 of 12
Regional Railways - Market Segments

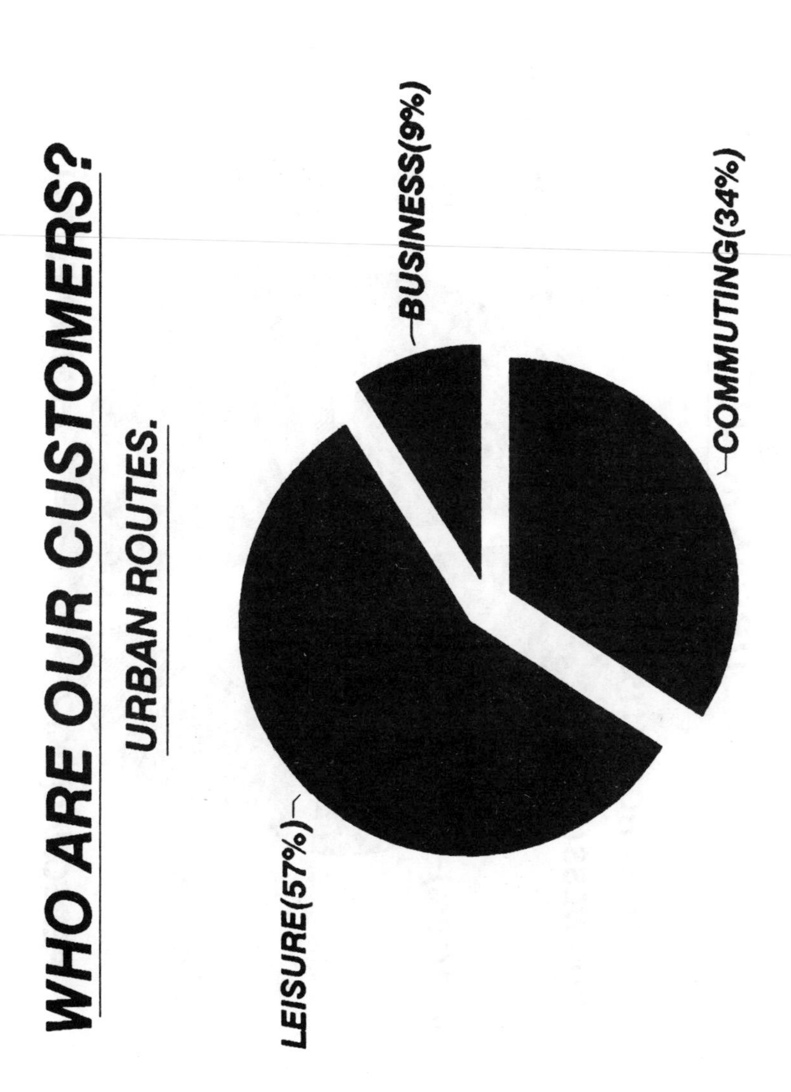
WHO ARE OUR CUSTOMERS?
URBAN ROUTES.
BUSINESS(9%)
COMMUTING(34%)
LEISURE(57%)

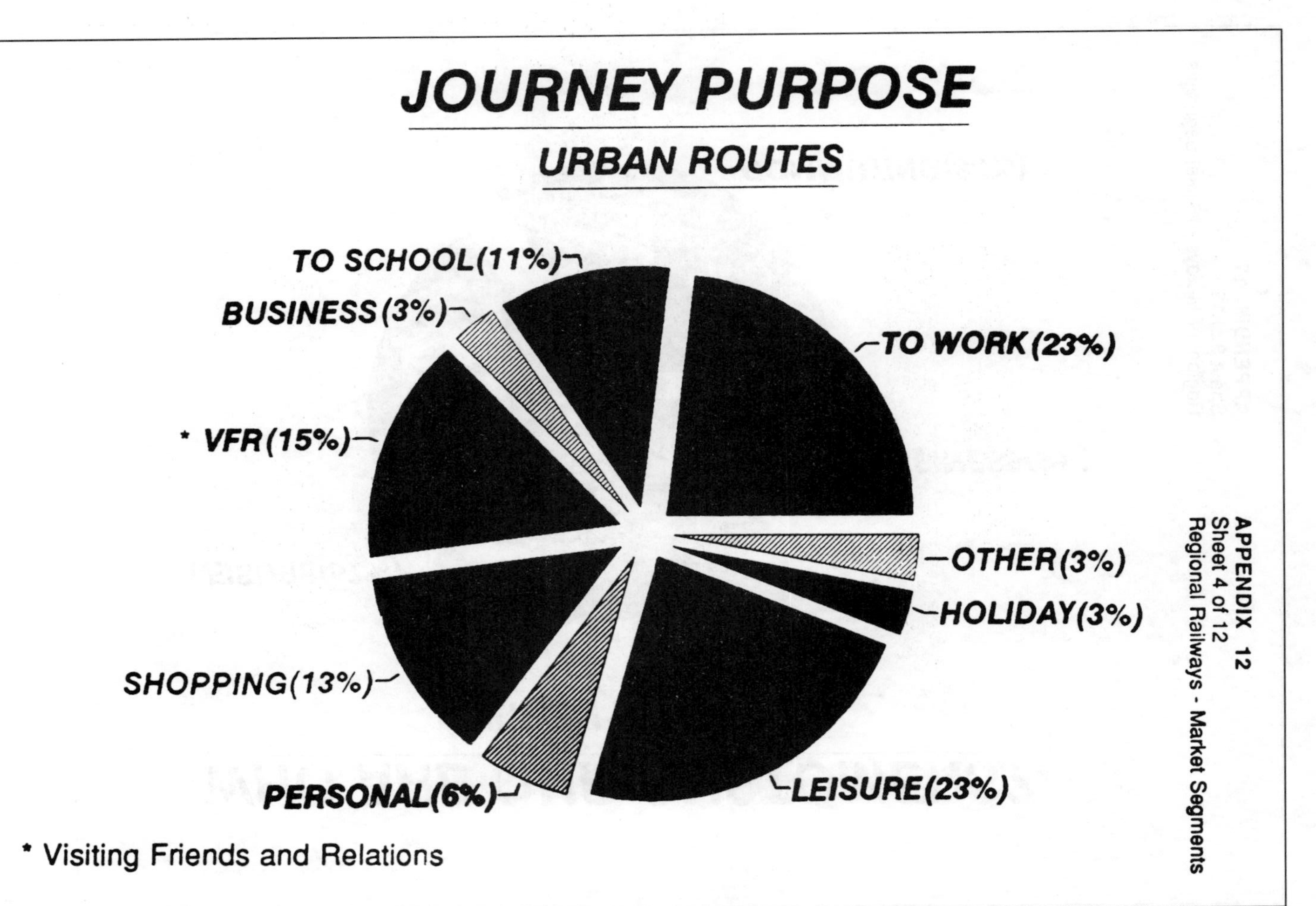
JOURNEY PURPOSE
URBAN ROUTES
TO SCHOOL (11%)
BUSINESS (3%)
* VFR (15%)
SHOPPING (13%)
PERSONAL (6%)
LEISURE (23%)
HOLIDAY (3%)
OTHER (3%)
TO WORK (23%)
* Visiting Friends and Relations
34
APPENDIX 12
Sheet 4 of 12
Regional Railways - Market Segments

APPENDIX 12
Sheet 5 of 12
Regional Railways - Market Segments

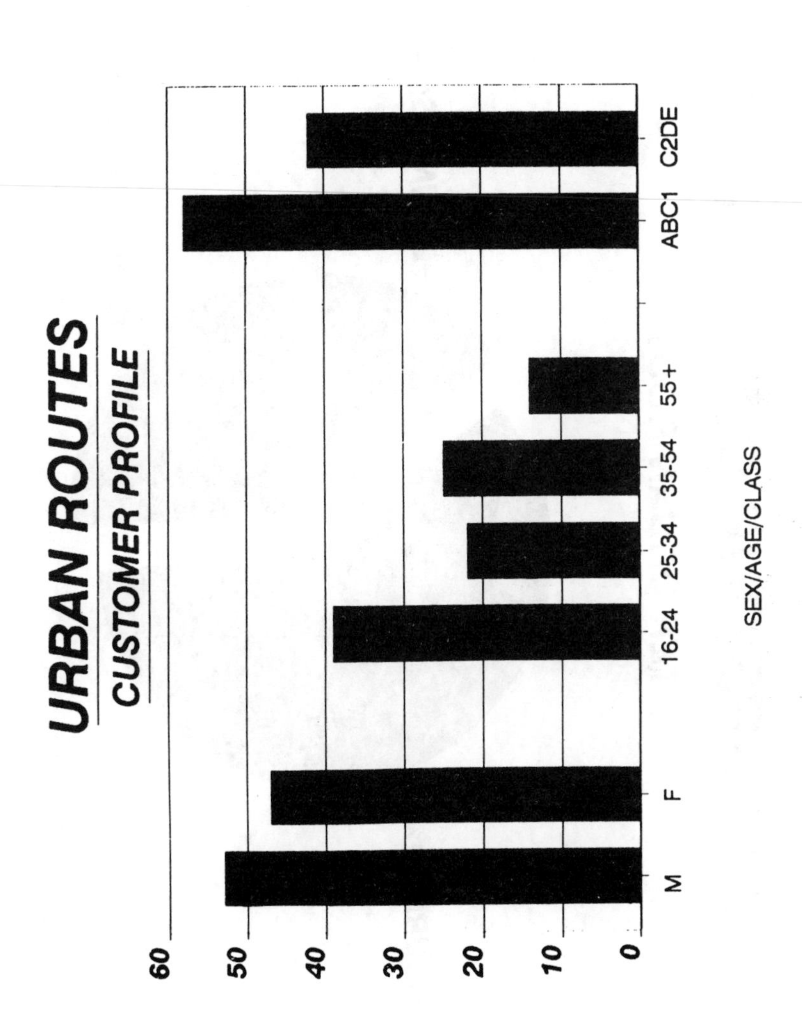

APPENDIX 12
Sheet 6 of 12
Regional Railways - Market Segments

WHO ARE OUR CUSTOMERS?

INTER URBAN ROUTES

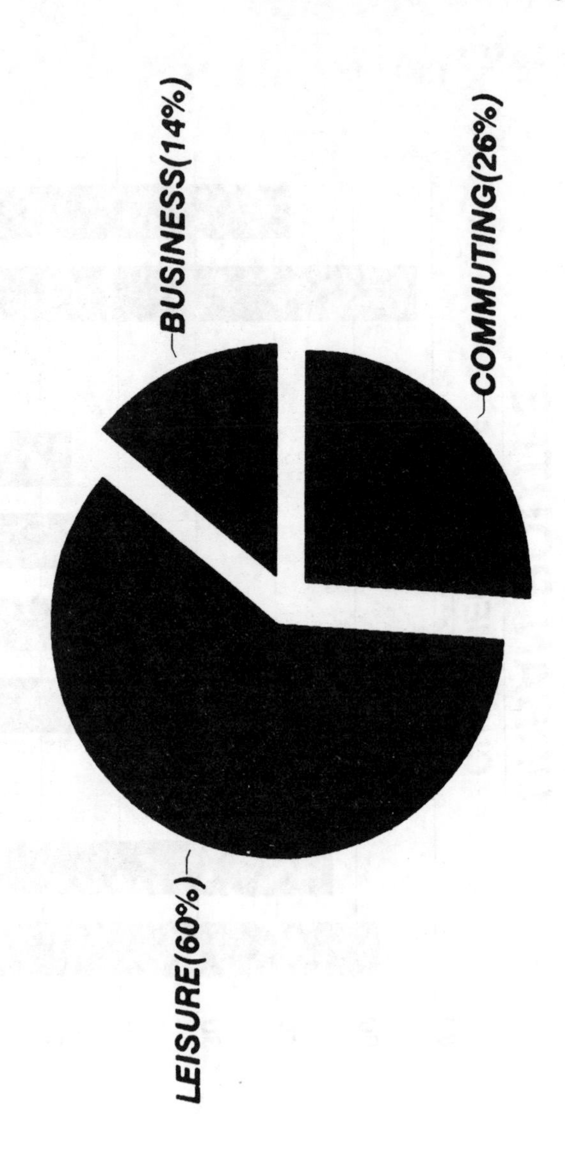

APPENDIX 12
Sheet 7 of 12
Regional Railways - Market Segments

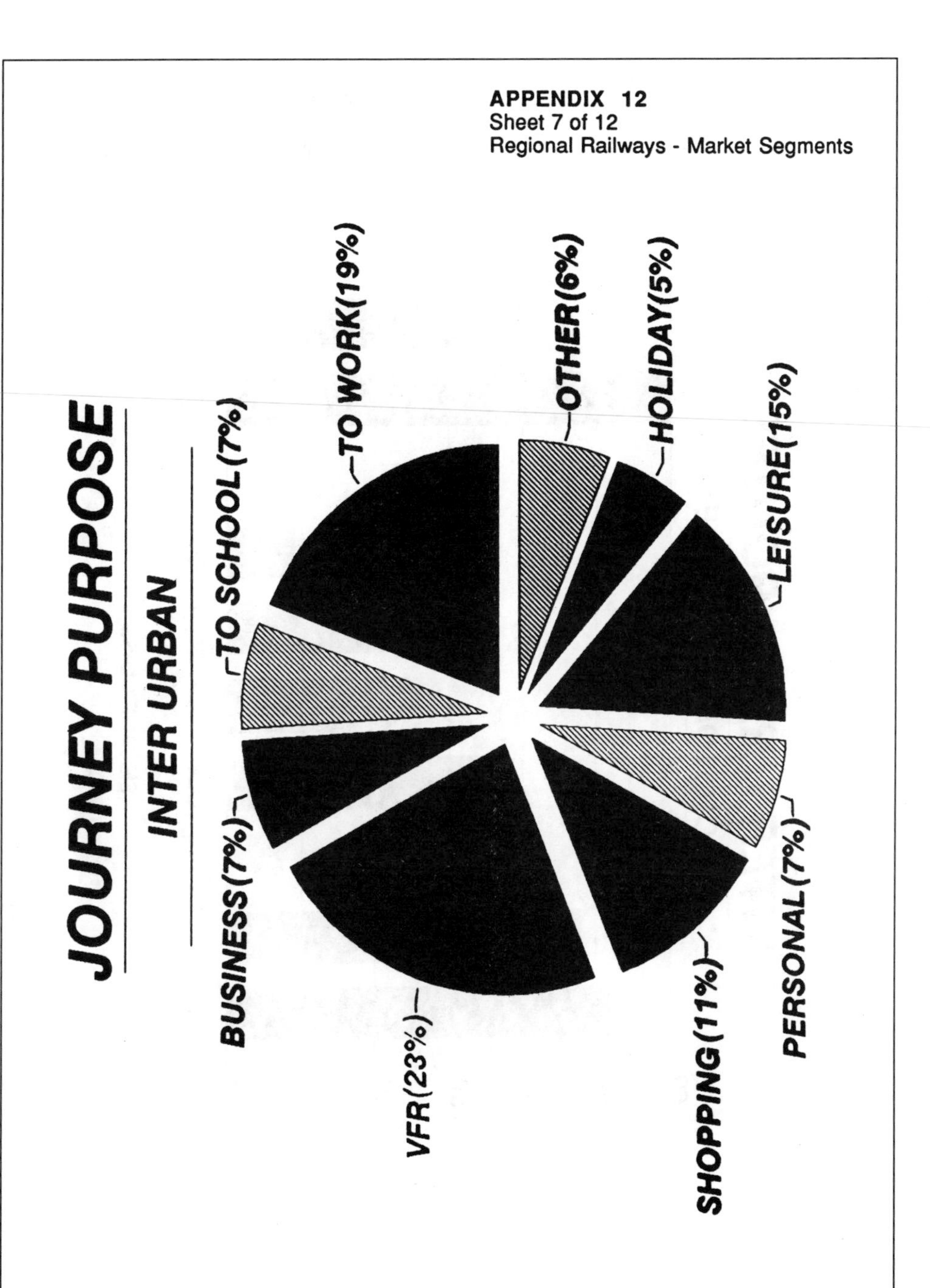

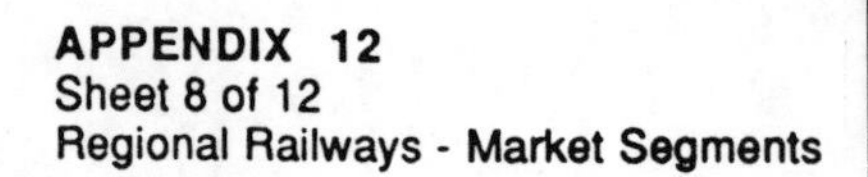
APPENDIX 12
Sheet 8 of 12
Regional Railways - Market Segments

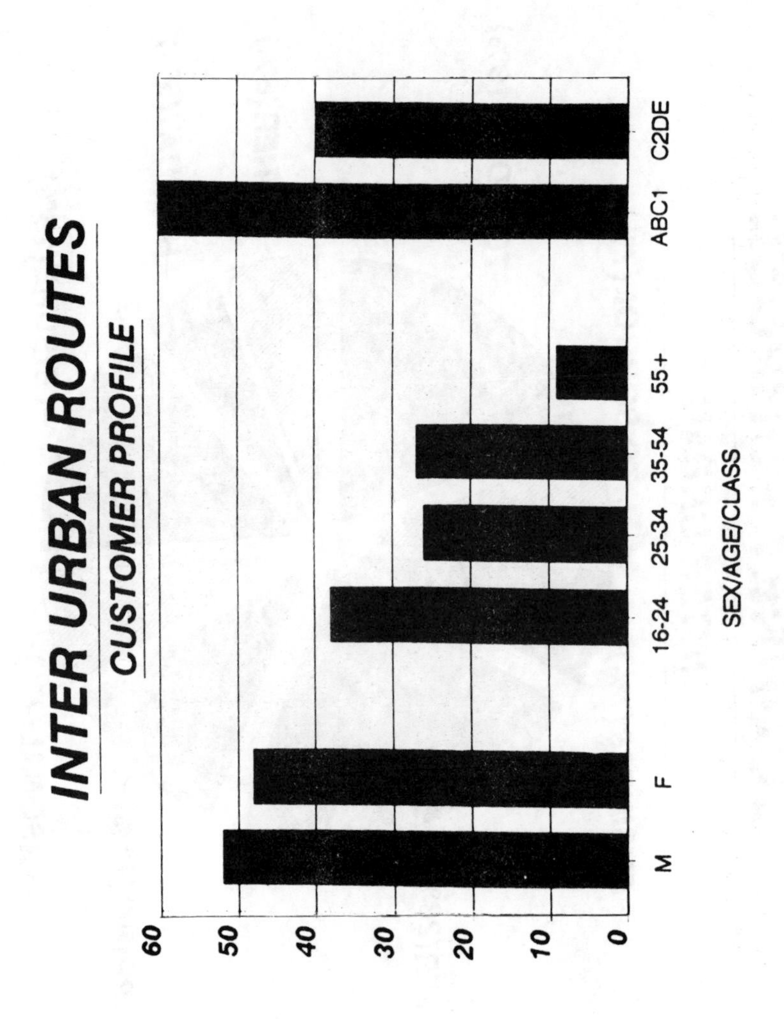
INTER URBAN ROUTES
CUSTOMER PROFILE
60
50
40
30
20
10
0
M
F
16-24
25-34
35-54
55+
ABC1
C2DE
SEX/AGE/CLASS

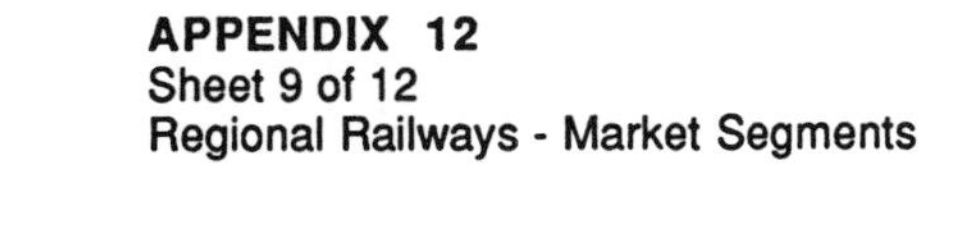

APPENDIX 12
Sheet 9 of 12
Regional Railways - Market Segments

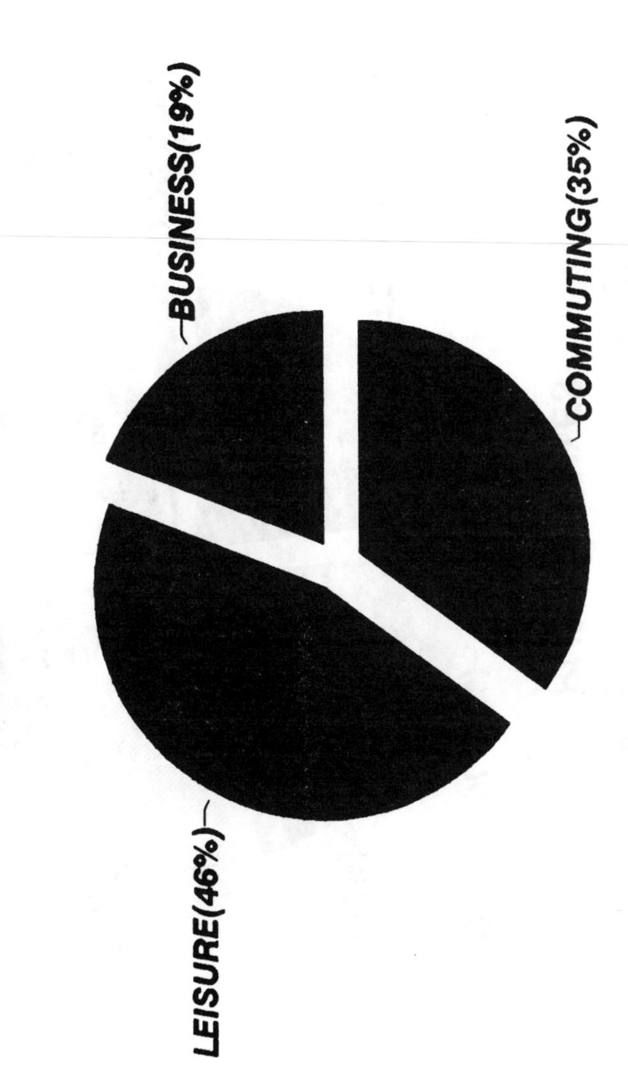

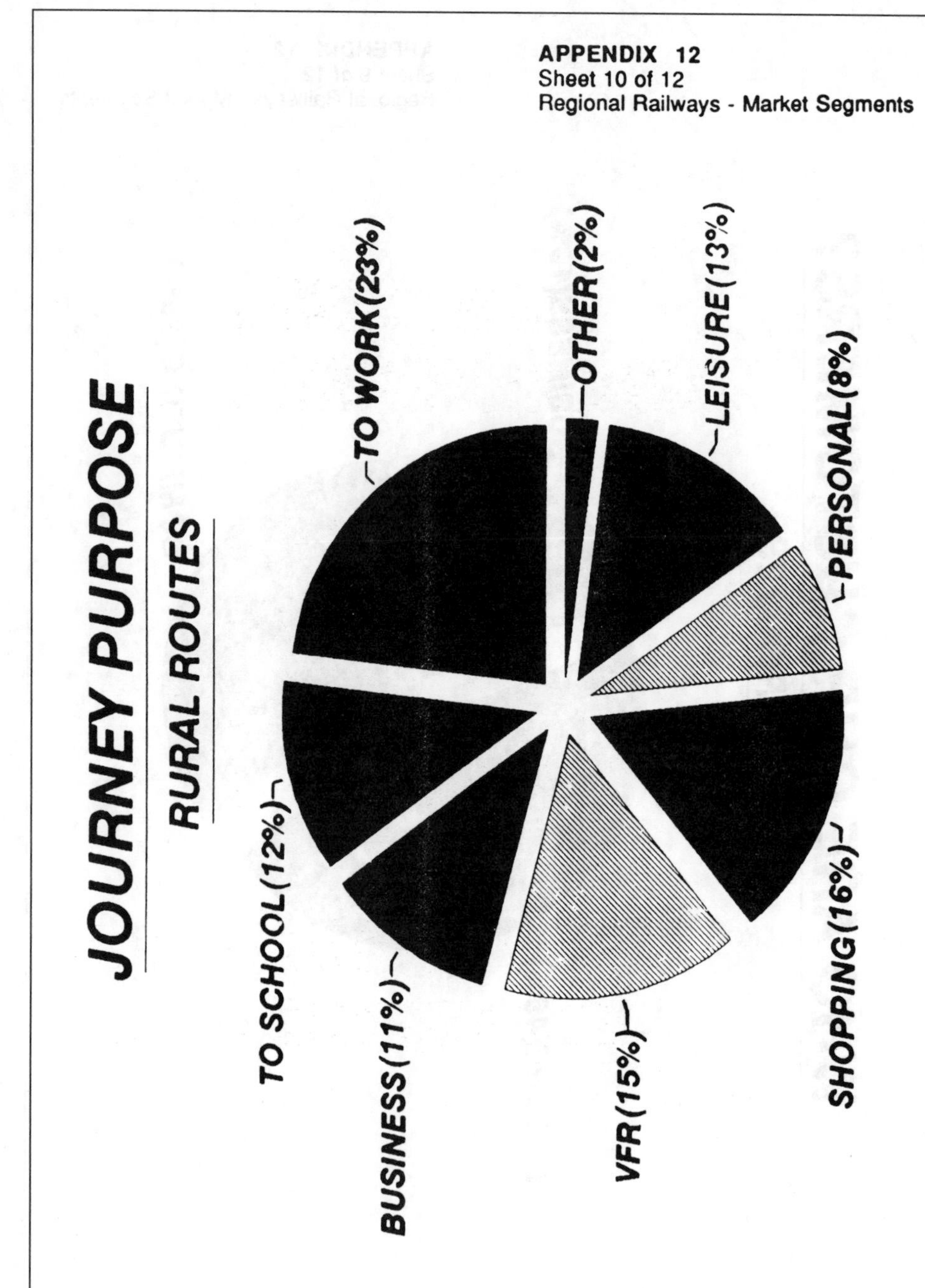
APPENDIX 12
Sheet 10 of 12
Regional Railways - Market Segments
JOURNEY PURPOSE
RURAL ROUTES
TO WORK(23%)
OTHER(2%)
LEISURE(13%)
PERSONAL(8%)
SHOPPING(16%)
VFR(15%)
BUSINESS(11%)
TO SCHOOL(12%)
40

APPENDIX 12
Sheet 11 of 12
Regional Railways - Market Segments

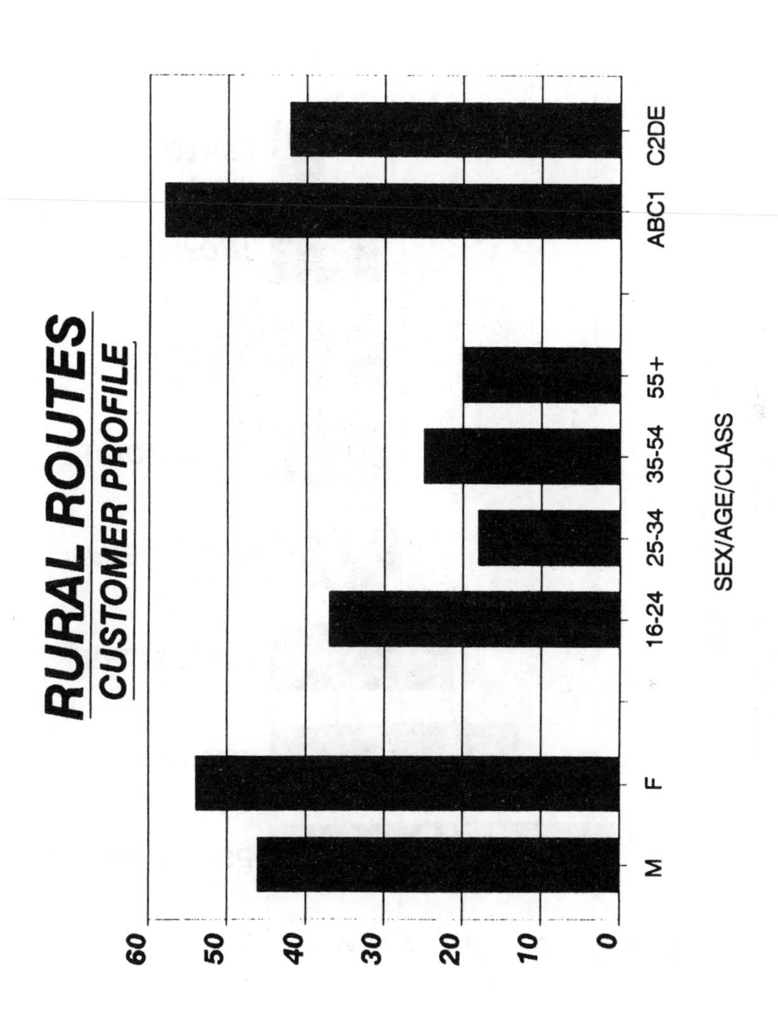

APPENDIX 12
Sheet 12 of 12
Regional Railways - Market Segments

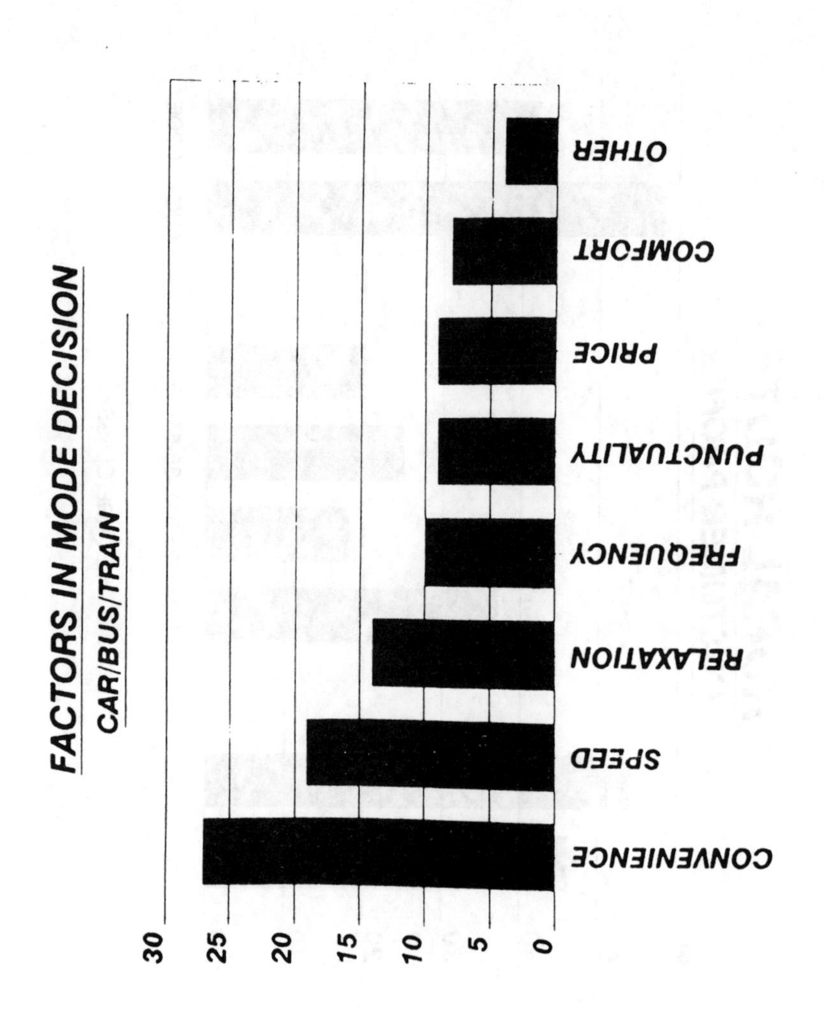

APPENDIX 13
Sheet 1 of 7
Regional Railways - Extracts, Proposed Advertising Campaign, Inter-urban Services

The Brief to the Advertising Agency

- Increase travel on Inter-urban services amongst B, C1, C2 adults.

  By:

  Raising Awareness
  Generating Trial

- Create a campaign with enough flexibility to:

  - work across every region, at a strategic level
  - easily translate into local tactical advertising
  - convey hard information, while also beginning to develop long term brand awareness.

Who We Want to Talk to - the Principal Audiences

Primary: Current non-users or lapsed users of rail for VFR (Visiting Friends or Relatives) or leisure trips.
Secondary: Infrequent users of rail for leisure; business users.

What Does the Consumer Currently Think of Regional Railways?

- doesn't know it exists
- doesn't know where it goes to or from
- doesn't know you don't have to change
- doesn't know how often trains go
- doesn't know it's moved on

What Do We Want Them to Think?

Short-term:

"Towards the Utterly Reliable Railway ..."

- Fast, direct, frequent services
- From a station near me
- To more places than I realised
- In modern, comfortable trains

Medium - Long Term:

Regional Railways is the Utterly Reliable Railway

- Train will always arrive on time
- Information easily available and accurate
- Staff competent
- Trains and stations acceptably clean

APPENDIX 13
Sheet 2 of 7
Regional Railways - Extracts, Proposed Advertising Campaign, Inter-urban Services

What Do We Want Them to Feel?

The Desired Brand Personality

- Friendly and responsive, not cold efficiency
- People matter rather than the machines (trains)
- Belongs to my part of the country, not a state bureaucracy

How it Should Fit Alongside InterCity

InterCity	Regional Railways
Flagship	Everyday
Civilised, cool	Friendly, no airs and graces
A to B	A to Z
(Super) Efficient	Reliable
Special	Normal
KNOWS ITS BUSINESS	KNOWS ITS CUSTOMERS

The Creative Brief for Inter-urban Services

Inform people about:

Routes; frequency; directness, modernity, better trains than you think.

In this tone of voice

Friendly, straightforward, down to earth, (just like you are). Not patronising!

BUT, Strike a balance between the need for credibility and the need for optimism.

The Creative Work : Print Executions

- Designed to work across all regions
- With a wide range of messages covering directness, frequency, new services
- Addressing the primary reasons for travel
- Addressing our potential and existing customers
- Flexible across all print media: 48 sheets, 4 sheets, press

Nine different photographic executions developed for 1992/93.

Media - 1992/93 Objectives

- Establish awareness and generate trial within catchment areas
- Begin to build a brand personality for Regional Railways

APPENDIX 13
Sheet 3 of 7
Regional Railways - Extracts, Proposed Advertising Campaign, Inter-urban Services

- Beyond 1992/93, as knowledge and awareness of the name Regional Railways, Inter-urban Services and what we offer becomes established, building the brand personality becomes more important in the mix

1992/93 Media Strategy

- Posters are the most effective medium to deliver 1992/93 objectives in England and Wales.

  Rationale:

  - impact and frequency
  - continuity
  - copy rotation
  - ability to target Inter-urban catchment areas
  - environment vs car/coach users
  - ability to target heavy congestion areas
  - cost efficiency

- Supported where site availability is low by local press

- Where affordable and where the delivery of the Inter-urban service allows, TV is used to begin to build the brand personality, and to complement the specific information of the poster campaign.

  TV is running on Yorkshire and Tyne Tees in June, and on Yorkshire and HTV in September.

- 40 second TV commercial "We'll take you there"

- Communicates
  - travel in comfort
  - direct services (from A to Z)
  - your local railway
  - friendly, relaxed atmosphere

- Regionalised by a computer-graphics end sequence showing Inter-urban services linking the major towns and cities for each Profit Centre/TV area

APPENDIX 13
Sheet 4 of 7
Regional Railways - Extracts, Proposed Advertising Campaign, Inter-urban Services

Execution F 'Seaside' (Days out/holidays at the seaside)

APPENDIX 13
Sheet 5 of 7
Regional Railways - Extracts, Proposed Advertising Campaign, Inter-urban Services

Execution G "Commuter" (Commuting)

YORK TO LEEDS IN JUST 38 MINUTES.
(For those who'd like a shorter working day.)
REGIONAL RAILWAYS

APPENDIX 13
Sheet 6 of 7
Regional Railways - Extracts, Proposed Advertising Campaign, Inter-urban Services

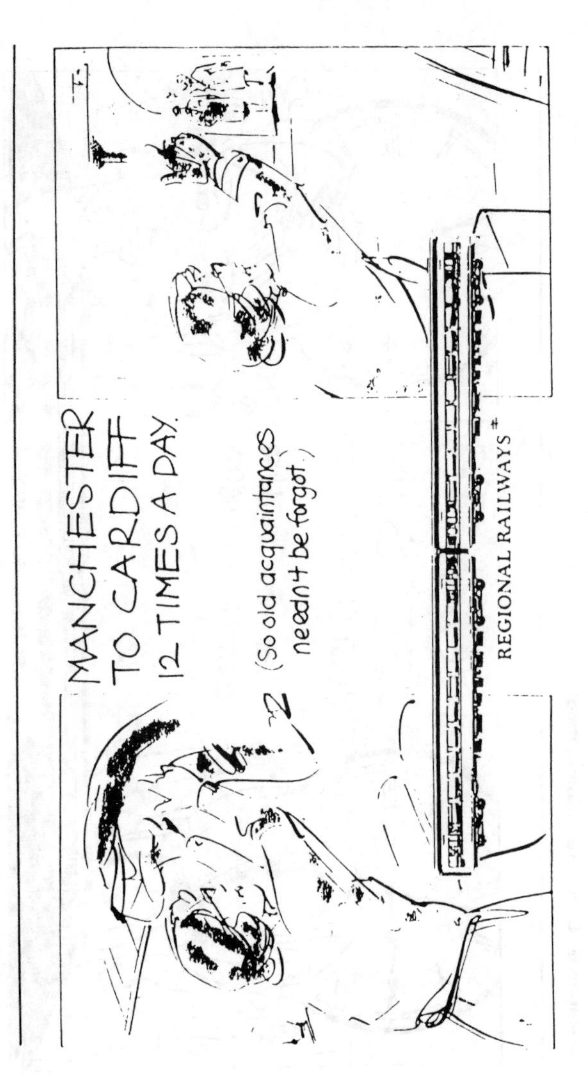

Execution H 'Lady' (VFR)

APPENDIX 13
Sheet 7 of 7
Regional Railways - Extracts, Proposed Advertising Campaign, Inter-urban Services

Execution I "Historic destination" (Days out - historical places of interest)

APPENDIX 14
British Rail Organisation

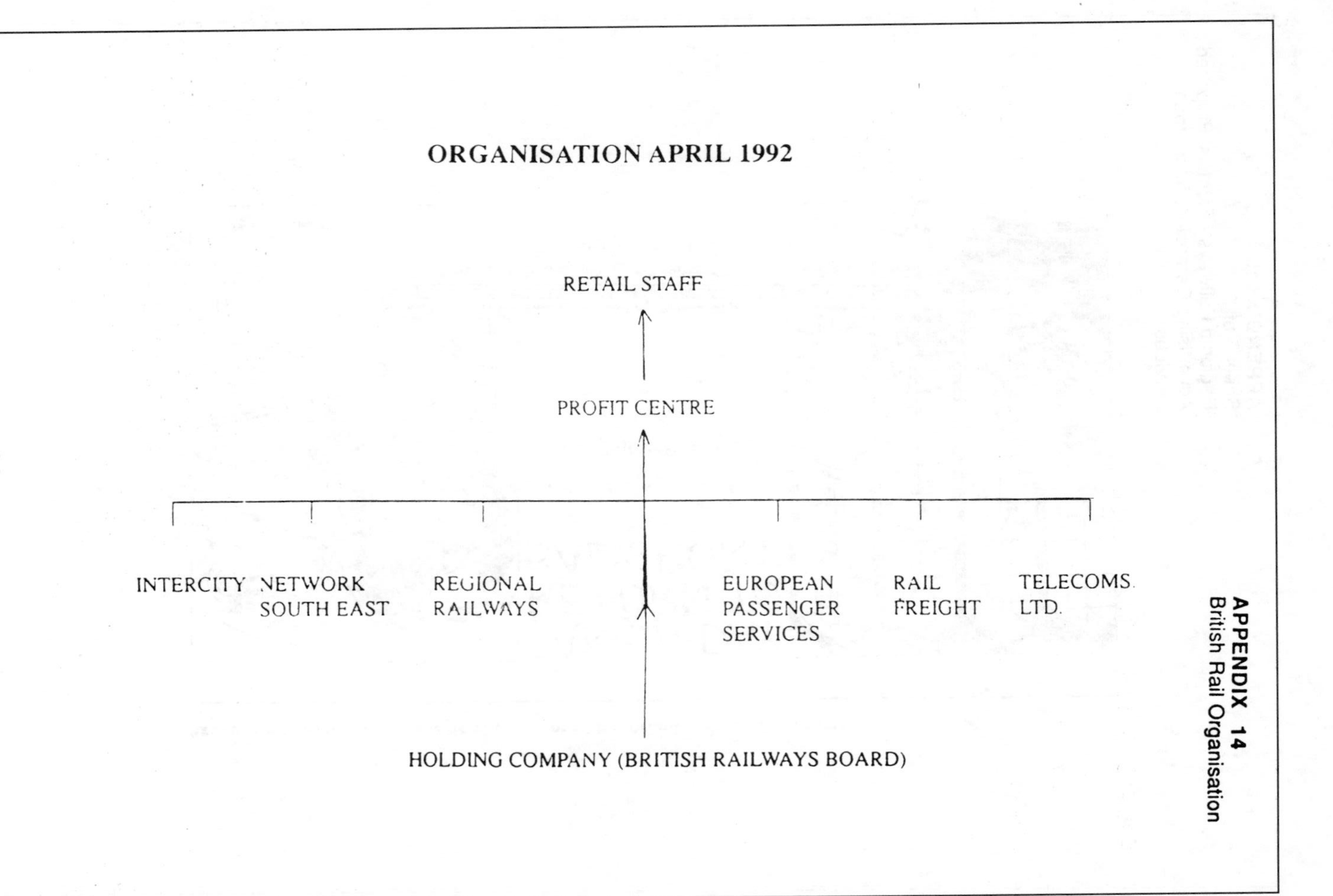

APPENDIX 15
British Rail - Comparisons with other Countries

EUROPEAN COMPARISONS 1991

SUBSIDY - As a % of GDP

Belgium	0.98%
Italy	0.89%
Spain	0.73%
European Average	0.70% or five times MORE than Britain
Germany	0.67%
France	0.66%
Holland	0.39%
British Rail	0.14%

PRODUCTIVITY - AS TRAIN KILOMETRES PER EMPLOYEE

Japan - Private Lines	4500
- Public Lines	4100
British Rail	3470
West Germany	2570
France	2460
European Average	2200
Italy	1520

APPENDIX 16
Sheet 1 of 10
British Rail - Compendium of Typical Press Articles 1992

ex. Daily Mail 8.1.92

Just the return ticket our railways need

THE Govern-ment's plan to sell off British Rail as a series of self-contained compa-nies — very like those op-erating before nationalisa-tion — will be hailed by the nostalgia buffs as a return to the golden age of trains.

Visions of the old Great West-ern Railway — God's Wonderful Railway, as its proud and loyal staff dubbed it — up and running once again, are exciting indeed.

I share that excitement — but at the same time acknowledge that there is a weight of opinion, not least in BR itself, which be-lieves the concept has no more substance than a cloud of long-gone steam.

It may have worked in the 19th century, they say, but the modern way is centralisation. After all, in 1923 it was deemed necessary to merge the 123 private railway companies, many of them then struggling to survive, into just four. And the logical extension of that trend was the single organi-sation which emerged on nation-alisation in 1947.

The corporatists grudgingly con-cede that privatisation is coming if the Tories get back in.

BUT their answer is to retain as much of the present central control as possible by selling off BR's two huge profit-making sectors, InterCity and Freight, and introducing a token of enterprise into the rest of the network by allowing com-panies to own and run their own trains.

Overseeing it all would be a 'track authority' — presumably still in the public domain — to decide how the trains operated.

That, in my opinion, would be the equivalent of selling somebody a sweet shop and then dictating to him which customers should be allowed in.

The track authority Big Brother would represent just the sort of dead-hand state control we do not need — which even the East Eu-ropeans now realise dulls initia-tive, kills enterprise and generates no employee loyalty.

Take that sort of mentality to its logical conclusion and you will end up with a single authority controlling railways across Europe — or one world airline serving everyone.

Continued

APPENDIX 16
Sheet 2 of 10
British Rail - Compendium of Typical Press Articles 1992

That is why, while joining in what is certain to be public enthusiasm over the separate companies, each with their own proud liveries, and uniforms, I welcome the Government's scheme for much more down-to-earth reasons.

The fact is that this is the *only* way to run a privatised railway. It was the very foundation of rail systems throughout the world when they emerged in the last century — a series of companies offering lines of route to diverse markets.

There are three main reasons why.

First, on the operational level. Despite nationalisation and reorganisation into divisions such as InterCity and Network SouthEast, British Rail still operates for practical purposes as a series of lines. Just as a passenger may use, say, the London to Brighton line every day of his life and never travel on another route, so staff and rolling stock are normally still dedicated to one line.

Moreover, morale is important for those who work on the railways. Many people had a pride and a loyalty in their job which was dissipated by nationalisation and then by years of neglect. And the individual companies will know exactly what their own customers want, be they passengers or freight shippers.

Second, the privatised railways will need massive investment. This will mean the entrepreneurial use of risk capital to develop new ideas for meeting modern demands profitably and reducing the subsidy from the taxpayer.

AND in terms of railway economics, the Channel Tunnel holds important lessons. Private capital will wish to invest in such projects only if it can be reasonably certain that it can generate revenue itself — in other words that the private sector can run its own trains on its own tracks.

This goes back to my sweetshop analogy. Nobody is going to put up vast sums of money if ultimate control rests in the hands of some non-capital-risking 'authority'.

Third, once the sell-off has taken place, the marketing of the new companies and what they can offer will be crucial. It is much easier for an advertising copywriter to sell the attractions of, say, an imposing-sounding Great Eastern Railway Company, than Network SouthEast with its drab uniformity.

I AM involved in just such a private project — which will breath new life into much disused and under-used track. A consortium of businesses intends to build a new freight line from a terminal near Leicester to the Channel Tunnel, providing it gets Parliamentary approval.

The beauty is that it will offer exactly the service the customers want, connecting the industrial heartland of Britain with the Continent and taking lorries off the roads. Like the Channel Tunnel — and any private railway — we shall welcome trains from other railways all over Europe.

The plan now being considered by the Government would allow the creation of many other such companies around the country — some self-contained, running all types of services from long-distance and local trains to freight and parcels, and others specialising in one aspect. All would compete with the roads, which would be good for the economy and the environment.

Staff will boast about the company they work for — and take it as a personal slight if customers are not satisfied.

The railways are in a mess and that is very serious. Of course, British Rail is cash constrained because it lies within the public sector. But merely tinkering with that public sector set-up by a half-hearted privatisation will not be a solution.

Splitting the railway up into a number of independent lines enables the badly needed investment in new infrastructure and train services to be identified by private capital, and provides the basis for the system to move into profitability.

If that means that the Great Western will rise again, most people will understand what is being offered and few will complain.

APPENDIX 16
Sheet 3 of 10
British Rail - Compendium of Typical Press Articles 1992

ex. The Times 13.1.92

Freeman dictates an apology to all typists

ARE you a typist? Have you always longed to have a senior government minister apologise to you? Your luck is in. Pop along to the Department of Transport at 2 Marsham Street, Westminster, collar Roger Freeman, minister for public transport, on his way into the office, and wait for him to say sorry.

A repentant Mr Freeman yesterday promised to apologise to all typists he meets today. He wants to make amends for his gaffe in suggesting on television that commercial operators who take over the rail network after British Rail is privatised could lay on "cheap and cheerful" trains for lowly typists, while civil servants and businessmen travel in style.

Mr Freeman's idea was that running "low fare, high density" commuter services could be attractive for commercial railway operators. The remark pleased nobody. Typists were furious at being classed as fit only for cattle class. Civil servants and businessmen were unhappy because, although they look forward to an improved rail service, Mr Freeman's outburst left it unclear whether the new Typist Class carriages will be on a par with current British Rail standards. Tha' would at least promise a better train service for non-typists in future.

But if today's haphazard standards of service and reliability on British Rail are to be the benchmark for Mr Freeman's Top Persons' trains, then civil servants and businessmen will still weep every morning into their *Traveller's Fare* Tea-Style Hot Liquid Beverage, even after BR is privatised. And typists would do better to travel to work by wheelbarrow.

Mr Freeman, now contorted into that appealing pose of *The Politician Who Has Made A Blunder And Is Squirming To Extricate Himself*, said yesterday: "I regret the phrases I used. They were clearly capable of misinterpretation. In no way do I think that typists are second class and I am going to apologise to all the typists I come into contact with on Monday."

But he said he stood by the principle of price competition on the railways, which would be similar to the pricing systems on airlines, but added that he did not want to imply there was to be two-tier, class-conscious services.

An airline-style train service would, of course, be a far more comprehensible concept to British Rail travellers, who are quite used to long waits in departure areas before starting their journeys.

APPENDIX 16
Sheet 4 of 10
British Rail - Compendium of Typical Press Articles 1992

ex. The Times 28.1.92

British Rail chief backs Major on citizen's charter

BRITISH Rail faces the same challenges whether or not it is privatised, Sir Bob Reid, chairman, told a conference in London. He admitted that at BR, despite successes, "much remains to be done".

Sir Bob spoke after John Major, the prime minister, had told the conference of his plans to strengthen the citizen's charter. BR, Sir Bob said, had been tackling the challenge of change since 1988 with a Quality Through People programme. He had carried forward that initiative after becoming full-time chairman in 1990.

"A new feature of change is the rapid rise in customer expectations," Sir Bob said. "We know that our customers' expectations rise faster than our performance. We also know that even in a recession, people are looking for quality as well as price competitiveness." The prime minister's charter enshrined the sort of expectations BR customers had, he added. BR had to meet the complex demands of its customers on safety, reliability, efficiency and environment.

Sir Bob said his vision of BR was of a quality organisation delivering a quality product and of a thriving industry contributing to the prosperity of the nation. He would not be drawn on privatisation, saying that whether or not the ownership of BR changed, its management's tasks remained the same.

Its safety programme was about quality leading on to safety and was an issue for all staff. Sir Bob said: "Our aim is zero accidents and we will achieve that by concentrating on the human factors . . . A quality railway will, by definition, be a safe railway, but a safe railway is not necessarily a quality railway." The tragedy of the 1988 Clapham disaster, on the one hand, and the bitterness of the 1989 strike, on the other, had driven BR to question what its management was about. If the quality programme had not been there, BR would have been forced to invent it, Sir Bob said.

BR in the Eighties had learned to control and reduce costs, yet something was missing. Reliability, cleanliness and information for the customer had remained deficient, particularly in certain places and at certain times. Staff morale was low. Sir Bob added: "We were not getting it sufficiently right. Sometimes we were getting it badly wrong."

Behaviour in the organisation was changing, he said. "We are moving from a situation where we were content to accept some margin of error to one where we get it right first time. Running a railway was "ferociously complicated".

Sir Bob believed the vision and the values were now in place but he added: "Much remains to be done. The organisational structure is high on the list." That meant matching staff numbers and skills to the task in hand.

Under-resourcing a project should not be confused with having a lean, mean organisation, he said, and added: "Exhausting our people, frustrating their best efforts and failing to recognise the limitations we have placed in their way is plain poor management. We have to ensure that it does not happen."

Vocational competence was also needed. It had been neglected but BR was keen to build ladders of opportunity for the workforce on vocational qualification lines. It would confer more workforce mobility, of both managers and staff, and give scope for talent in BR.

Making change work in BR in the past ten years had been "one of the great corporate management challenges anywhere".

The conference, on managing change in privatised industries and the public sector, was organised by *The Economist* Conferences.

Sir John Egan, chief executive of BAA, the former British Airports Authority, told the conference the company had for the time being rejected diversification as it met increased international competition and change on duty-free shopping.

His priorities were to see existing airports managed efficiently, with improved productivity and better quality of service. Retailing, especially, had to be improved, with initiatives such as the money back guarantee should an airport shop price be higher than the high street price.

Sir John said his company was in the business of satisfying its customers: the travellers who bought in airport shops (BAA's biggest single source of revenue) and the airlines that paid fees to use airports.

APPENDIX 16
Sheet 5 of 10
British Rail - Compendium of Typical Press Articles 1992

ex. The Sunday Times 9.2.92

BR's pledge on late trains heads for disaster

BRITISH RAIL'S pledge to compensate passengers for late trains is heading for disaster and is almost certain to result in an increase in fares to pay for the refunds.

The passengers' charter, itself running 13 weeks' late, will promise new levels of punctuality when it is unveiled later this month.

But a Sunday Times survey of 1,300 trains arriving at mainline stations over 24 hours last week found BR will be unable to meet its timekeeping targets. As a result it faces a tenfold increase in compensation claims.

When he announced the charter last summer, John Major, the prime minister, pointed to a target of 92% of trains arriving within five minutes of published times.

But the investigation of one in 15 train services between 4pm on Thursday and 4pm on Friday discovered that BR is already falling short of its existing 90% performance targets — even though, by the network's own admission, it was a 24 hours that should have been easy for BR. There were no alarms over the wrong type of snow, leaves on the line or trains slipping on wet tracks.

Nearly one in seven of the trains monitored arriving at eight main-line stations was late. Only 87% of local and regional trains arrived within five minutes of the scheduled time, while 12% of the longer-distance InterCity trains were more than 10 minutes late.

At Newcastle Central station, Charles Whitestreet, the assistant station manager, saw his InterCity trains delayed for up to 70 minutes because of signalling problems, level-crossing failures, a security alert and a body on the line. "This has been a good day," he said. "You should have been here last weekend when everything was late."

A catalogue of similar problems last year cost BR nearly £7m in payouts to passengers who took the trouble to complain. But under the charter it will be expected automatically to compensate those who suffer delays. Major has said that BR must "improve significantly" its terms of compensation.

Downing Street, BR and official rail watchdogs have spent months arguing over details. The charter was on the agenda nine months ago when Sir Bob Reid, BR's £200,000-a-year chairman, went to a meeting at Chequers, and it was due to arrive last autumn.

Under the charter, InterCity passengers who suffer unreasonable delay are expected to receive a refund of up to a third of the price of their ticket. But they must pay £2 for a reserved seat to get proof of travel. Commuters who travel on lines continually plagued by problems will get a discount when renewing season tickets. If a whole morning's services are cancelled, passengers will be given a one-day extension on their existing ticket.

The refunds threaten to double BR's deficit, which last year stood at £42.4m. If InterC passengers were repaid a third of their fares for late trains it would cost £34m, while if each commuter on Network SouthEast was given a month's extension on his or her season ticket BR would suffer another £40m in lost revenue.

The likelihood of large payouts to commuters was reinforced by delays at London's Charing Cross on Friday. Of 140 trains monitored, 43 or 30%, were more than five minutes late.

BR yesterday refused to speculate on the cost of the charter, but claimed that it would seek more subsidy to meet increased costs. However, the Treasury is unsympathetic and analysts expect the only solution wil be higher fares.

"The passengers' charter is heading for disaster," said Richard Hope, one of Britain's leading railway experts, last night. "It will end up like the poll tax. Just as everybody has to pay for the minority all passengers will have to pay for those who benefit."

The charter was attacked yesterday at Labour's local government conference in Blackpool by John Prescott, the shadow transport secretary. Labour's own calculation is that it could cost BR £1.3m a week on Network SouthEast alone. "The findings of The Sunday Times sur-

Continued

APPENDIX 16
Sheet 6 of 10
British Rail - Compendium of Typical Press Articles 1992

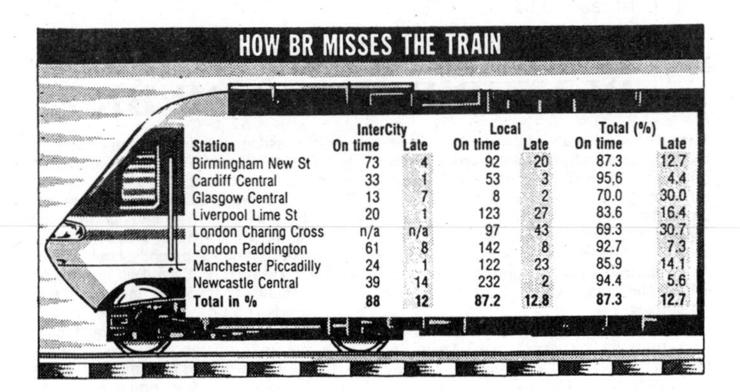

HOW BR MISSES THE TRAIN

Station	InterCity		Local		Total (%)	
	On time	Late	On time	Late	On time	Late
Birmingham New St	73	4	92	20	87.3	12.7
Cardiff Central	33	1	53	3	95,6	4.4
Glasgow Central	13	7	8	2	70.0	30.0
Liverpool Lime St	20	1	123	27	83.6	16.4
London Charing Cross	n/a	n/a	97	43	69.3	30.7
London Paddington	61	8	142	8	92.7	7.3
Manchester Piccadilly	24	1	122	23	85.9	14.1
Newcastle Central	39	14	232	2	94.4	5.6
Total in %	**88**	**12**	**87.2**	**12.8**	**87.3**	**12.7**

vey are staggering," said Prescott last night. "The charter will put BR into a spiral of decline with the quality of service going down and down."

However, BR's performance would be worse if it was not already disguising delays, according to Hope.

Two years ago it gave many regional trains an extra five minutes to reach a station before they were officially counted late. Its current figures are based on arrivals at a terminus, ignoring hold-ups at stations along the route.

In addition, BR builds a "recovery time" into its timetable for more leeway. Trains leaving Euston for the north are expected to arrive at Watford 16 minutes later, but trains travelling south to Euston are allowed up to 33 minutes for the same journey. "It seems they are cooking the books," said Hope, consultant editor of Railway Gazette, who helped analyse the results of the new survey.

Last week passengers were sceptical of the new charter's promises. After waiting 30 minutes at Newcastle for a train home to Scotland, Pat Beaumont, 37, a researcher, said: "The charter is going to be a real joke."

Joe Davies, 20, a student, was 97 minutes late arriving at Manchester Piccadilly on the 48-minute journey from Liverpool because of a points failure. "The service never seems to be on time. John Major's charter is purely cosmetic," he said.

Even BR staff admitted that the service was dire. Mohammad Ayub, 57, a leading railwayman at Leeds, said: "Trains are late and overcrowded. The service is a disgrace to fare-paying people."

● Forty-seven people were injured yesterday when a train collided with a lorry at a level-crossing on the A1123 near Ely, Cambridgeshire. The Stansted to Liverpool train was derailed.

Police were yesterday investigating an incident in which an InterCity train from Paddington crashed into a metal barricade placed on the line by vandals at Skewen, near Swansea, on Friday night. Nobody was hurt.

APPENDIX 16
Sheet 7 of 10
British Rail - Compendium of Typical Press Articles 1992

ex. The Times 7.5.92

BETTER ROUTE FOR BR

Queen's Speeches are rarely accurate guides to the route-march of a modern parliament. They are prepared in haste. Wise ministers strive to avoid repenting of them at leisure. Yesterday's was no exception. The postscript "other measures will be set before you" will doubtless have to work as hard as ever. Yet some glimpse of the forthcoming parliament could be detected by an assiduous Majorologist.

There is a clutter of minor measures left over from the last parliament. There are modest "supply side" measures on housing and industrial relations. But only two proposals carry ideological thrust in the tradition of 1980s Toryism, the bills on coal and rail privatisation. It is on these that Mr Major clearly wishes to peg the radical reputation of this important first session.

British Rail and British Coal merit long-service medals for surviving the 1980s intact. Both have kept their fates sicklied o'er with the pale cast of thought, confusing and finally defying Margaret Thatcher's privatisers. They, their unions and their Whitehall backers will fight against the novelties that Tory ministers have in mind for them. The test of the cabinet's resolve will be whether both corporate hierarchies manage to follow the big energy utilities and remain in being after privatisation, their salaries increased but the regulator not the market as the monitor of public accountability.

Of the fate of the coal industry, most people will be unconcerned. It lies in the hands of the politics of power generation. The extent to which it should be broken into regions or pits will largely depend on the view the government takes of vertical integration in the energy industry generally. Electricity, coal and railway freight are interdependent. The most relevant maxim is that small should be beautiful.

The railway is proving a far tougher test. Mr Major's last cabinet was besieged with doubt over the best means of privatisation. From that struggle there is a danger of the worst possible compromise emerging: of British Rail surviving as a track authority" running unprofitable tra[illegible]s with an undoubtedly soaring deficit while a new rail regulator offers odds and ends of profitable routes to franchisers. Some stations will also be for sale, but not, apparently, other aspects of the infrastructure. Even if all trains were thus franchised, track, signals and other fixed assets comprise some 60 per cent of railway costs. These would be charged to the various train companies. BR would continue to fix not just these costs but timetabling slots and also train rent and maintenance.

This is not privatisation. It is a recasting of the railway rather on the lines of the old Fleet Street, with the unions fixing overhead costs and hogtied managers passing them on to customers. The best that can be said for yesterday's announcement is that it is a temporary expedient. It will look like privatisation while ministers fight over whether the railway's assets of property and equipment should be split into the market's geographical components or managed by a national conglomerate. A better step in the right direction would be for the government to announce not one track authority but a dozen small ones covering different lines of route.

The prime minister is believed to favour a geographical break-up but he will have to fight for it. Unless local or regional train operators are free to manage the costs of their own track, signalling and stations, the bulk of their expenses will be subject to public-sector monopoly pricing. There is no practical obstacle to BR's recently suppressed southern, western or Anglian regions being resuscitated, with subsidy contracts for socially needed services. Private rail companies covering the main routes out of London (both commuter and inter-city), the conurbation networks, the rural and Scottish lines: all could be defined quite simply. The one obstacle is a vastly entrenched industrial and bureaucratic interest. That is the challenge that ministers were elected to overcome.

APPENDIX 16
Sheet 8 of 10
British Rail - Compendium of Typical Press Articles 1992

ex. The Times 27.5.92

Rail losses rise as executives go second class

BY MICHAEL DYNES, TRANSPORT CORRESPONDENT

BRITISH Rail is preparing to announce a substantial increase in group losses as businessmen cut back on their travel spending and property values slump in the recession.

InterCity profits are expected to fall from £49.7 million to £5 million, while Network SouthEast's losses have increased from £154.9 million to about £250 million.

Receipts from property sales and lettings, which have helped to cushion BR from the full impact of the recession in the past, are expected to show a further decline in the figures to be published in July, and falling demand for Regional Railways' services are expected to result in an increase in last year's £503.4 million operating loss.

Officials are still calculating the final figures, but they are expected to show a marked deterioration on the previous year's £10.9 million loss. That followed a £269.8 million profit in 1989-90.

InterCity's performance reflects a dramatic contraction in the business market, where many passengers who once travelled first class have traded down to standard or avoided travelling altogether. Leisure travel appears, however, to have held firm, and the electrification of the London to Edinburgh line brought in an extra £3 million.

The decline in Network SouthEast's performance reflects the reduced demand on most peak-time commuter routes, which give the network about 75 per cent of its income. "Most people come to London to work," a spokesman said. "If employment in central London falls, we get hit hard."

During the past three years, BR has offset declining income from fares with increased receipts from property sales and lettings. In 1989-90, for example, BR earned £412 million from property. But the next year, that declined to £223 million, and a further substantial fall is expected for 1991-2. "Property prices are so bad at the moment that its quite pointless to dispose of our assets," a spokesman said.

BR officials have already said that spending plans for this year made no provision for work to begin the modernisation of the west coast mainline, the Channel tunnel high speed rail link, the Kent Coast Networkers, and the second Channel tunnel terminus at King's Cross station in London. Most of the expenditure for these schemes will not be incurred for two to three years, although some preliminary works will have to be funded.

Government support for the railways has gone up from £1,446 million in 1991-2, to £2,096 million this year, and state support may be increased further in the next public spending round.

APPENDIX 16
Sheet 9 of 10
British Rail - Compendium of Typical Press Articles 1992

ex. The Times 4.6.92

Rail bill begins long haul on Commons track

Ministers have yet to convince critics and passengers that private enterprise can improve rail services, **Michael Dynes** says

PRIVATISATION plans for the rail network begin in earnest today when a bill to pave the way for ending British Rail's monopoly starts its committee stage in the Commons.

By granting senior rail managers the authority to hire consultants on the best way of transferring their functions to the private sector, the paving bill effectively provides BR with the right to help to bring about its own demise.

Before the summer recess, John MacGregor, the transport secretary, is expected to publish the long-awaited white paper outlining in greater detail how the government plans to proceed with privatisation, ready for legislation to implement the policy in the autumn. If ministers push for a fast-track approach, BR's 44-year monopoly to provide passenger and freight services could be over by the end of the year.

Ministers have portrayed privatisation as the panacea needed to revive a slumbering state-owned monster. But many awkward questions must be answered before the sceptics will be put at ease. Under the proposals as outlined so far, BR is to be divided into two authorities, one owning the infrastructure and the other operating the services. Freight and parcels will be sold off to the private sector along with commercially viable stations. Private companies will be authorised to run trains on BR's tracks, a policy known as open access, and the operation of BR's services will be franchised to private operators, reducing BR to the status of a state-owned track authority.

Ministers have insisted that privatisation will lead to a wholesale improvement in rail travel with the creation of stringent standards of punctuality and reliability for all rail operators, the maintenance of subsidies for socially-needed lines, the preservation of through ticketing, the creation of a regulator to ensure that all private rail companies have access to the network, and a monitoring system to ensure that franchise holders honour contracts.

The prospect of new commercial opportunities has brought an upsurge in private sector interest in the railways, leading to a new Stagecoach service between Aberdeen and London. Many other companies are waiting on the sidelines in expectation of running their own trains, incuding Richard Branson's Virgin Group, Sainsbury, Safeways, and National Power.

Roger Ford, technical editor of *Modern Railways*, says that such proposals are parasitical. "All of these enterprises depend on BR's involvement: they are essentially brand names plugged into the existing operational and administrative structure." In short, BR is left shouldering infrastructure costs, while private companies reap the marginal income by "cherry picking".

Proposals to divide BR into two, in effect separating fixed and rolling assets, has also attracted its critics. It has been pointed out, for example, that it would be difficult to turn rails into roads, with rival operators acting like competing coach companies. Such a division would risk creating duplication, waste and complexity.

Mr Ford said: "The idea of open access needs to be clearly developed, as a literal interpretation is incompatible with the integrated control which is the basic definition of a railway. The separate management of infrastructure and operations is hardly a novel idea ... but it cannot work in a state of open competition. Would Virgin be happy to take its place in an auction for train paths with infrastructure costs under someone else's control?"

The sale of service and station franchises could also be difficult to put into practice. Network SouthEast, for example, has nine groups of services, some of which are operated by 10,000 staff. Who is going to buy the franchises? Where is the new operator going to get staff and trains? A Network SouthEast route is not a McDonald's restaurant, so who is going to run the service other than those already doing it? Or does the government have in mind merely franchising the right to run senior management?

Finally, who will be responsible for overseeing investment schemes? Modernised lines are far more likely to attract private sector interest than lines waiting to be modernised. Privatisation may well have risen up the political agenda, but ministers have a long way to go before convincing their critics, not to mention passengers, that it will lead to a general improvement in the level and quality of rail services.

APPENDIX 16
Sheet 10 of 10
British Rail - Compendium of Typical Press Articles 1992

ex. The Times 30.7.92

Coach firm and BR staff seek railway franchises

BY MICHAEL DYNES, TRANSPORT CORRESPONDENT

STAGECOACH Holdings, a Perth-based coach company with ambitions to become a key private-sector rail operator, is to bid for the ScotRail passenger franchise, British Rail's Scottish operation.

The ScotRail franchise, described by John MacGregor, the transport secretary, at a business breakfast in Aberdeen yesterday, as an "obvious candidate" for one of the first franchises under the government's rail privatisation plans, would permit the franchisee to run passenger services on ScotRail's entire 1,700 miles of track.

Senior managers at InterCity, British Rail's profitable national passenger network, are preparing to bid for the franchise to run InterCity passenger services, in an effort to preserve the InterCity brand name and keep the national rail network intact.

InterCity managers fear that government plans to fragment the national passenger network into the five lines of route divisions, such as the east and west coast mainlines, would undermine the InterCity brand name, and waste two decades of building the network.

Instead, InterCity managers are experimenting with franchise options designed to reconcile the government's determination to bring private sector entrepreneurial skills into the railways, with the desire of rail managers to preserve the benefits of a national passenger network.

The Stagecoach bid for ScotRail, which is expected to be submitted by Stagecoach Rail, a subsidiary of the parent company, could face stiff competition from a buy-out team of ScotRail staff, which was described yesterday as a distinct "possibility" once implications of the government's rail privatisation white paper, including the likely level of government subsidy, are clarified.

Highlighting government support for management buy-outs, Mr MacGregor said he hoped that existing staff would be among those seeking franchises "once more details on the charging regime and the franchising conditions are published". The government was eager for franchises to reflect national or regional identities "wherever possible" in an effort to rekindle local pride in the railways, he said.

ScotRail, which runs 1,650 passenger trains between 315 stations and employs 11,000 staff, had turnover of £116 million last year and an estimated 50 million passenger journeys. It is heavily dependent on government subsidy for loss-making services.

Examiners' report

General comments

Overall, the results showed a pleasing continuation of recent improvements in the pass rate, in the level of financial literacy and in the standard of presentation. This position is particularly encouraging in light of the ever increasing number of candidates for this examination and would seem to reflect better teaching/learning techniques, possibly stimulated by the availabilty of more student aids, such as the subject manuals, 'Marketing Success' etc.

Having said this, too many candidates are continuing to fail because of poor allocation of time, lack of report format, inclusion of previous analysis rather than its application and particularly by not answering the questions set.

A worryingly large proportion of candidates made no obvious attempt to take account of the additional information included in the examination paper and for which a proportion of the marks available was specifically allocated. Candidates perhaps need to be reminded that there are reasons for such additional information, not the least of which is the demonstration of their managerial ability to deal with unforeseen developments.

On the matter of general structure and content, far too many candidates failed to make proper use of report style language, headings and sub-headings – resorting instead to essay type presentations or a series of unlabelled 'bullet' points.

Answers from some centres were lacking in knowledge of planning structures and failed to provide a single attempt to cost or schedule, despite specific instructions in the question to do so.

Candidates should adopt the structure suggested by the question (see comments on Question 1) and are strongly advised to think through the requirements of the question rather than write out a pre-prepared answer, the greater part of which is then irrelevant.

With regard to time management, distressingly large proportions of candidates produced two or three times more pages for Question 1 with 30 marks than they did for Question 3 with 40 marks. Often this was clearly because they had run out of time. This problem is often related to the wrongful adoption of essay style.

Question 1

The most common error in the answers to this question was that of not indicating the financial implications and the major problems involved, *for each opportunity given* as asked. Most candidates gave a list of opportunities followed by a list of combined financial implications/problems without clearly indicating under which of these two categories a given point was made. Worse still some candidates omitted to state any financial implications or major problems. Some candidates used headings such as 'Barriers' rather than those suggested in the question. Others simply copied out opportunities, threats and weaknesses from a pre-prepared SWOT analysis.

The best answers were those which used a systematic framework to explore opportunities (such as Ansoff), which reflected the time frame of the question (5 years), and which took account of the emphasis on the word *'major'*. Poor answers presented very short-term and tactical opportunities of a relatively minor nature. The weakest candidates were those who in addition to the above gave no indication of the financial implications or, if they did, limited these solely to the costs involved.

Question 2

Unfortunately, some candidates submitted a syndicated answer to a question which was not set i.e. they submitted a pre-prepared outline marketing plan, rather than the information needed for such a plan and the sources from which it might be obtained. Many candidates were relatively weak on the sources element of this question and some ignored this element completely and were failed. An effective marketing manager should have a good grasp of information sources and marketing research techniques.

Having said this, there were some excellently comprehensive answers which fully exploited the medium to long-term time span and which thoroughly deserved the distinction grade awarded.

These answers not only paid due regard to the additional information given in the examination paper but also included special information required for their communication plans as outlined in Question 3.

Question 3

The best candidates covered both internal and external use (separately) and gave sequence, timings and approximate costs, as required. Some candidates covered only one aspect i.e. either the internal or the external aspect and hence lost a lot of marks. The weakest candidates were those who, in addition to covering only the internal or external aspects, gave no indication of sequence, timings and approximate costs.

Disappointingly, many candidates proved unable to invoke a standard communications planning structure and therefore failed to cover important aspects such as the detail of the target audiences or the types of messages (copy/creative platform) needed to achieve the communication objectives.

Relatively few candidates submitted adequate media details and even fewer attempted to justify the media proposed.

The really good candidates were those who had thoroughly thought themselves into the scenario of post-acquisition and applied themselves creatively to this scenario.

6 The June 1993 Examination Case

Royal Mail (RM)

Examination paper

Diploma in Marketing

(12) Marketing Management (Analysis and Decision)

Tuesday 22nd June 1993 **Time: 14.00 — 17.00**

3 hours duration

This paper requires you to make a practical and reasoned evaluation of the problems and opportunities you have identified from the previously circulated case material. From your analysis you are required to prepare a report in accordance with the situation below. Graphing sheets and ledger analysis paper are available from the invigilators, together with continuation sheets if required. These must be identified by your candidate number and fastened in the prescribed fashion within the back cover of your answer book for collection at the end of the examinations.

READ THE QUESTIONS CAREFULLY AND ANSWER THE ACTUAL QUESTIONS AS SPECIFIED. CHECK THE MARK ALLOCATION TO QUESTIONS AND ALLOCATE YOUR TIME ACCORDINGLY. CANDIDATES MUST ATTEMPT ALL PARTS. CANDIDATES SHOULD ADOPT REPORT FORMAT. THOSE WHO DO NOT WILL BE PENALISED.

ROYAL MAIL CASE

EXAMINATION PAPER

ADDITIONAL INFORMATION - to be taken into account when answering the questions set for this examination, the effective use of which will be allocated up to 5 marks per question within the total marks available.

i Over the next 2-3 years the UK is expected to move out of recession into boom. The devaluation of sterling is expected to result in an improvement of Britain's competitive position within the E.C.and with regard to trade with the USA.

ii A number of European countries are expected to continue to experience economic problems, particularly Germany, France and most Eastern European countries.

iii Recent international research reveals that the British postal service is highly regarded on aspects of integrity and efficiency, by most businesses in most countries.

iv The major implications of the EC Green (Discussion) Paper for postal services in member nations are:

a Whilst the principle of 'reserved sectors' for the delivery of letters will be preserved so as to allow a universal service to be maintained by member nations at an affordable price - the extent and scope of competition in postal services should be the maximum possible ('reserved sectors' are those standard letter post services controlled by member nation governments and which are therefore protected to some degree from competition).

b 'Direct Mail' and mail coming from other countries inside and outside the EC are to be excluded from these reserved sectors and will therefore be open to competition.

c The Green Paper opposes but does not rule out cross-subsidisation from reserved sectors to non-reserved services (i.e. member states could, but should not, use profits from their postal monopolies to subsidise other postal services competing in the open market).

EXAMINATION QUESTIONS

Taking account of the additional information given above, present your proposals IN REPORT FORMAT to the Sales/Marketing Director on the following aspects:

1 Recommended and justified strategies for the replacement of business gradually being lost in traditional UK market segments due to growth in electronic data transfer, so as to maintain overall profitable growth. Your strategies should include European and other international dimensions.

(40 marks)

2 Potential new areas for data acquisition to assist in making strategic marketing decisions, with particular reference to Competitor Intelligence. Specify the information needed, giving justifications and indicating methods/costs.

(30 marks)

3 How you would seek to gain greater value from the corporate identity of Royal Mail and how you propose to solve problems caused by confusion between Royal Mail, service brands and service names.

(30 marks)

ROYAL MAIL

Candidates' Brief

You are one of two candidates who has won through a series of interviews for the new position of Marketing Manager, Royal Mail. You would report directly to the Sales/Marketing Director, Jim Lambert.

Both Jim Lambert and the Personnel Director, Joan Kay, find that there is little to choose between you and your rival candidate. They have therefore agreed to base their final decision on the best marketing proposals submitted in writing by the two candidates.

You have four weeks to prepare these proposals against the following information provided by Royal Mail, which is deliberately limited. You have been given strict instructions not to step outside the data limitations imposed. No credit will be given for work based on data outside these limitations.

You do of course comply with the requirements for this position which you will find in the job description in the data provided (see Appendix 12). Your name is John Solomon, age 30 with a degree in Travel and Tourism. You are currently finishing an evening course for the CIM Diploma examinations in June. Your career to date has been with the British Tourist Board where you started as a Management Trainee and gradually worked your way up to become Marketing Manager of one of the regional Tourist Boards.

You know very little about your rival candidate having met her only briefly in the preliminary interview rounds. She does, however, have a senior position in PR for a major European Airport and has an MBA which included a full marketing option.

This case material is based upon experience with actual companies. Alterations in the information given and in the real data have been made to preserve confidentiality. Candidates are strictly instructed not to contact companies in this industry, and are advised that some additional information will be provided at the time of examination.

ROYAL MAIL

Royal Mail is the largest of the three subsidiary companies belonging to the Post Office Group in the UK. The other two companies in the Group are Post Office Counters and Parcelforce.

The Post Office Group in 1991/92 made a profit of £247 million. This was made up of a profit from Royal Mail of £266m, a profit from Post Office Counters of £26m and a loss from Parcelforce of £24m (Group expenses amounted to £21m).

Royal Mail handles that section of the Post Office Business that we normally think of as letter post, both domestic and commercial, together with small parcels up to 1kg in weight. In this category, Royal Mail handles 60 million items per day.

Royal Mail is directed by Act of Parliament to provide a regular collection service, and a daily delivery to every address in the United Kingdom for a fair and equal charge. In return it has been the beneficiary of a protected monopoly status. In recent years the monopoly status has been partially lifted but only to the extent that items transported by an alternative carrier have to be charged at £1 each or more, compared with the present cost of a first class stamp of 24 pence for UK internal letters up to 60 grammes.

Royal Mail aims to provide next day delivery for first class post, and delivery within three days for second class post. That it fails to provide this completely is self evident, and probably unavoidable.

Nonetheless, the Royal Mail is fiercely proud of its record in deliveries, and that it has improved each year, in the past, over the projected target. It is also proud of the reputation that it has in the community and refers to high satisfaction rates shown in consumer surveys carried out by Royal Mail itself. In the absence of direct competition, assessment of these in-house surveys is rather difficult.

Royal Mail is also proud of its international record, handling mail to and from the EC, and all countries further afield. Royal Mail claims that its charges are lower in equivalent terms, than other countries' national Post Offices. It also quotes customer surveys comparing services with other national post carriers showing that it is preferred. Again, studies like this may be open to question.

There are organisations representing the consumer which are independent of Royal Mail. In particular the Post Office Advisory Committee (POAC) acts as a channel for complaints, when the Royal Mail Customer Care Department is either bypassed or unable to deal with them. Also the Post Office Users National Council (POUNC) is the independent statutory consumer watchdog body which produces very helpful and well balanced reports.

Royal Mail is aware that some customer criticism and complaint is inevitable and at times hard to anticipate and respond to, but it may well not be aware how significant this is. The company also knows that some big organisations, such as the mail order companies, use alternative carriers and is worried about the significance of this. It realises that customer attitudes may change with rapidly changing times, rapidly changing modern technology, and the threat of alterations in legislation with the Citizens' Charter and the EC Green Paper for postal services.

The Royal Mail realises that there are challenging times ahead offering opportunities on the one hand and threats on the other.

Royal Mail's history can be traced back to over 350 years. Important landmarks are as follows:

1635	King Charles I, introduced the first postal service for the public. Postage was calculated on the distance and number of sheets in a letter. The postage was paid by the person receiving the letter.
1660	Parliament established the General Post Office.
1840	Sir Rowland Hill introduced his major reforms by bringing out "Penny Black" postage stamps. The sender had to pay for the postage. Posting letter boxes were set up on the roadside.
1911	World's first scheduled Air Mail service.
1968	Launch of two-tier letter service, first class and second class mail.
1969	The Post Office became a Nationalised Industry and ceased to be a Government Department.
1972	Completion of the allocation of postcodes to all 20 million UK addresses (except Norwich re-coding).
1974	Postcoding of all 21.5 million addresses in the UK completed with the re-coding of Norwich using the new format.
1981	The Post Office separated from British Telecommunications, with effect from 1 October.
1985	350th anniversary of the public postal service celebrated.
1986	Reorganisation of Post Office into separate businesses.

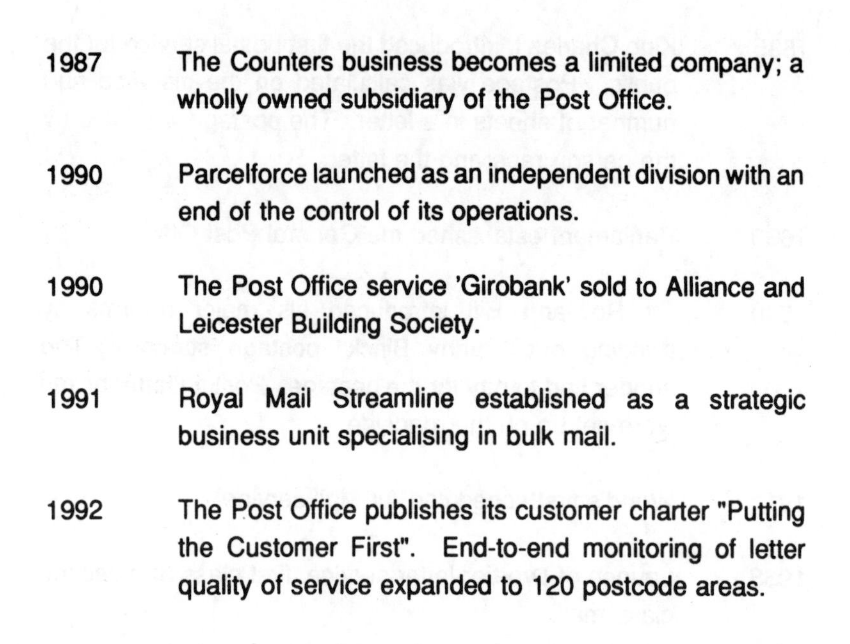

1987 The Counters business becomes a limited company; a wholly owned subsidiary of the Post Office.

1990 Parcelforce launched as an independent division with an end of the control of its operations.

1990 The Post Office service 'Girobank' sold to Alliance and Leicester Building Society.

1991 Royal Mail Streamline established as a strategic business unit specialising in bulk mail.

1992 The Post Office publishes its customer charter "Putting the Customer First". End-to-end monitoring of letter quality of service expanded to 120 postcode areas.

The organisation of Royal Mail has undergone radical change with most of the re-structuring completed with effect from April 1992. There are now nine geographical divisions operating under a central senior management functionally organised.

These nine geographical divisions replace 64 districts formerly organised into 4 territories. Each of the nine divisions has its own structure with a Director responsible for general management and a team of Directors responsible for finance, quality, processing, delivery, distribution, personnel, sales and facilities.

The nine geographical divisions are seen as operational divisions under the strategic direction of four newly created Strategic Business Units - see Appendix 4.

The distribution network is large and mail is transported by air, rail and road. Road transport is the main method in the UK and Royal Mail has a fleet of some 30,000 vehicles.

Cashco (a separate Royal Mail service for transporting cash and valuables) has about 170 depots of its own with a fleet of about 1,500 vehicles.

Parcelforce which is not part of Royal Mail also has its own distribution network and road fleet which is partially integrated with that of Royal Mail.

Royal Mail is a corporate brand which has become well known as a result of heavy promotion. It covers a wide and diverse range of services all of which have their own management and workforce. Some of these services have titles which substitute for brand names (such as Royal Mail Building Engineering Business [ROMEC] and Direct Mail). Some of the services have their own brand name such as Cashco, Quadrant and Presstream which are not very well known except to users. Recent research has indicated a considerable degree of confusion between the corporate brand, service brands and service names. A selection of these services is as follows:

1 <u>Direct Mail</u>
Rapidly growing advertising medium.

2 <u>Royal Mail International (RMI)</u>
With £450m annual turnover making a substantial contribution to overall profitability of the Royal Mail.

3 <u>Streamline</u>
For business customers who pre-sort their mail - 15 million items daily.

4 Presstream
For publishers distributing 2,500 magazines.

5 Royal Mail Stamps/Philatelic Service

6 Quadrant
Catering services

7 Royal Mail Engineering
Dealing with mail sorting, stamp cancelling machinery and developments.

8 Royal Mail Building Engineering Business (ROMEC)
Maintaining 2,500 properties owned or leased by Royal Mail.

9 Royal Mail Property Holdings
Responsible for the properties above.

10 Cashco
Transport service for cash and valuables.

11 Electronic Mail

Royal Mail are re-appraising their service strategy being aware that many traditional services are in decline whilst others are under threat from technological developments in telecommunications.

However, Royal Mail is itself innovative. One of its new services is Edipost which is designed to work with Electronic Data Interchange (EDI). Companies which have EDI systems can experience difficulties communicating with trading partners which do not have these. Barclays Bank for example needed a system which could deliver information quickly to non-EDI customers which would link smoothly with their existing EDI service. Edipost supplied the answer by allowing Barclays to divert electronic information to Royal Mail's Electronic Mail Centre in London. There the electronic messages are converted into print together with the customer company's logo, form design etc and delivered by first class post to non-EDI trading partners or customers.

Royal Mail are actively pursuing relationship marketing in the sense of creating a partnership approach to the solution of communication problems, as illustrated in the case of Barclays above.

Royal Mail's major market segment is businesses which accounts for approximately 80 per cent of the revenue. Household mail represents about 20 per cent of the revenue, decreasing.

The volume of international mail is relatively small but steadily increasing and showing a good return on sales.

Royal mail has some 500,000 account customers of which 160 represent 50 per cent of account turnover.

Royal Mail employs a large workforce, about 170,000 people. The new divisional structure will apportion the workforce equally to about 20,000 people in each division.

As is to be expected Royal Mail has many ways of achieving and maintaining good relations with the workforce. There are initiatives relating to Equal Opportunities, Employment of the Disabled, Career Breaks, Job Screening, Training and Developing, National Qualifications, Health and Safety, Welfare and Pensions.

The Royal Mail takes pride in offering a public service. The objective to deliver to every address in the country is a valuable service particularly to the isolated and the elderly. In isolated areas the post vehicle may also act as a Postbus for carrying people as well as mail.

Royal Mail supports the Citizens' Charter and has its own 'Customer Charter'. This puts the customer first and seeks continual response to consumers' needs and to continual improvement in service. The Charter does however envisage further changes in the future.

The company publishes a Code of Practice stating details of its services and explaining what to do if there are problems, the levels of compensation available and how to claim them.

Royal Mail publish a compendium of prices for all their services. The prices of some of its services are constrained by various watchdog bodies whilst other services have greater degrees of freedom on pricing policy.

Royal Mail employs all the elements of the promotional mix in its marketing operations and has recently embarked on a corporate advertising campaign using commercial television.

The Royal Mail conducts a fairly full programme of marketing research to inform its marketing mix decisions.

It also commissions surveys on attitudes towards Royal Mail services, eagerly publicising any improvements in customer satisfaction revealed, through its PR function.

As far as the international environment is concerned, the 1980s was a period of unprecedented change for postal administrations across the world. The driving force has been the desire to improve and assure the cost-effectiveness of services provided by postal authorities by exposing them to greater commercial pressures. Specific measures have included:

- incorporation as limited liability companies, albeit with the government as the sole shareholder

- identification of recognisable business units within the overall postal world, typically letters, parcels, retail and banking, each of which is run as a business in its own right

- restriction of monopoly powers to the letters business, and the promotion of competition in other areas, leading to the emergence of global express mail operators, remailers and other niche competitors.

National postal administrations have responded to these pressures in a variety of ways:

- they have recruited executives from the private sector, and introduced commercial systems and management practices

- they have introduced new and enhanced products, particulary in parcels, express mail and direct mail advertising; these generally make greater use of mechanisation and information technology

- they are making more entrepreneurial use of their retail network generally the largest in the country, to market a wide range of products and services. These range from the widespread "postshop" concept, through financial services, into leisure and lifestyle products such as packaged vacations and the UK's "Active Life" product for retired households.

The 1980s was also a period of relative financial prosperity for most postal administrations. The much heralded threat from electronic communications was slow to materialise, and any loss in traffic was more than offset by the dramatic growth in direct mail. This led to a steady increase in mail volumes and revenues, and to improved profitability.

So what about the prospects for the 1990s? The pressure for deregulation, and for reducing the scope of postal monopolies will intensify. International services will be opened up to competition, private operators will be allowed to provide trunking services and premium priced private delivery services will be permitted.

The European Community is formulating a strategic policy on postal liberalisation which will be published as a "Green Paper" (ie a discussion document). This concerns the future of postal and delivery services within the single market.

The preparation of the Green Paper is not straightforward due to differences in organisation of postal services in member states, and the demands of private courier companies to be allowed to compete in the market. However, the Green Paper will seek to eliminate differences in national regulations, and in quality and cost of service and will seek to ensure standards are met including deliveries to all destinations on all working days. There may be some protection of national monopolies, perhaps based on weight criteria, but these are likely to be less marked than at present. There is another large area of contention in the international business sector (where bulk mail is collected and sorted by a company in one country and re-injected into the postal system of another country). These steps will further encourage new entrants to target profitable segments of the postal business.

It is clear that the impending changes in regulations due to the EC Green Paper and the changes implied in the Citizens' Charter, offer opportunities in an expanding market but also offer challenges in alteration of monopoly status.

Also the traditional collaborative relationship between postal administrations is under considerable strain. The formation of private networks and the competition for international remail business demonstrate, if the trend amongst the world's telecommunications operators is a guide, a period of growing mistrust and greater competition can be expected.

Against this background of intensifying competition, there is the crucial issue of traffic volumes. Will mail volumes continue to grow through the 1990s, in which case will postal authorities have time to complete the transformation to fully competitive businesses? Or will saturation and electronic competition reduce growth rates and even cause decline in traffic, in which case the financial consequences will be profound and the pressure for dramatic change in working practices will be severe.

LIST OF APPENDICES

APPENDIX NUMBER	TITLE	PAGE No.
1	Mission Statements - Post Office Group - Royal Mail	13
2	Extract from Chairmans Report 1992 - Post Office Group	16
3	Extracts from Royal Mail Report 1992	19
4	Organisation Charts Royal Mail and notes	22
5	Service Range	27
6	Market Data	28
7	Some Marketing Research Findings	33
8	Special Report - The Electronic Challenge	38
9	Consolidated Profit and Loss Accounts and Balance Sheets for the Post Office Group and recent summary accounts for Royal Mail	44
10	Marketing Budgets	48
11	Compendium of Recent Press Articles	49
12	Copy of Recruitment Advertisement for your position	56

Mission Statements

APPENDIX 1
Sheet 1 of 3
MISSION STATEMENTS

THE POST OFFICE GROUP

MISSION AND VALUES

The Post Office Mission is to:

- anticipate and satisfy the requirements of our customers for excellent communications, distribution, financial and other agency services;

- create a positive working environment in which all our employees can find job satisfaction, take pride in our organisation, and feel that their views are valued;

- foster innovative product development and use of technology, and efficient working practices to give customers better value for money than can be obtained elsewhere;

- deserve national confidence as a responsible provider of a key part of the country's social and commercial infrastructure;

- and so to be recognised and respected as the world's leading provider of profitable, high quality postal services.

The mission will be achieved in manner consistent with the following Post Office Values:

- we care about our customers, and we shall at all times fulfil their expectations for;

  value for money
  reliability
  courtesy
  integrity
  security
  and prompt and timely service

APPENDIX 1
Sheet 2 of 3
MISSION STATEMENTS

- we care about our fellow employees;

- we care about the way we do our job and our role in the life of the nation.

- WE ARE PROUD TO BE PART OF THE POST OFFICE.

<u>ROYAL MAIL</u>

MISSION AND VALUES

<u>Royal Mail Business Mission</u>

As Royal Mail our mission is to be recognised as the best organisation in the World distributing text and packages.

We shall achieve this:-

- Excelling our Collection, Processing, Distribution and Delivery arrangements

- Establishing a partnership with our customers to understand, agree and meet their changing requirements

- Operating profitably by efficient services which our customers consider to be value for money

- Creating a work environment which recognises and rewards the commitment of all employees to customer satisfaction

- Recognising our responsibilities as part of the social, industrial and commercial life of the country

- Being forward looking and innovative

APPENDIX 1
Sheet 3 of 3
MISSION STATEMENTS

<u>Royal Mail Business Values</u>

We each care about:-

- Our customers and their requirements for:

  Reliability
  Value for money
  Accessibility
  Courtesy
  Integrity
  Security
  Prompt and timely response

- All our fellow employees and their needs for:

  Respect
  Training and development
  Involvement
  Recognition and reward

- The way we do our job and the way it affects our customers both inside and outside the Business

- Our role in the life of the community

- WE ARE PROUD TO BE PART OF ROYAL MAIL

Extracts from Chairman's Report 1992 for the Post Office Group

APPENDIX 2
Sheet 1 of 3
EXTRACT FROM THE CHAIRMAN'S REPORT

Extract from the Chairman's Report for the Post Office Group - 1991/92

CHAIRMAN'S STATEMENT

This has been, by any standards, a memorable year. Despite the recession, we have record profits, record volumes, the Post Office met its Group targets and, most important of all, independently measured standards of service to our customers have reached an all-time high. Nearly £300 million of capital investment was made to fund the future requirements for excellent customer service.

In summer 1991 the quality of the first class letter service topped 90% next-day delivery for the first time, averaging 89.8% through the year. This eclipses last year's record 85.5% and satisfies the demanding target agreed with the Post Officer User's National Council. Royal Mail confirmed its pre-eminent position in Europe when it again came first in an independent survey of first class letter reliability in leading European countries.

Although the recession slowed growth significantly, our customers posted still more letters than the previous year, a further 1.2% rise to new record volumes. We handled 61 million letters each working day through the year, rising to a record 122 million in the peak day before Christmas.

Counters and Royal Mail took the top two places in NOP surveys of value for money and quality of staff among public utilities.

FINANCIAL RESULTS

While Parcelforce's cost savings are the most spectacular, there has been improvement in efficiency right across the businesses. This has been a key factor in the Post Office Group comfortably beating its annual return on capital employed target, achieving 11.8% against the 11% target, and making a record profit of £247 million.

It is the 16th successive year of subsidy-free profit, a rare achievement among the world's postal services. This good financial result is vital to ensure we continue to generate the funds to sustain our high level of capital spending for the future.

APPENDIX 2
Sheet 2 of 3
EXTRACT FROM THE CHAIRMAN'S REPORT

The Post Office also beat its negative external financing limit target, contributing a further £74 million to Government funds. This brings the total contributed in this way over the past ten years to £750 million.

Royal Mail and Counters both achieved three-year targets to reduce real unit costs, a measure of their efficiency.

WHY THE IMPROVEMENT?

This encouraging picture has been taking shape over the past few years. One of my first important decisions when I took over nearly five years ago was to respond to customer demand for a new independent system of measuring the quality of the letters service. Instead of checking the letters ourselves from arrival on our premises to "ready for delivery", independent researchers now check "end-to-end" from pillar box to doormat.

This year we start to measure our performance for each of the 120 postcode areas, so that customers, wherever they are, know what service we are providing.

Another important move three years ago was the introduction of total quality management, a customer-drive strategy of change. We also introduced mission and values statements for the Post Office and each of its businesses. As a result, everyone is working to one clear objective - putting the customer first. This has been vigorously pursued throughout the Group and it is at the heart of the improvements we, as a team, have achieved. Team working at the top and spreading throughout the business has been a key ingredient for success.

THE WAY AHEAD

The results this year confirm that our strategy direction and the total quality management route are right. We shall continue down that path, in partnership with and listening to our customers, striving to give them the best possible service on all fronts. This commitment is backed by a planned £2,200 million five-year capital spending programme to boost services and keep pace with continuing growth.

APPENDIX 2
Sheet 3 of 3
EXTRACT FROM THE CHAIRMAN'S REPORT

Royal Mail not only set new record standards during the year but, determined to build on that success, the business reorganised, bringing its services still closer to the customer. It has begun the current financial year with its new structure in place and is continuing a planned £250 million programme of investment in the latest postal technology in support of the postmen and postwomen at the sharp end of the service.

Royal Mail is also eager to help British industry forge closer links with Europe through direct marketing supported by international reply-paid services, as well as encouraging European firms to post their foreign mail through Royal Mail International's unrivalled network.

Extracts from Royal Mail Report 1992

APPENDIX 3
Sheet 1 of 3
EXTRACTS FROM ROYAL MAIL REPORT

Extracts from Royal Mail Report for year ending 1991/92

The dedicated nationwide commitment to improving services has paid dividends for customers. Independent pillar boxes to doormat checks showed 89.8% of first class mail arriving the day after posting, compared with 85.5% in the previous 12 months.

This is the highest level recorded since independent checks began. The rise achieves the overall improvement target agreed with the Post Office Users' National Council and is equivalent to an extra 200 million letters a year arriving on time.

If is a far cry for the early 1970's when the postal service was considered to be in "terminal decline". Experts were forecasting the collapse of the letter service under pressure from technology - primarily telephones and fax machines - and the growth of private courier services. Sunday collections were stopped, service quality reached an all-time low and regular financial losses were incurred.

Today, despite the recession, volume of business continues to grow, totalling 61 million items each working day compared with 38 million ten years ago, while Sunday collections are fully restored. Pre-Christmas postings produced another record when, on Monday December 16, 122 million letters and cards were posted. In addition, 2.5 million mailings of BT shares were handled in the week before Christmas.

Another large posting was the 130 million items generated by the General Election during March and April.

By the end of the year, Royal Mail also reached an historic agreement with the Union of Communication Workers aimed at transforming industrial relations in the business - heralded as a benchmark for other companies and unions. In particular, it focuses industrial relations activity throughout the new organisation on key issues, improving communication and understanding and allowing Royal Mail to respond more quickly to customer and market needs.

APPENDIX 3
Sheet 2 of 3
EXTRACTS FROM ROYAL MAIL REPORT

FOCUS ON THE CUSTOMER

Royal Mail's Managing Director led a massive communication exercise under the banner "Delivering For You". He visited employees around the UK and talked with 3,500 managers about the need for continual pursuit of excellence, setting and achieving fresh goals, and giving customers value-for-money, reliability and improved service.

The focus on the customer was further strengthened when the foundations were laid for a Royal Mail restructured into nine geographical divisions.

There will be independent monitoring of quality service for each of the 120 postcode areas, instead of the 63 postal delivery districts, setting improvement targets and publishing results quarterly.

In January 1992, Royal Mail refined the process of strengthening its partnership with business customers through the Postal Business Partnership, a forum in which trade associations and other organisations representing groups of customers work with Royal Mail to develop improvements in services.

Royal Mail has already established an award-winning customer-supplier partnership with Kodak Limited in Hemel Hempstead, where teams from both businesses meet on a regular basis to maintain and improve quality of service. Kodak, which posts more than two million items a year, awarded a Quality First certificate to Royal Mail Oxford. Other major customers, such as BP, also at Hemel Hempstead, are discussing a similar Royal Mail partnership.

INTERNATIONAL MAIL

Royal Mail International (RMI) handles 50% more mail to the rest of the world than any other European country. It has more direct flights to other countries and is one of the few operators to have its delivery times independently monitored.

APPENDIX 3
Sheet 3 of 3
EXTRACTS FROM ROYAL MAIL REPORT

With potential growth of the European market, RMI is concentrating on UK customers with contacts overseas as well as encouraging overseas companies to base their mailing operations in the UK. RMI helps customers by publishing guides on finding, making and keeping contact with potential clients, and encourages closer links with Europe through its Twin Town Awards scheme.

DEVELOPING THE NETWORK

The start of the financial year saw the launch of Royal Mail Streamline, a new strategic business unit within Royal Mail, which was set up to focus on the needs of customers with mailings of more than 2,000 letters at a time.

Mailsort, the largest Streamline service, illustrated the success of this customer driven initiative when it attracted 1,500 new customers during the year. Mailsort 3, the service for non-time-crucial direct mail and other items grew by 13%.

Eight regional centres dedicated to handling customer-sorted mail, Mailsort and Presstream, were also brought under Streamline management control during the year. In total, 16 such centres, many purpose-designed and built will be operational by mid 1993.

Streamline's relaunched Reponse Services - a combination of Freepost and Business Reply - also bucked the recession achieving 5% growth to more than 430 million items annually.

INVESTMENT AND AUTOMATION

Royal Mail is one of the world's biggest buyers of the latest postal equipment, and aims to spend £250 million on sorting technology over the next five years as part of a planned £1,600 million investment to improve service.

IMPROVING THE NETWORK

The year also saw the elimination of leaded petrol from Royal Mail's vehicle fleet in a number of environmentally friendly innovations. The concept of left-hand drive vehicles for safer in town deliveries was agreed.

Organisation Charts
Royal Mail

APPENDIX 4
Sheet 1 of 5
ORGANISATION CHARTS

PREVIOUS ORGANISATION

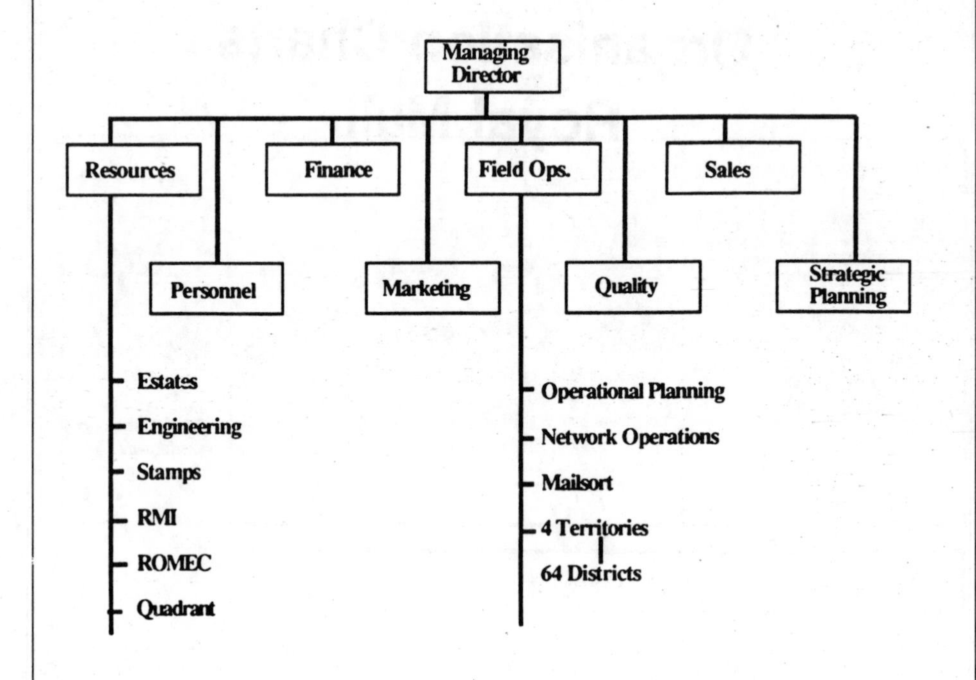

APPENDIX 4
Sheet 2 of 5
ORGANISATION CHARTS

NEW ORGANISATION STRUCTURE

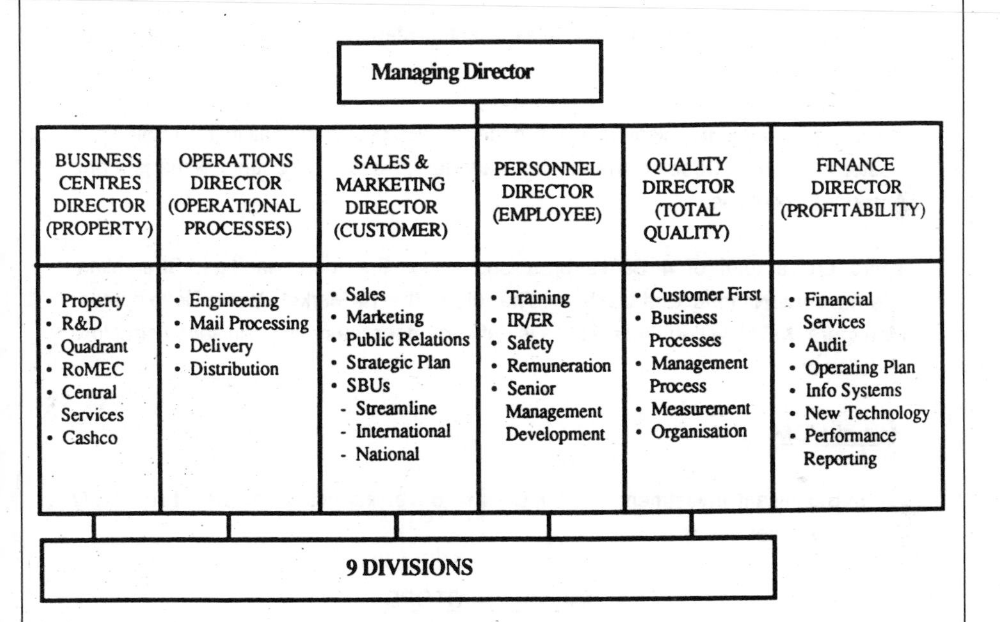
Managing Director
BUSINESS CENTRES DIRECTOR (PROPERTY)
OPERATIONS DIRECTOR (OPERATIONAL PROCESSES)
SALES & MARKETING DIRECTOR (CUSTOMER)
PERSONNEL DIRECTOR (EMPLOYEE)
QUALITY DIRECTOR (TOTAL QUALITY)
FINANCE DIRECTOR (PROFITABILITY)
• Property • R&D • Quadrant • RoMEC • Central Services • Cashco
• Engineering • Mail Processing • Delivery • Distribution
• Sales • Marketing • Public Relations • Strategic Plan • SBUs - Streamline - International - National
• Training • IR/ER • Safety • Remuneration • Senior Management Development
• Customer First • Business Processes • Management Process • Measurement • Organisation
• Financial Services • Audit • Operating Plan • Info Systems • New Technology • Performance Reporting
9 DIVISIONS

APPENDIX 4
Sheet 3 of 5
ORGANISATION CHARTS (NOTES)

Notes on the marketing and sales organisations of Royal Mail

Strategic Business Units (SBU's) come under the general jurisdiction of Strategic Headquarters and for Sales/Marketing under the Sales and Marketing Director (Customer).

Each SBU has its own Marketing/Sales Director, Market Development Manager and Product Managers.

There are nine geographical Divisions in the UK. Each Division has its own Sales and Customer Service Director, Area Sales Managers, National Accounts Managers and Account Executives.

There are a total of 4 SBU's organised under the four headings; Streamline, International, National and Cashco. The role of the 14 Market Sector Development Managers (MDM) within these SBU's is defined under the new organisation structure as follows:

Role of MDM

- Significant investment in 14 MDMs to drive product development to satisfy customer needs

MARKET SECTORS

*	STREAMLINE = 5	:	MAIL ORDER FINANCE COMMERCIAL PUBLISHING GOVT. DEPTS & UTILITIES
*	INTERNATIONAL = 3	:	ENGINEERING/MANUFACTURING DISTRIBUTION/WHOLESALE EDUCATION

APPENDIX 4
Sheet 4 of 5
ORGANISATION CHARTS (NOTES)

*	NATIONAL = 5	:	ELECTRONIC PERSONAL MAIL (RETAIL STAMPS) POSTCODES SMALL/MEDIUM BUSINESS SERVICES PREMIUM
*	CASHCO = 1	:	CASH IN TRANSIT BUSINESS

- MDMs will discuss with customers at a strategic level their future needs

- Visits to customers will be done in conjunction with or knowledge of accounts managers within the divisions

Account Managers are responsible for selling to, developing and servicing the customer leaving MDMs to understand future customer requirements and drive product development.

MARKET SECTOR REVIEW PROCESS

- MDMs responsible for producing a sector review.

- Each market sector would be teamworked with Divisions to produce a plan to take advantage of opportunities and counter threats. The sector would be reviewed twice a year.

- MDMs will interface with Divisons normally via National Account Managers or Sales and Customer Service Managers and possibly with Account Executives.

- The MDM Divisional interface would teamwork within the Divisional sales function to provide input to the particular sector review. All customers are now additionally identified with a market sector code eg Finance to ease this process.

APPENDIX 4
Sheet 5 of 5
ORGANISATION CHARTS (NOTES)

The MDMs sector plans will form part of the SBU Business Plan and MDMs will input to the new product development process.

SBU AND DIVISIONAL RELATIONSHIPS

The organisation is flexible, dynamic and evolving. The following guidelines determine the potentially complex relationship between the four SBU's and the nine Divisions:

- the relationship depends upon partnership
- sales priorities will be largely determined by the SBU's
- sales deployment/operations will remain the responsibility of the divisions
- SBU's will only have direct access to customers through account managers

Royal Mail's Service Range

APPENDIX 5
Sheet 1 of 1
ROYAL MAIL'S SERVICE RANGE

ROYAL MAIL SERVICES

PRODUCT GROUP LISTING

Postage Rates	UK Postage Rates International Postage Rates Weight Allowances
Priority Services	Intelpost Special Delivery
Insured Services	Cash on Delivery Consequential Loss Insurance Recorded Delivery Registered Post
Office Services	Collection and Delivery Franking Private Boxes Redirection Selectapost
Volume Mailings (Discount and Contract Services)	Electronic Post Mailsort 1, 2 3 Postage Paid Symbol Presstream 1, 2 Printed Postage Impression
Direct Marketing and Response Services	Admail Business Reply Direct Mail Freepost Household Delivery Postcodes
International	Airstream International Business Reply International Direct Marketing International Insured Service International Registered Post Printflow Air Printflow Airsaver Printflow Surfacesaver Swiftair

Market Data

APPENDIX 6
Sheet 1 of 5
MARKET DATA

Top twenty customers for Mailsort/Presstream revenue in rank order, by business category

SIC CODE	BUSINESS CATEGORY
8140	Banking and bill discounting
6560	Mixed retail businesses
4752	Periodical publishers
8395	Business services not elsewhere specified
4754	Other publishing
8150	Other financial institutions
6330	Retail distribution of books, stationary and office supplies
6190	Wholesale non-food
6540	Other specialised retail distribution (non-food)
4751	Printing and publishing
8200	Insurance - not compulsory social security
9611	Social welfare, charitable and community services
8380	Advertising
9631	Trade Unions, business and professional associations
4930	Photographic and cinematographic processing laboratories
8360	Accountants, auditors and tax experts
9111	National government service not elsewhere specified
8393	Business services
8394	Computer services

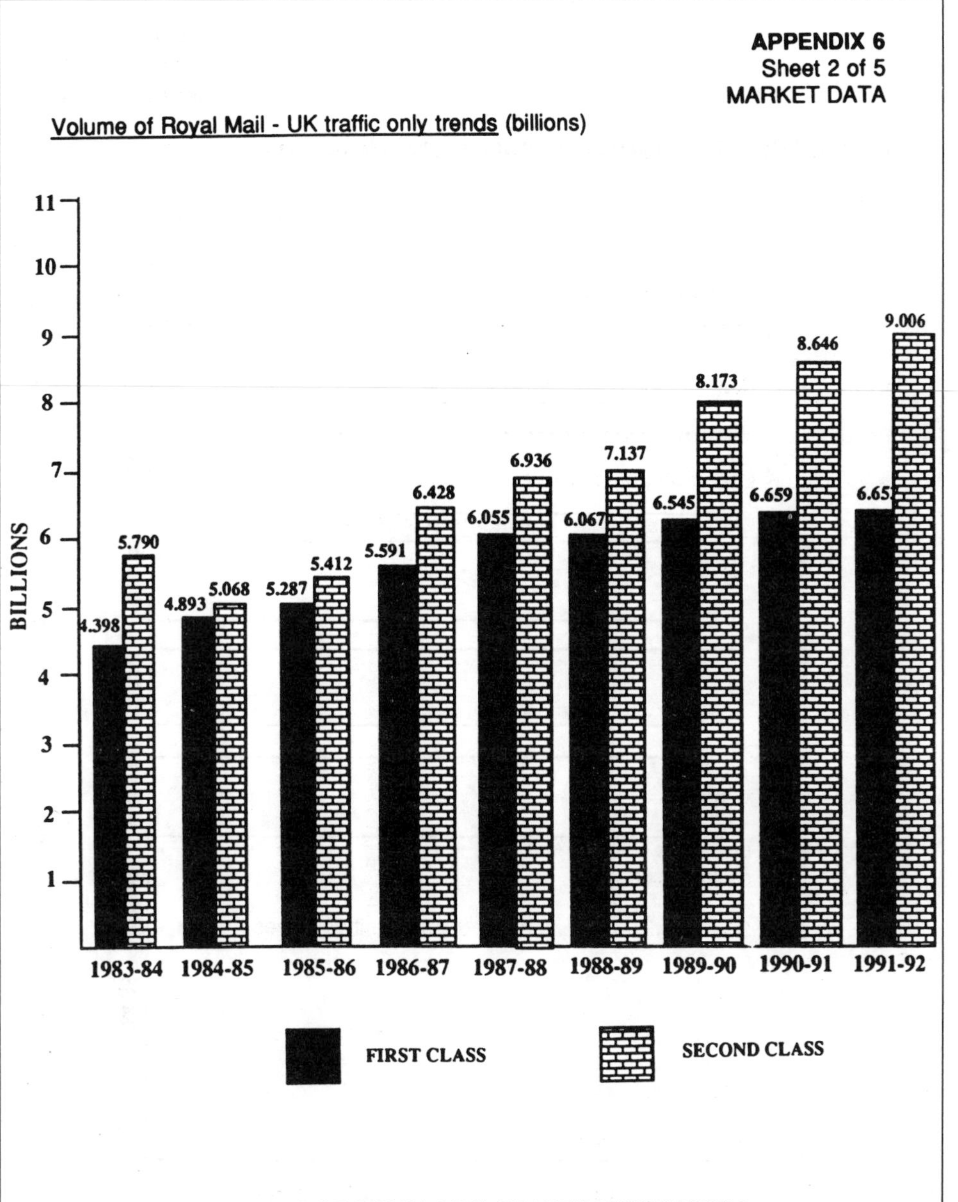

VOLUME OF ROYAL MAIL TRAFFIC/TYPE/ANNUM
(FIRST CLASS - SECOND CLASS)

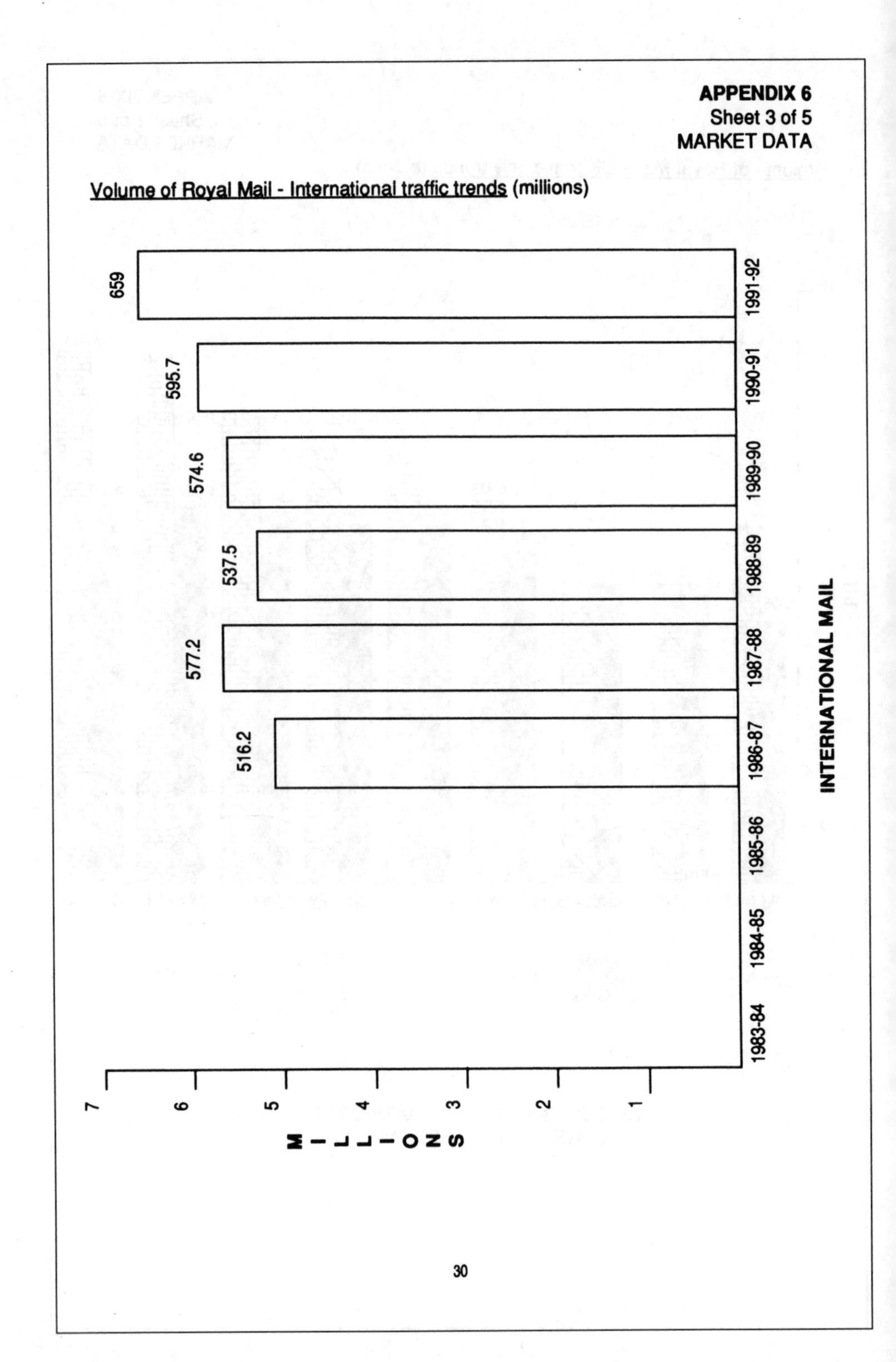

APPENDIX 6
Sheet 3 of 5
MARKET DATA

Volume of Royal Mail - International traffic trends (millions)

30

APPENDIX 6
Sheet 4 of 5
MARKET DATA

Royal Mail income/payment methods 1990/91

Total Income £3573.2 million

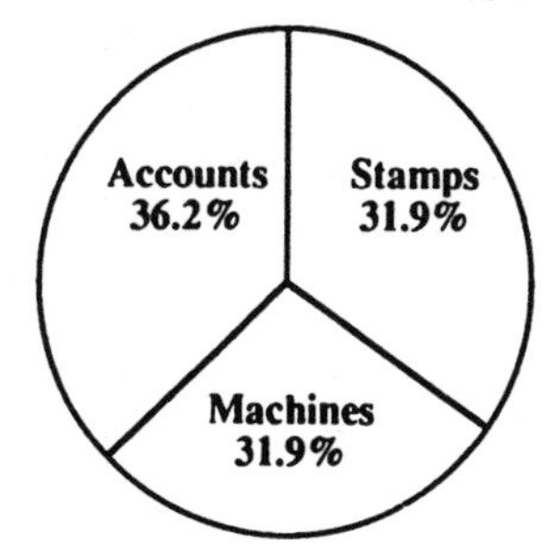

2nd Class Income £1736.6 million

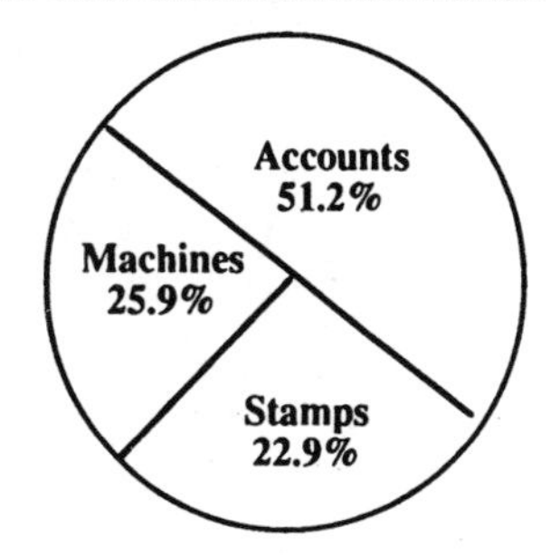

Other Items Income £207.2 million

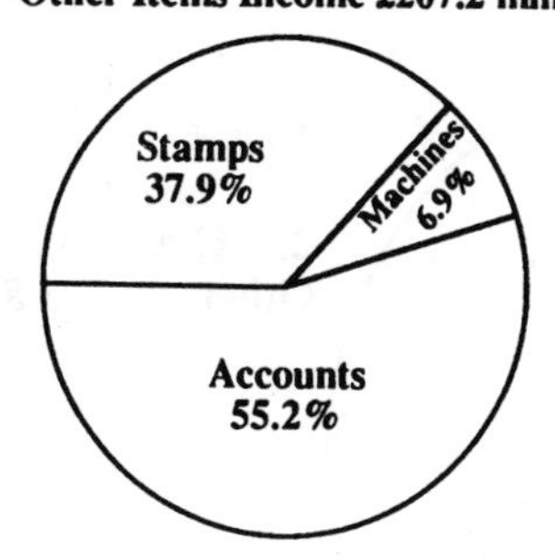

1st Class Income £1629.4 million

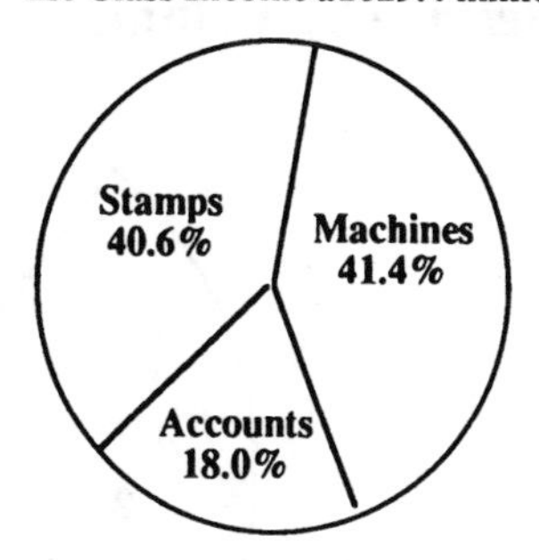

APPENDIX 6
Sheet 5 of 5
MARKET DATA

Royal Mail turnover by value and volume 1990/91

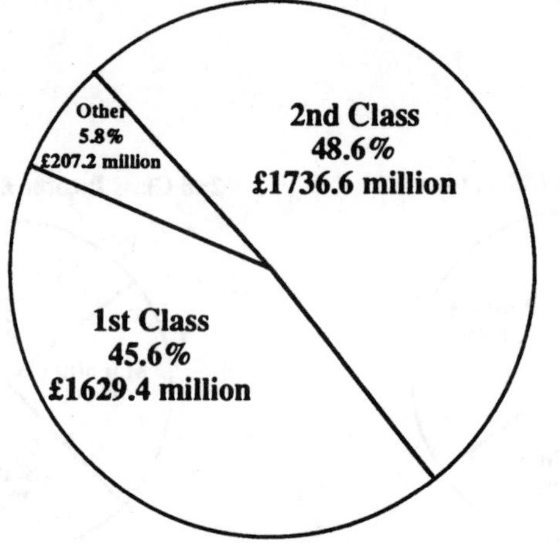

Service by Volume

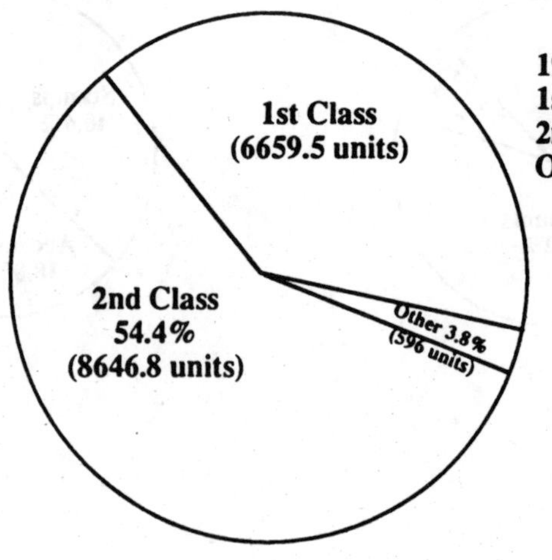

Marketing Research Findings

APPENDIX 7
Sheet 1 of 5
MARKETING RESEARCH FINDINGS 1991

Business Customer Survey

- 17% of customers surveyed utilize Royal Mail's Presstream program
- 50% of customers surveyed were aware of Royal Mail's Presstream program
- 8% of customers surveyed utilize Royal Mail's Streamline program
- 42% of customers surveyed were aware of Royal Mail's Streamline program
- 68% of all businesses surveyed required next day delivery to their customers
- 66% of all businesses surveyed said they use a different carrier than Royal Mail for next day letter delivery

APPENDIX 7
Sheet 2 of 5
MARKETING RESEARCH FINDINGS 1991

Business Customer Survey

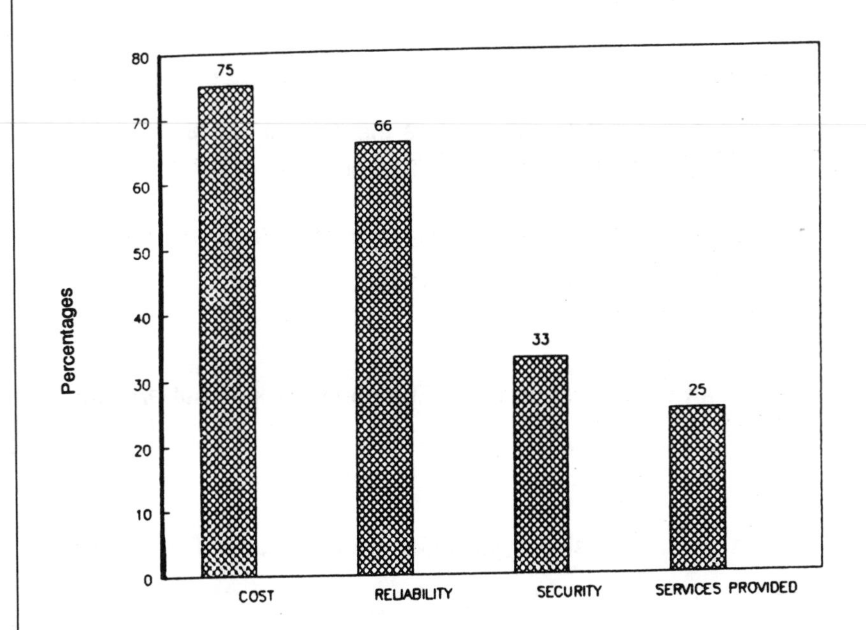

The above graph illustrates the customers primary consideration when choosing a next day delivery carrier

APPENDIX 7
Sheet 3 of 5
MARKETING RESEARCH FINDINGS 1991

CONCLUSIONS

Royal Mail provides a high quality service but has yet to realise full potential.

Royal Mail's "2nd Class" delivery achieves the highest success against stated aim - though the title suggests a different image.

Royal Mail has been protected by monopoly status.

Royal Mail has an opportunity to enter European markets but appears unprepared.

Royal Mail is a labour intensive organisation with poor utilisation of fixed assets.

Royal Mail marketing does not create adequate customer awareness of specialised services.

Royal Mail's quantified quality exceeds that perceived by the customer.

Royal Mail's potential customers show a high dissatisfaction rate with defection to other carriers.

APPENDIX 7
Sheet 4 of 5
MARKETING RESEARCH FINDINGS 1991

Threats

Potential Competitors

Analysis of a small sample of likely competitors, with networks and infrastructures which could pose a threat to the traditional letter services of the Royal Mail, was undertaken to see how they saw their role and the future for their business. The sample consisted of TNT, Federal Express, ANC, Group 4, Pony Express.

The first three companies we believe could pose some direct threat to the Royal Mail's first class service, whilst the remainder would be in direct competition with the Mail's Cashco company.

The Survey Suggests

1 All companies gave a 24 hours next day guarantee service.

2 All companies listed customer care, reliability and security as major features of their business.

3 Two of the companies gave a standard no quibble money back/cancellation of fee if delivery did not arrive on time.

4 All companies collected the items for delivery from customers.

5 When asked to rank their competitors in order as they saw the market, only one saw the Royal Mail as a competitor and that was TNT. Although two others saw "Parcel Force" as a direct competitor positioned at second and third place.

APPENDIX 7
Sheet 5 of 5
MARKETING RESEARCH FINDINGS 1991

6 All companies are currently focused on different market segments but could in our opinion compete for growth in other segments, given a worsening economic situation.

7 All companies saw Europe as a big opportunity for growth as well as technology, satellite tracking, computerisation etc. The security based companies also consider secure warehousing as a growth market.

ONE COMPANY SEES EUROPEAN, INCLUDING UK, POSTAL SERVICES AS A MAJOR GROWTH MARKET.

That company is TNT who have already formed a joint venture with a 50% holding with the Post Offices of Germany, France, Sweden, Holland and Canada holding the balance between them. In addition, TNT have operating companies in the twelve European community countries as well as the seven countries that make up the European Free Trade Association (EFTA), and are therefore well positioned to develop postal services throughout Europe, AND MUST BE CONSIDERED A MAJOR THREAT.

Special Report
The Electronic Challenge

APPENDIX 8
Sheet 1 of 6
SPECIAL REPORT

The Electronic Challenge

Over the past decade any threat to the postal industry for the electronic exchange of documents has been more than offset by overall growth in trade and the development and exploitation of opportunities such as direct mail. This has been true with high penetration of electronic services such as facsimile where, for example, over 60% of all companies in the developed world now have fax machines.

However, there are signs that this situation is changing as information technology becomes every more pervasive. Firstly, the direct substitution of documents which are currently carried by post, for example invoices, cheques or letters by electronic communications, with or without a paper copy being produced is increasing, and could extend to private households. Secondly, business practices are changing in ways which eliminate the need for transferring documents by post. Examples of this include the integration of suppliers and/or customers into the business process through joint computer systems enabling just-in-time (JIT) manufacturing, the use of smart cards to collect local taxes and the establishment of fully integrated order processing, invoicing and payment systems.

The key electronic services likely to impact the postal industry directly or indirectly over the next decade are briefly reviewed below:

Electronic Document Transfer

In the past, lack of standards has restricted the manipulation of revisable documents to single computer systems or applications environments. Increasingly, though, there is a need to transfer documents between different environments, or different vendors' equipment, both within an enterprise and with other organisations. This need is driven by the recognition that there are considerable cost savings, as well as productivity and business performance improvements, to be obtained from successful implementation.

So far progress in this area has not been sufficient to meet users' needs in full, although standards such as ODA (Open Document Architecture) have been ratified and individual vendors have also produced proprietary solutions.

APPENDIX 8
Sheet 2 of 6
SPECIAL REPORT

We expect very significant advances as open system concepts become more fully implemented across a wide range of businesses

Electronic Mail (E-Mail)

Most usage of E-Mail today is within an enterprise based on proprietary systems, but there is a growing trend to implementations based on the international E-Mail standard, X.400, which was defined in 1984 as a means of ensuring compatibility and allowing global inter-connection of different messaging systems. The standard was extended in 1988 to provide additional facilities including store and forward, security, and conversion from E-Mail to telex, fax and mail services.

However, although there is a wide availability of X.400 products and services, take-up has, in general, been slow to develop, mainly because of the existing use of proprietary internal messaging systems and the relatively slow growth in demand for public messaging services in Europe.

The strongest demand for X.400 is being generated by the public sector. For example, the UK government is an X.400 user and current projects include the Inland Revenue Office and Management Support Services (OAMSS).

Major private companies are also committing to X.400. Hoechst in Germany has standardised on X.400, and has implemented links to each of the office automation packages.

Electronic Data Interchange

Electronic Data Interchange is the electronic transfer of commercial data between computer systems, structured according to agreed standards.

EDI provides a means of replacing the commercial paperwork that is exchanged between trading partners, allowing data to flow from the point at which it is generated to the point where it is to be processed, without manual intervention. The dominant

APPENDIX 8
Sheet 3 of 6
SPECIAL REPORT

applications are high volume transactions such as orders, invoices, delivery instructions etc, although a wide range of transaction types can be exchanged. Organisations are using EDI to reduce costs, improve productivity, be more responsive to their trading partners' requirements and introduce new business processes.

The vast majority of EDI applications today are batch and run over third party value added networks (VANs). The benefit of using VAN is that only one connection is required to communicate with all trading partners (assuming that they are all connected to the same VAN). Also all transmissions can be batched together and submitted to the VAN, without the need to synchronise communications with the trading partners.

EDI has evolved on a sector and community basis, with standards being developed to support specific sectors and communities. Examples of important groups of users include:

- the major retailers in France
- the motor manufacturers in the UK
- the pharmaceutical industry in the USA
- the travel and transportation industry using, EDI for communication with their distribution channels and major users.

EDI is also used in other sectors including other manufacturing companies, finance and insurance, energy, engineering and the public sector-likely to be one of the largest users. The scale of public procurement means that potentially there are considerable savings to be gained from improving the efficiency of the supply chain, and in the UK the National Health Service in particular is putting a substantial amount of effort into the use of EDI.

APPENDIX 8
Sheet 4 of 6
SPECIAL REPORT

EDI is currently still in its infancy. Its rapid deployment is severely hindered by two key factors:

- lack of agreement on standards which prevent interworking even at a basic level

- the requirement to change working practices in order to achieve cost effective implementation.

Nevertheless EDI is achieving tangible benefits for those companies who have got it right and significant growth is expected during the 1990s.

One further consideration needs to be highlighted. So far EDI have generally focused on the automation of the order/invoice cycle: payment has largely continued to be effected by paper-based transactions, particularly where transborder payments are required. One the other side, interbank payment systems are fully automated. Completing the EDI loop by allowing EDI-based payments and associated data to be exchanged directly with banking systems is a development which is under serious consideration. Effective implementation may take some time to be achieved but the eventual impact on postal traffic could obviously be considerable.

Facsimile

Over the last ten years facsimile has moved from being a marginal, new technology to being indispensable to most businesses in many countries. The vast majority of the business population in the developed world can now be reached by fax, and the trend is for ever smaller workgroups to have their own machine.

Surprisingly, this rapid adoption of the technology by businesses worldwide has had less discernible impact on postal traffic than was feared. Most faxes have, until recently, been followed by higher quality hard copy in the post.

APPENDIX 8
Sheet 5 of 6
SPECIAL REPORT

However, there are signs that this is beginning to change. Users are becoming accustomed to the poorer quality of fax and are less worried about receiving follow-up hard copy. As a response to this companies are beginning to encourage users not to use both fax and post but to choose. Additionally we are seeing the emergence of fax enhancements including:

- plain paper fax

- computer to computer fax

- fax services providing multi-addressing, broadcast facilities

Already fax is being used by some companies as a new way of delivering direct mail - a move which the postal industry worldwide will regard as a threat to its own lucrative business in this area and one which becomes even more serious if the emerging trend to faxes in the home takes off.

Plain paper and computer to computer fax both remove the problems of poor paper quality duty standards and technical complexity. Inertia from the massive installed base of conventional equipment and price are still considerable barriers to significant uptake.

Cable TV

Interactive cable TV coupled with card technology could provide a new route for telemail and direct marketing as well as opening up access to other applications eg. home banking, televoting, on-line games. Most countries do not yet have well enough developed or sophisticated enough systems to support these types of developments in the short term, but the longer term threat is definitely a reality.

APPENDIX 8
Sheet 6 of 6
SPECIAL REPORT

CAD/CAM

The storage, manipulation and interchange of large-scale drawings, graphics and maps is an important but rather specialised application. The growth in cost-effective broadband telecommunications services will facilitate on-line document interchange but the impact on postal traffic is likely to modest.

Mobile Technologies

Analogue cellular radio telephony has enjoyed very significant growth during the 1980s. This growth is set to continue as digital cellular systems are adopted during the 1990s and data capabilities become a reality. The addition of mobility to data capture and processing could have major effect of work practices in some industries, for example insurance where direct capture of policy information by agents could increase efficiencies and reduce paperwork. This in turn could reduce the need to send this information by post if it becomes simpler to communicate on-line.

Conclusions

A recent UK survey showed that 80% of managers now use a PC and produce some if not all of their own correspondence. Companies are looking for efficiency in all their business processes and many regard the order/invoice/payment/goods cycle as a key one to improve. Direct mail has been hugely successful but companies are now looking for new ways to make an impact on potential customers.

These changes are brought about by the continuing developments in the computing and communications industries. The challenge for postal administrations is to understand how to benefit from these changes rather than succumb to them.

Consolidated Profit and Loss Accounts and Balance Sheet Royal Mail

APPENDIX 9
Sheet 1 of 4
CONSOLIDATED PROFIT AND LOSS ACCOUNTS AND BALANCE SHEETS

1 **Consolidated Profit and Loss Accounts and Balance Sheets 1989/92**
Post Office Group - £ million

	1989 Mar 29	1990 Mar 28	1991 Mar 31	1992 Mar 29
Property	1,481.4	1,575.0	1,528.0	1,439.0
Other tangible fixed assets	423.0	497.0	580.0	602.0
Other fixed assets	298.0	281.0	348.0	341.0
TOTAL FIXED ASSETS	2,202.4	2,353.0	2,456.0	2,382.0
Stock	24.1	18.0	25.0	27.0
Debtors	339.2	317.0	462.0	359.0
Cash and securities	1,114.5	1,299.0	1,024.0	1,061.0
CURRENT ASSETS	1,477.8	1634.0	1,511.0	1,447.0
TOTAL ASSETS	3,680.2	3,987.0	3,967.0	3,829.0
Shareholders Equity	1,977.3	2,234.0	2,114.0	2,122.0
Non-current liabilities	131.6	122.0	120.0	83.0
Long and medium loans			32.0	32.0
NET ASSETS	2,108.9	2,356.0	2,266.0	2,237.0
Creditors	1,490.5	1,502.0	1,555.0	1,437.0
Current tax due	80.8	129.0	146.0	155.0
CURRENT LIABILITIES	1,571.3	1,631.0	1,701.0	1,592.0
LIABILITIES AND EQUITY	3,680.2	3,987.0	3,967.0	3,829.0
PROFT AND LOSS				
Sales	3,535.6	4,053.7	4,719.0	5,149.0
Operating expenses	3,441.6	4,005.9	4,719.0	4,918.0
OPERATING PROFIT	94.0	47.8	.0	231.0
Other income	66.8	38.0	47.0	30.0
PROFIT BEFORE INTEREST	160.8	85.8	47.0	261.0
Interest charge	19.6	.0	.0	14.0
PROFIT BEFORE TAX	141.2	85.8	47.0	247.0
Tax charge	52.7	34.5	16.0	95.0
EARNINGS	88.5	51.3	31.0	152.0
Employee numbers (FTE's - 000's)	198.5	204.2	207.4	201.9
Staff costs (£m)	2,518.1	2,850.2	3,113.0	3,233.0

APPENDIX 9
Sheet 2 of 4
CONSOLIDATED PROFIT AND LOSS ACCOUNTS AND BALANCE SHEETS

Consolidated Profit and Loss Accounts and Balance Sheets 1989/92
Post Office Group - £ million

	1989 Mar 29	1990 Mar 28	1991 Mar 31	1992 Mar 29
GROWTH RATES (%)				
Sales growth		14.65%	16.41%	9.11%
Earnings growth		-42.03%	-39.57%	390.32%
PROFITABILITY				
Return on net assets	6.70%	3.64%	2.07%	11.04%
Net profit margin	3.99%	2.12%	1.00%	4.80%
Return on equity	4.48%	2.30%	1.47%	7.16%
Staff costs/sales	71.22%	70.31%	65.97%	62.79%
Staff cost per employee (£'000s)	12.7	14.0	15.0	16.0
Sales per employee (£'000s)	17.8	19.9	22.8	25.5
ASSET UTILISATION				
Sales/net assets	1.7	1.7	2.1	2.3
Sales/properties	2.4	2.6	3.1	3.6
Sales/other fixed assets	8.4	8.2	8.1	8.6
Stock days	2.6	1.6	1.9	2.0
Debtor days	35.0	28.5	35.7	25.4
Creditor days	158.1	136.9	120.3	106.7
Net assets per employee (£'000s)	10.6	11.5	10.9	11.1
LIQUIDITY MEASURES				
Current ratio	.9	1.0	.9	.9
Liquid ratio	.9	1.0	.9	.9
Cash days	115.1	117.0	79.2	75.2
FINANCIAL STRUCTURE				
Total debt/total assets	.4	.4	.4	.4
Long term debt/total assets	.0	.0	.0	.0
Interest cover	8.2	.0	.0	18.6

APPENDIX 9
Sheet 3 of 4
CONSOLIDATED PROFIT AND LOSS ACCOUNTS

ROYAL MAIL

Profit and loss account for the year ended 29 March 1992	1992 £m	1991 £m
Turnover	3,911	3,575
Staff costs	(2,671)	(2,561)
Depreciation & other amounts written off tangible fixed assets	(85)	(66)
Other operating charges	(948)	(822)
	(3,704)	(3,449)
Profit on ordinary activities before interest	207	126
Interest receivable	59	45
Profit on ordinary activities before exceptional item	266	171
Exceptional item	-	(50)
Profit on ordinary activities before taxation	266	121
Taxation	(96)	(42)
Profit for the financial year	170	79

Statement of reserves
for the year ended 29 March 1992

Reserves at 1 April 1992	1,368	1,393
Net revaluation of tangible fixed assets	(118)	(104)
Profit for the financial year	170	79
Reserves at 29 March 1992	1,420	1,368

APPENDIX 9
Sheet 4 of 4
CONSOLIDATED PROFIT AND LOSS ACCOUNTS

ROYAL MAIL

Balance sheet at 29 March 1992	**1992** £m	**1991** £m
Tangible fixed assets	1,442	1,497
Current assets		
Debtors	228	290
Inter-business balances	606	437
Cast at bank and in hand	13	11
	847	738
Current liabilities		
Creditors - amounts falling due within one year	(661)	(673)
Inter-business balances	(156)	(48)
	(817)	(721)
Net current assets	30	17
Total assets less current liabilities	1,472	1,514
Creditors - amounts falling due after one year	(22)	(98)
Provisions for liabilities and charges	(30)	(48)
	1,420	1,368
Capital and reserves		
Revaluation reserve	484	629
Profit and loss account	936	739
	1,420	1,368

Marketing Budgets

APPENDIX 10
Sheet 1 of 1
MARKETING BUDGETS

Royal Mail Marketing Budgets 1992/93 - £ millions

New Product Development			20
Marketing Research			3
Promotion			
Above the line (inc production costs)			
T.V.	5		
Press	2		
Radio	0.1		
Cinema	0.2		
Poster	5		
		Total	12.3
Below the line			
Literature	3		
Direct Mail	3		
Incentives	2		
Exhibitions	2		
Other	1		
		Total	11.0
Public Relations			5.0
Salesforce			5.0
		GRAND TOTAL	56.3

Compendium of Recent Press Articles

APPENDIX 11
Sheet 1 of 7
EXTRACTS FROM RECENT PRESS ARTICLES

Carol Leonard discovers the new chief executive of the Post Office

The Post Office, that huge monolithic organisation with an annual turnover of £5.5 billion and 220,000 employees, has a new boss. Two days ago, Bill Cockburn took over from Sir Bryan Nicholson as its chief executive.

Cockburn who has come up through the Post Office ranks, is the son of a hospital porter and is neither nervous, shy nor daunted by his new job. His reputation in business - and unusually for a nationalised industry - is as a man manager driven by customer service. Although he repeatedly gives the impression that his own world begins and ends with the Post Office, that, from his perspective, the rest of the world revolves around *it*, when it comes to examining the external view of the Post Office and its services he seems able to detach himself sufficiently to cast a critical eye.

He becomes increasingly animated as he discusses it "I suppose I do have a strong sense of ownership towards it and what is wonderful now is it's mine. It's my great big train set and I can do what I want with it. Yes I am passionate about it and I expect the same passion from the people who work here. But it is not all consuming. I can visualise myself doing other things."

Some people might find that surprising given the hours he puts in at the Post Office. He says he does not know if he can be accurately classified as a workaholic. "The hours are long" he says "I get in at 8.30 am and if I'm home in time to see the 9 o'clock news then I'm doing well. I go to dinners maybe three evenings a week."

At work, he prides himself on being a visible boss "I like meeting our front-line employees. What they can tell me is far more important than what I can tell them. I have worked with various bosses who have been very rank conscious and I never wanted to model myself on people like that. Perhaps that's because I'm still young enough to remember what it is like to work for that type of person. You must fight against grandeur and self-importance. It's very easy to get seduced by it."

Cockburn's appointment is for a three-year term, his fourth successive such term since being made a director. "I would want to stay for as long as it was felt that I genuinely added value," he says. Does that mean that in three years he might consider a fresh challenge? "Oh I think so" he replies. "Yes, there is another job in me. I'm quite good at running large, service businesses and I know from experience how to manage cultures and how to find the levers and buttons of change."

Times
24 October 1992

APPENDIX 11
Sheet 2 of 7
EXTRACTS FROM RECENT PRESS ARTICLES

ROYAL MAIL LAUNCHES GIFT MAGAZINE SUBS SCHEME

The Royal Mail is to launch its own gift magazine subscriptions scheme through newsagents - despite pulling out of a similar venture last year.

The national scheme, developed with the Periodical Publishers Association, will offer selected titles through a voucher available at the newsagent, from which the recipient can pick a subscription. The idea, being test-marketed regionally before a national roll-out later in the year, aims to boost subscription sales.

PPA circulation executive Jackie Fay says: "The vouchers will be like a stamp book, restricted to a few titles at first, but ultimately there may be a voucher for each sector from which recipients can choose their favourite".

UK subscriptions represent less than ten per cent of sales, one of the lowest in Europe. In research, the Royal Mail found that 24 per cent of adults were very likely or quite likely to buy a gift subscription.

Newsagents have previously expressed concern over the growth of subscriptions, which may eat into retail sales. However, industry insiders say the National Federation of Retail Newsagents' gift subscriptions programme - also organised with the PPA - failed last year after the Royal Mail decided to withdraw funding to prepare the present scheme.

Newsforce Marketing director Mike Howard, who worked on the NFRN/PPA scheme, says: "The idea needed a big injection of cash, but without support it never got off the ground".

Marketing Week
13th March 1992

APPENDIX 11
Sheet 3 of 7
EXTRACTS FROM RECENT PRESS ARTICLES

BRITAIN'S LETTERS ARE FIRST PAST THE POST
By Nicholas Watt

Britain has the quickest postal system of the European Community's six major countries, with 90 per cent of first class letters delivered on time. Italy trails in last place with 14 per cent arriving on time, according to an independent survey published yesterday.

Announcing the survey results, Bill Cockburn, Royal Mail's managing director, said: "This confirms (our) position as the fastest and best value for money postal service in the EC". Britain's nearest competitor in the survey was Holland, with 81 per cent delivered on time. Germany, which charges the equivalent of 34.8p for next day delivery, compared with Britain's 24p, managed a rate of 75 per cent.

Italy's performance was even worse on long-distance letters that should arrive overnight, with none delivered on time, compared with 85 per cent in Britain.

Royal Mail hopes the results will help entice multi-national companies to Britain.. "We want to sell Britain strongly as the mailing centre of Europe", he said.

It was a considerable improvement on Royal Mail's performance four years ago, when 74.5 per cent of first class letters arrived the day after posting. But Mr Cockburn said he was still looking for improvements and Royal Mail would be spending more than £1.6 billion over the next five years.

He unveiled a £1.5 million computerised laser system that will link the Royal Mail with the postal systems of France, Germany and Ireland. Royal Mail sends 217 million letters and packets to the three countries each year and the system, known as Computer Aided Post in Europe, will track mail bags at each stage of their journey.

Mr Cockburn said that Royal Mail had completed its most ambitious computer-system to improve deliveries across Britain. The £11 million scheme - Delivery by Air, Road and Rail Transport - has been installed in every main sorting office and will iron out bottlenecks and delays.

Times
11th June 1992

APPENDIX 11
Sheet 4 of 7
EXTRACTS FROM RECENT PRESS ARTICLES

MAIL BONDING WITHOUT TEARS

Believe it or not, the UK postal service is the best in Europe, and its Continental counterparts have a lot of catching up to do.
By Michele Martin

The chief executive of Italy's direct marketing association used to meet regularly with his opposite number at the Italian Port Office. The topic of conversation was always the same -why did it taken ten days for a first class letter to get to Milan from Rome?

The chief executive would be sent away with the same empty assurances ringing in his ears. To soothe his nerves, he often snatched a rest on the bridge that spanned the Tiber outside the post office's head-quarters.

One day his attention was caught by a particularly colourful carnival of flotsam heading downstream. Peering closer, he realised that the mass of paper and envelopes bobbing towards him looked horribly familiar. It was a mailing his agency had sent out two weeks before, supposedly to 40,000 homes across the country.

Even if the delivery system in Italy has improved in the five years since this incident - and many say that it has not - the story is a timely reminder of how problematic sending a letter can be. In the UK we have become used to what is arguably Europe's best postal service, where 86 per cent of letters are delivered the day after postage. In Germany that drops to 68 per cent, France 65 per cent and Spain 15 percent. Italy is second from bottom of the league, with next day deliveries for 17 per cent of post.

For once, direct mailers in the UK are in accord with the bureaucrats of Europe. Both have realised the need to standardise the community's postal system.

The truth is that there are no easy solutions to the problem, but this has not prevented some good compromises being reached. Direct mailers will eventually get a more reliable, customer-led service which will make pan-European campaigns easier to do. But in the short term at least, no one has been able to find an answer that pleases both the user and all the postal providers of Europe's 12 states.

At the moment, each country has a different system of prices, weights, delivery times and even mail-pack regulations. Each has a state-regulated letters monopoly which ensure a universal service at a set price and includes domestic direct mail, but each defines its monopoly differently. In France, for example, it applies to all items weighing up to one kilogram while in the UK it applies to any document costing less than £1 to send.

APPENDIX 11
Sheet 5 of 7
EXTRACTS FROM RECENT PRESS ARTICLES

Beyond the monopoly, countries vary enormously in the services they offer. In Germany and France, the state post offices have a virtual strangle hold on the delivery of parcels, printed matter and express documents. Whereas countries such as the UK, the Netherlands and Ireland have accepted that independent carriers can compete.

The Irish Post Office has been a semi-privatised operation since 1984, and caters for direct mailers with Postaim, its version of the Royal Mail's Mailsort. It also markets to business users with special offers from time to time.

Royal Mail International faces competition from services such as TNT's Mailfast and DHL's World Mail for international business with private companies. But the prices and quality of delivery it offers means that it still carries the vast majority of mail, and is even wooing international mailers for bulk remail contracts. It wants to double its £500m worth of international mail in the next five to ten years.

The Netherlands has perhaps the most radical postal system in Europe. More of a facilitator than a carrier, it will speculate in any associated area that can make it a profit. This has led to interests in storage businesses in the past, and it also works with TNT on some international remail work.

Between the two extremes of ratecard state monopoly and semi-privatised business, there is little middle ground. This is the problem which faces the user, who has to sort out the logistics of an international direct mail campaign, and the commissionaires, who are trying to legislate a way through.

At least direct mailers in the UK know what they want, even if they are not sure how to get it. The same demands come up again and again; a universal service which guarantees delivery to every part of every country, a selection of carriers and therefore competitive prices, and access to customers through door to door service within a reasonable time. Individual users prioritise different elements of the list, but universal service is an absolute. If you have spent so much time and money getting your mailing list right, you need to know you can reach the people on it.

"No one wants a system that reduces the level of service", says David Rogers, manager of distribution and postal affairs for leading European direct mailer Reader's Digest. "Users want deliveries to every address, once a day, six days a week, at a uniform price. Who provides it is less important. I don't envy the person who has to say how it should be done".

Rogers' observation encapsulates the problem, because it raises two almost irreconcilable differences. To get competitive prices, you need competition. But a postal service run solely on price will affect the quality of service offered to rural areas - which is why monopolies are attractive.

APPENDIX 11
Sheet 6 of 7
EXTRACTS FROM RECENT PRESS ARTICLES

Most postal systems make heavy losses but are propped up by the telecommunications arms of their business. The Royal Mail is the only EC service to have made a consistent profit without subsidy for 15 years. Banning cross-subsidies would be the first step towards a customer-led European system. Survival would depend on the right product at the right price.

If monopolies were at least less restrictive, and postal services run like businesses, European direct mailers would have some say in what they got. Ian Hughes of Mail Marketing, one of the UK's leading mailing houses, believes customers can have a better influence on quality of service than either regulation or deregulation.

"There are certain advantages in terms of quality of service to having restricted areas, but there has to be competition, rather like with BT", he says.

"There has to be something which forces post offices to give value for money. That's one of the benefits of having large volume mailers - they are in a position to say 'I won't have this level of service'".

Direct marketing consultant Dick Thomas of Richard Thomas and His Friends agrees. "As the EC opens up and post offices become more competitive and privatised, big mailers will be able to shop for the postal system they like best", he says. "Postal rates would pretty much go out of the window, and services would have to pull their socks up. The well organised ones are going to beat the others hands down".

There is already evidence that companies with large regular mailings want to put contracts out to tender in the same way that they already do with print and fulfilment. At the moment, though, the quality of service available from the kind of post offices which will do mailing is unpredictable.

If professional, responsible postal services can offer this kind of service, they would arguably not need subsidies. The UK's Royal Mail, as one of Europe's more commercial operations, already realises this.

"We already have a lot of international mail coming into this country - about 50 per cent more volume goes out of the UK to the rest of the world than from our nearest rival Germany - we would like to see that grow", says Simon Chisnall, European business development manager for Royal Mail International.

"We are talking to large companies about terms and what they want from posting. We are also talking to postal administrations, so that we can make up mail under their conditions, sort letters as they want, even frank them in a certain style. In that way, Royal Mail International operates as a sort of clearing house, making sure post goes into a state's internal domestic system as easily as possible".

APPENDIX 11
Sheet 7 of 7
EXTRACTS FROM RECENT PRESS ARTICLES

Harmonising interstate mail traffic is only the first step to what users want, however, and arguably the second goal can only be reached with the help of legislation. Many mail producers feel that, for the good of the internal market and encouraging mail from beyond Europe, a single fixed tariff must be the next objective. Some say this can be achieved by setting up a central authority which puts redefined licenses up for tender.

Leading direct marketing agency Wunderman Worldwide, now Wunderman Cato Johnson, handles many European clients including American Express, and managing director John Shaw advocates greater standardisation.

"There are very few pan-European mailings done from one point, most of it is done market-by-market, because of the different needs of countries, and also because the postal rates are so different. The industry is crying out for a uniform postal system and one rate throughout Europe", he says.

Thomas also believes that such a move would increase mailings from non-European states, particularly the US. "The combined EC market is about 320 million, and the US has only 250 million people. The US is looking at us with tremendous envy. But then people realise that they would have to deal with 12 different post offices as well as 12 different printers, and the prospect doesn't look quite as attractive anymore. It would be better to get some rationalisation. It would be particularly good for the US to deal with one centralised body", he says.

Marketing Week
20 March 1992

Copy of Recruitment Advertisement for your position

APPENDIX 12
Sheet 1 of 1
ADVERTISEMENT

COPY OF RECRUITMENT ADVERTISEMENT FOR YOUR POSITION

Marketing Manager

£37K + Car + Benefits

As evocative as it is familiar, the Royal Mail insignia is a symbol of tradition and innovation, and is an integral part of everyone's life. The business of the Royal Mail is serving its customers. Led by their demands, the Royal Mail is dedicated to anticipating and satisfying market needs.

The Marketing and Sales function of the Royal Mail strategic headquarters covers Strategic Business Planning, Sales, Public Relations, Marketing and Quality. As Marketing Manager, your role is to develop strategic marketing plans over a broad range of products and services.

You will take responsibility for the Royal Mail brand, develop strategy, manage policy, oversee brand development and raise the profile of the Royal Mail and its services brands in the marketplace. You will contribute to the highest level of decision making over a broad range of related business issues.

This is a new position within the Royal Mail, and it will be the responsibility of the successful candidate to develop his or her role in strategic headquarters to maximise the marketing effort, in close co-operation with the four strategic business units to ensure timely delivery of marketing initiatives.

This role calls for the candidate to have the ability to quickly and clearly identify key success criteria to resolve issues between business units, challenge traditional ideas and accepted practices if necessary, and work independently and effectively while under pressure.

Candidates will be of graduate calibre with a structured marketing background, including at least 5 years' experience in a senior role gained within a substantial service or manufacturing industry. Quality and accuracy in both written and verbal communication, including a flair for speechwriting, are essential, as is the ability to influence decisions in a tactful yet decisive manner.

To apply, please send a detailed CV, including work and home telephone numbers to LJ Associates, Recruitment Consultants, 12 Celbridge Mews, Porchester Road, London W2 6UE, quoting reference number 09/382.

Royal Mail positively encourages Equal Opportunities

ROYAL MAIL

Examiners' report

General comments

Most students in most countries appear to have related well to the postal service setting and to have grasped the essentials of the somewhat complex situation.

Comments made before bear repeating in that a good case study should, upon rigorous and competent analysis, yield its key issues. These key issues should normally form the basis on which the examination questions are set so as to preserve the integrity of the case. Most candidates (no doubt ably assisted by tutors) appear to have conducted a thorough enough analysis to have been able to anticipate the likely question areas.

Unfortunately, however, standards varied considerably between centres and within centres with some students clearly having conducted very little analysis, presumably hoping to be able to waffle their way through the paper, but failing miserably.

Most students adopted the role well and phrased their answers from the viewpoint of the candidate – John Solomon. However, far too many candidates submitted answers in inappropriate and time wasting essay style despite endless warnings that not to adopt report format is courting failure. People reading this examiners' report are urged to consult the recommended principal text for examples of proper report format and techniques to adopt which save valuable time (therefore offering the opportunity of more marks being earned with the spare time available).

A further example of unnecessary time wasting is the practice of many candidates of writing out report lead sheets *for each question*, sometimes detailing every sub-section and even giving relevant page numbers. What we really want you to do is to answer the questions. All that is necessary is to state who the report is to (The Sales/Marketing Director) who it is from (John Solomon), the date (22.6.93), the heading (e.g. Marketing Proposals in Support of Application for the Post of Marketing Manager) and the broad contents (e.g. Section 1 = Growth Strategies, Section 2 = Information Needs and Competitor Intelligence, Section 3 = Corporate Identity and Branding).

Another general time wasting practice is that of candidates writing out a pre-prepared analysis of the case rather than using this to answer the questions set. 'SWOTITIS' namely the irresistible obsession to write out a pre-prepared SWOT analysis regardless of the questions, seems to be endemic. Perhaps worse in this case was candidates for the post of Marketing Manager telling their Sales/Marketing Director things he obviously already knew rather than what he really wanted to read – namely some good ideas to ensure continued profitable growth for the Royal Mail.

Some overseas candidates even wrote out full 'fictional' CVs prior to attempting the questions set. Quite apart from the fact that the Candidates' Brief clearly states that a series of interviews has already taken place (i.e. we are well past the CV stage), this examination is on Marketing Management:

Analysis and Decision not on CV writing. It sometimes seems that some candidates will write anything rather than answer the questions set.

Those examinees who attempted to 'dump' their entire pre-prepared marketing plan in answers to Question 1 had very little time left to attempt the other two questions and consequently failed.

We need to continue to urge candidates to stick to the questions set and to ensure these are *fully* answered. Far too many candidates apparently ignore key words e.g. the word 'justified' in Question 1, the word *'new'* in Question 2 and the word 'confusion' in Question 3. This apparent myopia can and does often extend to entire parts of the question e.g. Competitor Intelligence in Question 2 and solutions to brand confusion in Question 3.

However, those candidates who had prepared well and so gained a real understanding of the situation appeared to have anticipated the nature of the additional information provided on the examination paper and were able to apply this in their answers to the questions set. This demonstrates a pleasing ability to think in the examination room and to adapt to new information given on the spot. The device of providing additional unseen information on the examination paper itself, the use of which carries a proportion of the marks available – has been adopted to catch out those candidates who blindly copy out previously prepared answers.

Question 1

Perhaps the most predictable of the questions but also the most difficult. Weaker candidates lacked any strong strategic conceptual framework in their answers. Ansoff would have been the obvious choice but any reasonable structured approach would have sufficed. The question clearly specified that recommended strategies should be *justified*. A worrying proportion of students ignored and/or were unable to do this. Other students failed to include European and other international dimensions in anything but the most superficial way. Good candidates had well-structured answers, with clearly delineated and justified strategies. The best answers also demonstrated a strong practical grasp of the realities of the situation and were creative but at the same time showed cognisance of the resource implications of their suggested strategies.

Question 2

This was a reasonably straightforward and predictable question which simply required candidates to demonstrate an understanding of the sort of information required for strategic marketing decisions plus an appreciation of how to organise its collection.

Surprisingly then, some candidates seemed to have no idea how to proceed on this question. Of the three questions on the paper this second question generated the most 'blank sheets' and subsequent zero or near zero marks. Some candidates focused on commenting on the market research/data already collected and contained in the case rather than looking at *new* information. Many candidates had no practical grasp of the realities of Competitor Intelligence, the sorts of information it can yield or the ways in which such information might be gained. Again better candidates had answers which were well-structured, which justified the new data acquisitions proposed and which showed an appreciation of appropriate methodologies and costs.

Question 3

Weaker candidates trotted out pre-prepared communication campaigns with detailed budgets, schedules and so on, almost irrespective of the specific question set. Better candidates had practical ideas on how to build on the corporate identity of Royal Mail and reduce the confusion between Royal Mail, service brands and service names. Few candidates made use of the additional information provided which pertained to this question. Overall, however, this question seemed popular and was on the whole handled well and creatively by most candidates.

[illegible] collected and [illegible] in [illegible] rather than [illegible] tion. Many candidates [illegible] group [illegible] Consequently [illegible] information [illegible] which [illegible] might be [illegible] which [illegible] were [illegible] and which [illegible] an appropriate [illegible]

Question [illegible]

Most candidates [illegible] with [illegible] the [illegible] how to [illegible] the [illegible] candidates [illegible] and clearly [illegible]